In the Ruins of the Reich

By the same author

In the Ruins
of the Reich

DOUGLAS BOTTING

London
GEORGE ALLEN & UNWIN
Boston   Sydney

George Allen & Unwin (Publishers) Ltd
40 Museum Street, London WC1A 1LU, UK.

George Allen & Unwin (Publishers) Ltd
Park Lane, Hemel Hempstead, Herts HP2 4TE, UK.

Allen & Unwin Inc.
Fifty Cross Street, Winchester, Mass 01890, USA

George Allen & Unwin Australia Pty Ltd,
8 Napier Road, North Sydney, NSW 2060, Australia.

First published in 1985

ISBN 0 04 943036

Set in 10 on 11 point Plantin by Fotographics (Bedford) Ltd
and printed in Great Britain by The Anchor Press Ltd, Tiptree, Essex

Contents

'Enjoy the war – the peace is
going to be terrible.'

*Graffiti on a Berlin wall,
March 1945*

Introduction

Though this book has a lot to do with armies it is not a conventional war book. Nor is there much about actual fighting — the Battle of Berlin apart — though there is a great deal about the consequences of Hitler's war. The story of the conquest and occupation of Germany in the havoc years between 1945 and 1949 is a remarkable one. Never before had four civilised industrial nations tried to work together to govern a country inhabited by a fifth. Never before had one great modern state been laid quite so low.

This book is about how victors and vanquished alike deported themselves among the ruins of that ravished battleground. It is not an exhaustive account. Indeed the canvas is so vast I doubt if there ever can be a definitive account of Germany under the Occupation within the compass of a single volume. The reader will not find much here about the new trade unions, or the rebirth of the German church, or the reform of the German financial system, or other worthy but specialist aspects of the subject. But he will find the big events and the characteristic phenomena which made occupied Germany a unique place to be in: the 'Third Man' world of the black-market dealer, the ubiquitous Fräulein, and the crook in a foreign uniform; the armies of refugees; the Pooh-Bah sahibs of a new kind of Raj grappling with the heavy responsibilities of waging peace, building democracy and dispensing justice in a land (so some thought) of yahoos. In presenting a selective view of Germany under the Occupation, I have tried to recreate the special flavour of the place and time during a little-known lacuna of history between the collapse of the Third Reich and the foundation of the new Germanies.

I first started gathering material for this book in 1973. At that time the book was intended to cover much wider ground, including the Cold War and the whole of eastern Europe. Between 1981 and 1983 I also worked on two other books set partly in the same occupied Germany at the same moment in history — *The Aftermath: Europe* (the final volume of *The Time-Life History of World War Two*) and *Nazi Gold*, the story of the robbery of the Reichsbank reserves, which was written with Ian Sayer. Here and there both these books drew on similar source material and inevitably there are a few small overlaps between those earlier books and the present one. *In the Ruins of the Reich* was finally written in order that it could be published in Great Britain in time for the fortieth anniversary of VE Day. But as the reader will discover, there are not many of the romantic heroics of war and victory to be found here. The war (and its aftermath) as experienced by the countless millions of continental Europeans on all sides was a very different and very much more terrible war from that experienced by the British and the Americans. Not for them the career-enhancing Anglo-American concept of 'a good war', or the stirring patriotic airs of the Dambusters' March. So this book does not celebrate VE Day in a conventional festive sense, for it knows all too well what was to follow the day after, and the day after that.

I am grateful to my publisher, Adam Sisman, and my agent, Andrew Hewson, for their firm encouragement when resolve was wavering. I am also grateful to Michael Cuddy, who delved for several months among the files of the Public Record Office to help research the book; to Patsy Meehan, for drawing my attention to certain hard-to-come by papers relating to the British administration in Germany; and to my copy-editor Rupert Christiansen, for his judicious expertise in preparing the manuscript for printing. Above all I am grateful to the following individuals who gave up their time to talk to me or write to me or help in other ways during the preparation of this book: Bill and Kathleen Allen, Gwendoline Baehr, Professor Robin Barbour, Eberhard Bethge, Peter and Christabel Bielenberg, Col. Biggs, Jan Boesman, Col. Karl Heinz Boettger, Theo Botting, Rev. Michael Bourdeaux, Major-General Denys Buckle, Dr Jane Caplan, Len Carpenter, Lt-Col. Reggy Chip, John Clarke, General Lucius D. Clay, Lt-Col. H. H. Cook, C. A. J. Cox, Ingrid Cranfield, Ernest and Sadee Crasson, Captain William H. Craydon, Brigadier Gerald H. Cree, Michael Cuddy, Lt-Col. John Dale, Edward Dean, Marlene Dietrich, Peter Fabian, John Falconer, Mrs J. Fawcett, Lt-Col. Will Fenwick, Alfred Foertsch, Jon Fuhn, Frank C. Gabell, Lt-Gen. Sir Alexander Galloway, Col. J. M. Grant, Dr Glenn and Ursula Gray, Karl-Gunther von Hase, Roland Hill, Elizabeth Hook, I. Hordijchuk, Patrick Howarth, Tom Howarth, Mrs Thelma Hughes, Basil and Elizabeth Carew-Hunt, Isabel James, Dr Otto John, Charles L. Jones, Jan Josten, Ian E. Kaye, Hans Kehrl, Adele Kramer, Jerome Kuehl, Christopher Leefe, Lt-Col. Alec D. Malcolm, James J. Mallen, Frank Masters, Phil May, Patricia Meehan, Yehudi Menuhin, Metropolitan Police Archives, New Scotland Yard, Edmund Milewczyk, Jiri Mucha, Freddie Nunn, Brigadier James Oliver, Eric Orbell, Stephen V. Patterson, Monika Pietrek, Major W. H. Pitkin, Suska Podolska, Heinz Propper, Jesco von Puttkamer, Lady Edith Robertson, Peter Saabor, Ian Sayer, Peter Sheppard, Mrs M. H. Simpson, Gertrude Sington (*née* Kafka), Anthony Smith, Miroslav and Olga Smutny, Dr Lumin Soukup, Brigadier Nigel I. B. Speller, Dr D. A. Spencer, Colonel Graf Berthold Schenk von Stauffenberg, Dr Jessica Stolterfoht, A. Stypulkowski, Zbigniew Stypulkowski, Herbert and Beate Sulzbach, Charlotte Tangerding, Field Marshal Sir Gerald Templer, Anthony Terry, Major Urban-Smith, Lord Gordon-Walker, I. Warner and Frank Wright.

I would also like to thank the Estate of Victor Gollancz for permission to quote from *In Darkest Germany* (Gollancz, 1947); Lt-Col. W. Byford-Jones and Hutchinson & Co. for permission to quote from *Berlin Twilight* (Hutchinson, 1947); and Wolfgang Leonhard and William Collins & Co. for permission to quote from *Child of the Revolution* (Collins, 1957).

One of the above — Frank C. Gabell, of Arizona, who survived the war but found his life in ruins — has penned a fitting envoi: 'My voluntary participation in World War Two cost me some $700,000, everything I had attained, including home, furnishings, car, bonds, even my wife (divorce), my senior partnership in a large accounting firm, my advisory job to a large law firm — well, just everything.

'I do have a few decoration ribbons, having been in six different battle campaigns. But my most valued award is etched on my brain and heart. It reads: "WAR STINKS! MAY ALL POLITICAL AND RELIGIOUS WAR-MONGERS BE CONSIGNED TO ETERNAL HELL"!'

1

Pursuit

All through the last winter of the war Dr Goebbels's graffiti officers from the Reich Propaganda Ministry had been busily scribbling along the German frontier beyond the Rhine. On the walls of the border towns and on the huge concrete dragon's teeth of the Siegfried Line, Nazi sign-painters had plastered slogans in white paint facing both east and west. Those facing west were intended to strike a chill into the heart of the four million troops of the Allied Expeditionary Force now gathering for the last great offensive against the Reich: SEE GERMANY AND DIE, they read; DEATH TO THE INVADERS; UNSER HASS—ANGLO-AMERIKA (Our hate—Anglo-America). Those facing east exhorted German soldier and civilian alike to a final fanatical defence of Hitler's kingdom: SIEG ODER SIBERIEN, the slogans cried, VICTORY OR SIBERIA; IF YOU WANT THE V-2, THEN WORK; IF YOU WANT THE V-4, THEN WORK; THE SA IS HERE AGAIN; and everywhere the ubiquitous ES LEBE DER FÜHRER—(Long Live the Führer).

The great bomber fleets could not see the west-facing slogans as, daily and nightly, they droned eastward to flatten the cities of the Rhineland and the Ruhr. They could not see the east-facing ones either, as they flew back to their bases in England to rearm and refuel. Instead they dropped slogans of their own, millions of leaflets concocted by the copy-writers of the Psychological Warfare Division, a paper blitz, verbal saturation bombing. YOU ARE NOW CUT OFF, the leaflets read, YOU MUST GIVE UP OR DIE. And again, ominously and persuasively, after the Allies had launched their February offensive, the drive to the Rhine:

THEY ARE COMING
with their steel monsters, fighter-bombers and flame-throwers

THEY ARE COMING
because nobody and nothing can stop them

1

THEY ARE COMING
because now Northern and Central Germany lie open before the Anglo-Americans and Russians. The greatest fraud of the world is almost over:

What became of the German miracle weapons?

What became of the strategic reserves?

What became of the Party members and high officials who always advocated fanatical resistance? The Allied Armies are taking Germany by storm.

THEY ARE COMING
to exterminate militarism once and for all

THEY ARE COMING
to bring war criminals to justice

THEY ARE COMING
to set up a state based on justice, lest the world's peace be disturbed again.

And as they came, this vast land armada of Americans, British, Canadians and Frenchmen, hell-bent for the Rhine and the first great cities of the Reich, the Germans opposed to Hitler and Nazism—the socialists, communists, democrats, and anti-fascists who had evaded the Gestapo and the camps—crept out of the ruins and broke twelve years of silence, scrawling their own salvos in the graffiti war: USE TERROR AGAINST THE NAZI TERROR; WOMEN—KEEP YOUR MEN AT HOME; EVERY HUMAN BEING IS A PRECIOUS GIFT FOR GERMANY. As Cologne, then Bonn, then Koblenz fell, and the Allies began their great leap across the Rhine, ordinary people, tired of the war, the bombs, the sacrifice and the lies, rose up with paint-brush and whitewash bucket and made their voices heard more plainly than since the heady days of Hitler's rise to power: WEG MIT HITLER! the walls screamed. WEG MIT KRIEG! 'Down with Hitler! Down with war!'

It was not what the Yanks and the Tommies had been led to expect. It was not what General Eisenhower, the Supreme Commander of the Allied Expeditionary Force, or his commanders or intelligence staff had been led to expect, nor the Joint Chiefs of Staff who controlled the military direction of the war in Washington, nor their political leaders, President Roosevelt and Prime Minister Churchill.

After the D-Day invasion and the Anglo-American liberation of France in the west, and the Soviet advance through Germany's territories in the east, the Allied leaders could have reasonably expected a rational German leader of a normal civilised state to have cast about for ways of ending the war. But Hitler was not a rational leader and Nazi Germany was not a normal state, and any German inclination to sue for peace was dashed by the Allied leaders' insistence on unconditional surrender—a recipe for total German prostration which ensured that the Nazis would fight to the finish. 'The more the English prophesy a disgraceful peace for Germany,'

The Greater Reich at its maximum wartime extent, showing annexed or administered territories

Goebbels had written in his diary, 'the easier it is for me to toughen and harden German resistance.' As the Anglo-Americans and the Russians closed in upon the Reich, the German people and the armed forces rallied to support the reign of the very man who had led them to the brink of ruin and defeat. Along the Siegfried Line and the banks of the Rhine the German Army fought in the main with great courage and skill. But among the civilian populace the arrival of the Anglo-Americans seemed to produce a reaction quite different from what was anticipated. Where were the Werewolf bands of stay-behind fanatics, the hate and enmity in the streets? The Allied soldiers moved into the Third Reich amid scenes of incongruity and startling paradox.

These paradoxes occurred in the very heat of battle. The fighting could be savage, especially at the beginning of the battle for Germany, at the frontier and along the Rhine. But even then, in the thick of the fray, there was something not quite predictable about it.

At Homberg, for example, on the west bank of the Rhine, American artillery was bombarding German concentrations in Duisburg, on the east bank. A grocer's shop had been turned into a company HQ, where the company commander directed operations amid an aroma of tea, thyme and soap. Two hundred yards away American snipers with telescopic-sight rifles were shooting anyone who presented a target among the twisted girders on the opposite bank. While the Americans blasted away with their guns and rifles, and the Germans answered with scattered shell-fire, the German children played in the streets, ignoring the soldiers' pleas that they go home. Then a lorry-load of dusty German prisoners drove up and stopped while the driver asked the way. German housewives and American soldiers came out to look, and suddenly the Americans began to throw packets of K-ration cigarettes to their erstwhile enemies, and the housewives went into their houses and came out with hunks of bread and cheese and glasses of water to give to the prisoners. The prisoners smiled and shouted their thanks in German and English and the Americans grinned back: 'Don't worry, you guys. You're out of it. You're lucky Joes.' The housewives laughed, the lorry started off, and the housewives and the Americans stood together and waved as it drove away. Then the housewives went back to their houses, as the Americans gave wolf-whistles and called out ribald remarks before returning to their posts. That night the housewives sent two boxes of cigars and three or four bottles of schnapps to the American company in the grocery store. 'If General Patton hears about this, they'll hang me,' the company captain exclaimed. 'First time I've got a bottle of liquor in Germany without shooting someone for it.'

Major Frank C. Gabell was a Military Government officer in Homberg at this time. He recalled:

I had accompanied the Infantry to this town. The first thing we did was to loot the SS headquarters. I came out with a large Nazi flag, a parade flag, with the big swastika and name of the town. The next thing, I had my photograph taken by a German photographer. Still have it. Then I heard a lot of shooting in a bank, so I went in and found a GI tommy-gunning the bank vault.

The GIs had a big secret from the top brass: Germany Army on the Leverkusen side of the river, US Army on the Homberg side. The local phone line had not been destroyed and there was a very live telephone conversation between the two armies across the Rhine. We maintained very friendly communications with the Germans across the river. Before they shelled Homberg they would let us know in advance the exact time.

Before we shelled Leverkusen we would let the Germans know in advance. So everybody took cover ahead and nobody got hurt.

One day three US officers came to me and said they wanted to row out on the Rhine, make like they were fishing, and wanted to be the first of the US Army to be on the Rhine River. They asked if we could ask the Germans not to fire at them while they were out there taking pictures, etc. We called the Germans on the 'secret line' and they agreed not to fire. Our officers went out rowing a small boat, took their pictures and fooled around, and not a shot came from the Germans. They stuck to their agreement.

War reporter Leonard Mosley recorded: 'Wherever we drove through the Rhineland those first weeks in April the feelings of the German people were unmistakable. The war was not yet over but they knew it was lost, and they were engaged in an instinctive effort to save something from the wreck. The mass of the people were casting off National Socialism like an old coat, almost without grief or regret, determined to forget it and to work to recreate, in co-operation with their conquerors, the things that had now been destroyed.' There was no Werewolf underground, no sabotage campaign behind the Allied lines. The great industrial centre of München Gladbach had been torn to rubble by Allied bombers and artillery, Mosley found, yet wherever he drove, by day or by night, through this great industrial area, he could find no sign of resentment: 'The men and women we stopped on the streets to ask the way were polite and helpful; they gathered round in bunches when they heard us speaking German, and bombarded us with questions: "How far had we advanced? When would the war be over? Where were the Russians?" '

Again, in the fighting for Koblenz on the middle Rhine the soldiers of both sides were inclined to hit the bottle when they could. The Germans filled their water-flasks with cognac. The Americans broke into the cellars and the sideboards of houses and drank whatever they found there. Sometimes soldiers from both sides shared the same building and made merry in different rooms. In one house during the fighting for Koblenz a group of American soldiers held a drinking party in a room on the first floor, while a group of German soldiers were doing the same on the second floor. When the tipsy Americans came out into the dark hall to find the bathroom, they bumped into some of the equally tipsy Germans who had come downstairs for the same reason. ''Scuse me. Beg your pardon,' one GI found himself saying as he fumbled in the dark. 'Wanna get through there.'

Out in the streets intoxicated American infantrymen lurched past, firing anywhere, pursued by over-excited German girls who ran after them through the artillery barrage, dodging the avalanches of falling tiles, longing for love. The GIs were not slow to respond. When one member of a stretcher-party ducked into a house to escape the German shelling, he found another member of the stretcher party in the dining-room riding out the barrage having sexual intercourse with the woman of the house.

Across the Rhine in Wiesbaden, an American intelligence officer, Captain Saul K. Padover, found the streets packed with German civilians, many of them in their best clothes. 'There were a lot of pretty girls,' he noted, 'and they smiled at us broadly.' It was no different in other German cities. 'Everywhere women, some of them beautiful and most of them young, accosted us and whispered invitations. They would pass slowly, give us a long sideways look and murmur, 'I live by myself; would you like to come up and see me?' This went on all the time.' The German women, Padover thought, were the easiest white women in the world.

The Supreme Headquarters of the Allied Expeditionary Force—SHAEF—had imposed a strict non-fraternisation rule on its troops: no contact with Germans except in the line of duty. Any American soldier found violating the ban was fined $65—so inevitably the propositioning of German girls became known as 'the 65 dollar question'. Few soldiers heeded the ban. 'Copulation without conversation', they claimed, 'is not fraternisation.' Even the officers indulged when opportunity offered: 'Sororisation', the academics among them suggested, 'is not fraternisation either.'

Far from the front line and the quirky realities of the battle for Germany, Higher Intelligence Staff in Paris, their heads full of Werewolves and Fifth Columns, took a dim view of friendly German females and issued a prim warning to the Anglo-American troops in a pamphlet that served to inflame the situation rather than douse it: 'Do you know German women have been trained to seduce you? Is it worth a knife in the back? A weapon can be concealed by women on the chest, between the breasts, on the abdomen, on the upper leg, under the buttocks, in the muff, in a handbag, in a hood or coat. How can you search women? The answer to that one is difficult. It may be your life at stake. You may find a weapon by forcing them to pull their dress tight against their bodies here and there. If it is a small object you are hunting for, you must have another woman to do the searching and to do it thoroughly in a private room.'

But the problem was not just the girls—it was the whole German population. Children waved, adults smiled, everyone was anxious to help the Allied soldiers in any possible way. In a lovingly tended cottage flower-garden at the edge of Krefeld, an old man tending his shrubs raised his hat, gave a courtly bow and greeted Captain Padover and his party with the words: 'Good morning, gentlemen. I am making all this pretty for our liberators.' And he told them: 'The people sigh with relief and say at last it's over. It is better to live under the American Occupation than under the whip of the Nazi bandits.' When Padover asked a 10-year old ex-Hitler Youth what he thought of Adolf Hitler now, the boy replied laconically: '*Der Führer kann mir den Arsch lecken*' (The Führer can kiss my arse). To the man in the street Hitler had become '*der Kerl*' (that fellow) and the Nazis '*die Goldfasane*' (the golden pheasants) or '*Parteibonzen*' (party bums). Not even the German Army was exempt from such seditious views. 'Praise be to God,' an officer was heard to exclaim before surrendering the Rhineland village of Titz without a fight, 'the Americans are here.' And Padover was told, with ardent, if mistaken, enthusiasm: 'Now things will be all right. Now we'll have an English government.'

But some Allied observers believed that the Germans' joy at their liberation was as *ersatz* as their coffee, the fake emotion of opportunists who saw that now was the time to change sides. There were few signs among average Germans of responsibility for Nazism, the war, or any real awareness of what the Allied conquest was all about. Not all the Allied soldiers went in for fraternisation with the enemy, and some, who were embarrassed by the unctuous comradliness of the civil populace, decided that dignified aloofness was to be their approach—an attitude the Germans found bewildering.

Though the Anglo-American armies had fought their way to the German frontier by the autumn of 1944—Aachen, the first German city to be occupied and submit to Military Government rule, fell to the US First Army on 21 October 1944—it was not until February 1945 that the Allies began the first phase of the battle for Germany—the great advance through the frontier defences known as the Siegfried Line to the Rhine. After clearing a large part of the west bank of the lower river, and capturing major Rhineland cities like München-Gladbach and Cologne, the Allies began the second phase of the campaign, the crossing of the Rhine, last great natural obstacle to the heartland of Nazi Germany.

On 7 March the US 9th Armoured Division, in a major feat of arms, seized the only bridge over the Rhine which the Germans had not yet demolished and with remarkable swiftness pushed three corps of General Bradley's Twelfth Army Group across into a bridgehead ten miles deep on the opposite bank. Further south, in a combined offensive of startling dash and drive by the Third and Seventh Armies, the Americans advanced on the Palatinate, smashed through the Siegfried Line defences and on 23 March boldly pushed a division of Patton's Third Army across the Rhine at

Oppenheim in a surprise move which cost only eight lives. That same evening Eisenhower launched the main set-piece operation on the north flank of the Rhine front. In a massive and carefully prepared ground and airborne assault under Montgomery's overall command the Second British Army, the First Canadian Army, the Ninth US Army and the First Allied Airborne Army—1,250,000 men with 300,000 tons of supplies—crossed the Rhine near Wesel after an annihilating air and artillery bombardment on the German positions. All resistance on the west bank of the Rhine now ceased and the huge Allied forces stood poised for a break-out across the Reich eastwards towards the Elbe and (so it was thought) Berlin. The Germans meanwhile had lost over 350,000 men, more than a third of the forces which had been deployed against the Allies at the start of the offensive six weeks before.

The end of the war was now barely six weeks away. Never again were the British and the Americans to fight a set battle against the Nazis in Germany. Henceforth the conquest of Germany became a mopping-up operation, a series of skirmishes accelerating to a headlong pursuit as Hitler's army in the west melted away under the sheer weight of men and material under Eisenhower's command, culminating in the destruction of a modern state on a scale without precedent. The Western Front was wide open. Between Eisenhower and Berlin there was nothing that need now impede the drive to the capital—no natural barriers, field armies, or prepared defences, no lack of transport or supplies. For the last six months it had been assumed that the main Allied effort would be a rapid thrust to Berlin under Montgomery.

But it was not to be. On 28 March Eisenhower announced a radical change of plans. The Allied main effort was not to be a drive to Berlin by Montgomery's 21st Army Group but a thrust through the centre of Germany by forty American divisions of Bradley's 12th Army Group aimed not at Berlin but at the Leipzig–Dresden area to the south of the capital. The role of Montgomery, who was convinced he could have taken Berlin before the Russians, was now a subsidiary one: instead of driving headlong east to the capital he was now to cover Bradley's left flank and swing north-east to secure the German North Sea ports of Schleswig–Holstein and beat the Russians to the Baltic port of Lübeck, thereby cutting off the German forces in Norway and Denmark. Denver's 6th Army Group was to protect Bradley's right flank and advance down the Danube and secure the so-called Alpenfestung or National Redoubt before the Germans could organise a last stand of the Third Reich there.

The British were outraged. They believed that the Supreme Commander had acted wrongly in going over the heads of Churchill and Roosevelt and their governments, that he had unilaterally broken a joint agreement to make Berlin the main objective of the Allied campaign in Germany, and that, military considerations apart, his decision was politically naïve and ill-considered and would have disastrous consequences for Europe after the war (as indeed it did). In Churchill's view, Eisenhower had far exceeded his brief and moved out of the area of military strategy, for which he was authorised, into grand strategy, for which he was not.

Eisenhower argued that militarily Berlin was no longer an overriding objective. His mission was not to capture places but destroy Hitler's armed forces. In his view the industrial complex around Dresden and Leipzig, which contained all that was left of Germany's heavy industries, was more important than the capture of the capital, which was now no more than a prestigious symbol. Since the Russians were only 35 miles from Berlin and American spearheads still had 285 miles to go it was highly probable the Russians would get to Berlin first. If the British and Americans did beat them to it the cost in Allied lives—100,000 dead in Bradley's view—would be insupportable. In any case, soon after capturing the city the Allies would be obliged to withdraw westward to their zones of Occupation agreed by the political chiefs at Yalta. Since Berlin was deep inside what was designated as the future Soviet zone it seemed logical that the Red Army should take the prize. Above all, US military intelligence reported active preparations for a fanatical Wagnerian last stand by the Nazis in the Alpine regions of Southern Bavaria and Western Austria—a stand led by the Führer himself from his bunker complex on the Obersalzberg at Berchtesgaden, his 'second capital'. Determined resistance in such impenetrable terrain could lead to a prolonged campaign which would delay the end of the war for an incalculable period—and Eisenhower was under pressure from General Marshall, the American Chief of Staff, to end the war in Europe as soon as possible so that American troops and material would be switched to the Pacific theatre. For all these reasons Eisenhower decided to leave Berlin to the Russians and turn the armies of General Patton and Patch southwards towards the prettier picture-postcard country of southern Germany.

In vain the British argued with their American allies that with the war almost over the important thing now was not military objectives but the post-war balance of political power. The best way to secure this balance was to keep the Soviets as far to the east as possible by pushing the Allied armies forward into central Europe as far and as quickly as possible—to Berlin, to Prague and even beyond. If the Americans had their way, the British argued, not only would the Soviets advance far into Western Europe, but they stood the chance of overrunning Denmark and gaining access to the North Sea and Atlantic by the capture of the North German ports—an eventuality which British foreign policy had sought to prevent ever since the days of Peter the Great. In any case, British intelligence believed—correctly—that the Americans had greatly exaggerated the threat of the National Redoubt.

Eisenhower's controversial decision was backed by the American Chief of Staff, General Marshall. But there were dissenting American voices. When Patton urged Eisenhower to take Berlin, Eisenhower replied, 'Well, who would want it?' At which Patton put his hands on the Supreme Commander's shoulders and said: 'I think history will answer that question for you.'

Eisenhower had now no less than eighty-five combat divisions at his command, two-thirds of them American, the rest British, Canadian and French, totalling some four million men in seven armies. His new plan was to deploy these armies in a series of huge loops and encircling movements advancing eastward along a broad front. To the north, at the top of the line, was Crerar's Canadian First Army, whose job was to seal off the V-weapon sites and German forces in Holland and relieve the starving Dutch. Next in line came Dempsey's British Second Army, advancing north-east towards Schleswig–Holstein and the Baltic in a movement intended to cut off the great North Sea ports of Bremen and Hamburg and the whole of Denmark. Münster, Osnabrück and Minden fell in the first fortnight after the Rhine crossing, then the British wheeled north-east towards Lüneburg Heath, in the direction of Bremen and Hamburg.

On the British right came two American armies, Simpson's Ninth and Hodges' First, which in one of the most brilliant operations of the campaign swung from north and south round the Ruhr pocket, which Hitler had ordered to be defended as a fortress, and linked up on its eastern side, thus trapping inside the industrial heart of Hitler's Reich the whole of German Army Group C under Field Marshal Model and two corps of Army Group H, comprising some twenty German divisions in all. When the Ruhr pocket was finally liquidated on 18 April, thirty generals and 325,000 soldiers were taken prisoners, in the largest mass surrender of the war up to that date—even larger than the German surrender at Stalingrad.

By then Simpson and Hodges were already in full cry towards the Elbe, pouring in an unending stream across the Reich towards the Russians advancing from the east. Further south Patton's Third Army, with Patch's Seventh Army on his right flank, was also racing into the German interior after turning south-east at Kassel; while at the bottom of the line the First French Army, which had crossed the Rhine at Phillipsburg on 1 April, captured Karlsruhe and drove the German forces on the Upper Rhine into the Black Forest.

The greater part of Hitler's forces were distributed along Germany's Eastern Front in an attempt to contain the Soviet advance towards Berlin, and the German C-in-C in the west, Field Marshal Kesselring, outnumbered three to one and desperately short of ammunition, food, transport and fuel, could offer little resistance to the Allied tide which now swept over central Germany from the west. Many of his divisions were little more than battlegroups composed of hotch-potch jumbles of weary

Wehrmacht soldiers, SS troopers, recruits, officer cadets, local police, Hitler Youth, Home Guard, sailors, airmen, labour force conscripts, convalescents and stragglers from sick-parade units like the 281st Stomach Ailment Battalion. Though Hitler had ordered all towns and cities to be defended to the death and all surrenders punishable by summary execution, many of the German soldiers saw no future in giving their lives for a lost cause at the eleventh hour. Some units, like the 1st Parachute Army and the 15th Panzer Grenadier Division, maintained their cohesion to the last. Here and there pockets of resistance held by improvised battle-groups fought with fanatical courage until annihilated by the sheer weight of the artillery bombardment poured down on them.

But over large areas of the Western Front the broken and disorganised German Army melted away or gave itself up in droves. German prisoners-of-war were surrendering at the rate of 30,000 a day. By the second half of April there were two million in American hands alone, and by the end of the month nearly eight million in captivity in the west.

For more than sixty million civilian Germans the moment of conquest produced a confused range of emotions and reactions. This is how the conquerors came and the occupation began for a few.

One of the first big cities to fall to the Allies during the big push to the Rhine was Krefeld. Uncertain how the Germans would react, the Americans were taking no chances and had confined the hundred thousand inhabitants indoors—most of them below ground in cellars. Driving through the deserted streets at night, war correspondent Alan Moorehead could see nothing until he caught sight of a faint glow coming out of the earth. This was the entrance to one of Krefeld's vast underground shelters, where a large part of the population had fled as soon as the first American tanks appeared in the streets. American sentries now stood guard at the entrance to make sure nobody came out of the shelter. Accompanied by a GI escort, Moorehead walked down into the light—the first enemy to appear in the Germans' midst below. He reported later:

> A wall of suffocating, foetid heat, a tangible thing full of the smell of human bodies, came up the ramp and seemed to close round behind us as we went on. We were in the middle of a great concrete room filled with Germans. Germans sleeping and eating. Germans playing cards, feeding their children, lying and sitting on the concrete floor. Mothers washing their children, young men playing a concertina, and the old men and women sitting vacantly in row after row along the benches. And beyond this another room, again filled so densely with humanity that there was no space for everyone to lie down. And beyond that another room and another and another.
>
> As soon as we were seen, the American and British uniforms, all activity ceased, and for a moment one was conscious only of thousands of staring

eyes. They stared as though some kind of revelation were going to come out of us. We were the first of the enemy they had seen, standing here with guns, having absolute right of life and death, and we were the first real vision of men behind the Nazi propaganda posters. They stared as though we were creatures from another world.

As Moorehead and his companions walked slowly through these concrete chambers towards the central office, German men stood to attention or touched their foreheads in salute, the children stopped playing and fell silent, and the women shrank back—a wall of faces pressing in from all sides and from behind and in front. 'Like dumb, herded animals in a cage, the crowd stood still and waited to see what we could do.'

In Krefeld the Germans were fearful: but in Cologne they welcomed their American conquerors. Beerhalls and restaurants offered them free drink. Crowds lined the streets and shouted: 'For years we've been waiting for you for years!' And so it went on. As the resistance of the German forces in the Ruhr began to collapse, the cordiality intensified. Germans in their 'Sunday best' lined the streets to greet their conquerors, cheered and waved, brought wine, schnapps and biscuits, bombarded them with questions, got drunk and sang. 'The conquering army rode into the Ruhr and thus sealed the doom of Nazi Germany,' reported Leonard Mosley, 'and the German workers, for whom this was defeat, cheered our coming and celebrated it in practically every city we visited.'

Peter Saabor was still a boy when the war front came to Halberstadt, one of the oldest towns in Germany, and a railway junction on the Americans' direct line of advance to Magdeburg on the Elbe. Saabor was a very junior member of the Hitler Youth at the time—though his mother was English and his father a German–Jewish refugee in London. The days of the German collapse are indelibly etched in his memory:

First there was the daylight air attack on the railway station. There was a munitions train in the station and I could hear cannon fire and wagons blowing up one by one. About a hundred people were queuing up outside my aunt's tobacconist shop in the main square of Halberstadt while the raid was going on. Cigarettes were very scarce in Germany by this time and my aunt had just had a delivery and people were not going to miss out on them even if there was an American raid overhead. Then as the planes flew off they came very low over the town and machine-gunned the main square as they went past. I remember one plane coming over and heading straight for the queue outside my aunt's shop. Then an extraordinary, really quite hilarious thing happened. There was one of those *Plakatsäule*—those continental-style advertising kiosks—in the square, and as the plane headed at them the people in the queue, who were very anxious not to lose their place, simply swung round in a very orderly straight line behind the kiosk and adjusted the angle so that the kiosk was dead between them and the plane; and they just stood there as the plane opened up on them, and when it had gone over—it was so low I remember I could see the pilot's face quite clearly, he looked like a black man—there they still were, not a person out of place, waiting for their cigarettes as if nothing had happened.

Things soon got much more serious. One Saturday morning, I think it was, planes came over and dropped leaflets on the town. The leaflets stated that Halberstadt lay in the way of the Allied advance, and to avoid unnecessary destruction and loss of life the town should surrender without a fight and fly a large white flag from the top of the Rathaus. A plane would fly over the next morning and if the white flag was flying the Allies would know that the town had surrendered and move through it, but if there was no white flag they would wipe it out. Well, the Nazi Kreisleiter refused point blank to surrender the town and when the plane came over on Sunday there was no white flag. So that evening Allied bombers came over and bombed the town to bits.

It was fantastic, that raid. There were no defences and they just bombed at will. I went down into the cellar with my family and all I could hear was the bombs falling and getting closer and closer. Then they hit the house over our heads. There was a tremendous crashing of falling masonry and the cellar was full of choking dust and everyone was coughing because it was impossible to breathe properly. There was a barrel of water in the cellar, I remember, and I tore strips of cloth and dipped them in the water and gave them to people to put over their mouths and noses. We were very lucky because the cellar staircase was still standing and when the air raid was over we managed to get out. We were in a great state of shock. I remember legs poking out through the rubble, and people screaming and everything burning. Then my mother said she was going back into the cellar to get a suitcase of valuables she had left behind and I became completely hysterical. I refused to let her go down. I was in such a state that my mother had to walk with me through the ruined streets to the edge of the smoking town.

The Allies came back the following night. Halberstadt was in such chaos I don't even remember any air-raid sirens going off. I refused to go down into the cellar of the house where we were staying. So my grandmother went down and my mother and I went into an open field. I remember lying in between the furrows in this enormous ploughed field and watching it all go on, the growling of the planes in the sky and then the Christmas trees—the target markers dropped by the pathfinders—falling slowly down. They literally looked like Christmas trees—like huge, very bright, silvery fir trees hanging in the sky, four of them, one in each corner of the square, which was the target, Halberstadt. The planes came over and just bombed into the middle of it and there I was, lying in the field, watching this eerie spectacle.

Halberstadt was such an inferno, it took three days before anybody could go into the town. The Allies laid it absolutely waste. Then one very sunny morning we saw across the fields a convoy of vehicles coming, and as they came closer we saw they were Americans, with little white stars on the side. There was a jeep up front and then tanks and troop carriers, and the bloke in the jeep had both his hands up, and in one hand he had a loaf of bread and in the other a lump of cheese. They came on very slowly, I remember, and as

13

they came the Home Guard threw down their weapons and rushed towards the Americans, and my mother leapt up and started racing over the fields, with me about two hundred yards behind her, straight towards the American column. The man in the jeep turned out to be a very fat American sergeant, and my mother threw her arms around his neck and kissed him and hugged him in absolute joy and relief. It was all over.

On the morning of 25 April the church bells of the town of Salzwedel began to ring the alarm and the air-raid sirens howled ceaselessly over the town as a motorised column of the American 84th Division drew near. The shops were locked and shuttered, the windows of the houses shut, the doors bolted. The only people who dared to come out in the streets that morning were the erstwhile prisoners of the place—some two thousand slave-labourers of various nationalities, a transport of Allied prisoners-of-war, several hundred women from a nearby concentration camp, and a group of Jewish women who had emerged from hiding. They heard the crump of artillery fire, saw columns of dust and smoke rising everywhere, watched the jeeps racing down the road into the town and the squadrons of planes roaring over on their way to distant targets in the east—and knew that the longed-for moment of liberation was at hand. At noon the clouds rolled away, the sun came out and the day promised to be a glorious one. But it did not proceed as they had imagined, and there were those among them who, having survived their many years of captivity, did not outlive their first day of freedom.

Appropriately the first liberating American to reach the tatter-demalion assembly of ex-slaves and prisoners outside the Rathaus was himself a descendant of slaves, a well-built black soldier in steel helmet and shiny brown boots, who drew up in a jeep to an effusive welcome. Frenchmen broke into song, Italians blew kisses, Poles and Ukrainians bowed low and wept, and Hungarian women kissed his hands. The soldier pushed them aside without a word, forcing his way through the crowd. He saw little significance in the occasion or his own role in it. He had a simple task to do and he did it. Walking up to the nearest traffic pole, he nailed up a traffic sign which read: SLOW. Then he took off his helmet to fan himself, paddled his way back through the crowd to his jeep, jumped in, blew his horn and drove off. Thus were the prisoners of Salzwedel delivered out of Nazi hands—and the first dreadful hours of liberty began.

More American liberators followed, rumbling down the streets of the captured town in trucks and tanks. Broad-shouldered young men gazed blankly at the cheering crowds of prisoners, casually returned their greetings by raising their leather gloves to their helmets, and tossed packs of Chesterfield cigarettes from their armoured cars. The Nazis had gone. Though the Stars and Stripes had been hoisted on the Rathaus, the Americans had not taken full charge of the town. The ex-prisoners and slaves seized the opportunity of this short interregnum to give full rein to their pent-up passions, the overriding one of which was a thirst for vengeance against the Germans. Gangs of women smashed windows with their bare fists. Barefoot Rumanians hurled buckets of marmalade out of a smashed shop-front. A wild Russian peasant grabbed handfuls of herrings out of a barrel. A wounded SS man was dragged out of his hiding-place under a car in a garage, was trampled, torn and bitten to death by the mob of ex-prisoners that fell upon him. Mobs poured into houses and threw radios, clocks, mirrors and portraits of German soldiers out of windows. Even the sick dragged themselves from their deathbeds, crawling on hands and knees along the pavement behind the main body of the mob, driven on by an irresistible urge to participate in this ritual act of hatred and revenge.

In the Protestant cemetery the Nazi mayor and his wife and young daughter had been smoked out of their hiding-place in the family vault by a rampaging mob of Russians. The mob tied the mayor to a tombstone, then stripped his wife and daughter almost naked and pulled them by their hair across the grass, while the mayor bucked and screamed like a cock crowing. An elderly, well-mannered Russian in a pilot's jacket and a looted derby hat directed the proceedings. He made the mayor's wife crouch on her hands and knees like an animal and formed the younger Russians into a queue in front of the mayor's huddled daughter. Then he shouted to the mayor in broken German that his own wife had suffered a similar fate in Kharkov during the German advance. There was a moment's silence, then the first man in the queue, a squat Mongolian from Siberia, went down on the young girl and forced his way into her. The mayor uttered a last cry, then tore the tombstone to which he was bound clean out of the ground, and fell dead. His body, still lashed to the tombstone, was thrown into the family vault, the next in line took their turn with his screaming wife and daughter, and the elderly Russian in the derby walked impassively out of the cemetery and left them to their fate.

Christabel Bielenberg, a niece of Lord Northcliffe, the Press baron, was an English woman who had lived in Germany ever since her marriage to a young Hamburg lawyer, Peter Bielenberg, in the year following Hitler's assumption of power. Ever since 1943 she had lived with her three small sons in the remote Black Forest village of Rohrbach, where she had settled down to await the end of the war in an inn called the Gasthaus zum Adler, far from the nightly terror of the air raids on Germany's cities. In February 1945 her husband, who until recently had been confined in Ravensbrück concentration camp because of his membership of the anti-Hitler resistance, fled to Rohrbach and went into hiding high up in the woods on the other side of the valley. There, the Bielenbergs waited as the war drew steadily nearer.

Weary soldiers—exhausted boys in outsized uniforms—were pouring through from the west. Travelling only by night because Allied fighter-bombers made movement by day impossible, they lay up in the Adler till dark, sleeping on the floor with their bazookas on the breakfast table. One dawn, after a night full of the clamour of rumbling wheels and shouts of command, day broke on an extraordinary scene. The 719th Infantry Division had moved in, and with it three generals called Seeger, Bader and Dormagen.

'Overnight the village had become an armed camp,' Christabel recalled.

Every farmhouse had some army vehicle, ingeniously camouflaged with logs and firs, nestling under its protective eaves ... The heavy artillery pieces were drawn by horses and even oxen. Their attendants followed on bicycles, in farm carts, or in small stretcher-like conveyances drawn by Alsatian dogs. Some trudged along on foot, not looking to the right or to the left, not even when two large Mercedes cars forced them with peremptory hooting to stumble on in the ditch. The cars drew up outside the Adler. '*Jawohl, Herr General. Sofort, Herr General!*' Click click, zack zack, three stiff figures, their faces almost hidden by the huge fur collars of their greatcoats, climbed out of the cars. Flashes of scarlet braid and highly polished boots, and they disappeared inside the *Gaststube*.

It seemed the three generals were planning a last-ditch stand. Day after day, while the bored soldiery played interminable games of *Skat*, the generals conferred behind the closed doors of the *Gaststube*. For the Adler their presence brought some compensation, however, in the form of sacks of coffee beans, meat, smoked sausage, bacon and flour. Then one night the Army disappeared as suddenly as it had come, leaving behind its motor transport, drained of petrol and tipped into the fields, and a flotsam of provisions and equipment. After they had gone, the valley that night was alive with scavengers—dancing shadows in the bonfires that flickered as far as the eye could see. A huge white sheet hung from a makeshift flag-pole at the mouth of the valley. It was said that the French were in Furtwangen: there was nothing to do but wait for the conquerors to arrive. 'This longed-for moment,' Christabel Bielenberg wrote later, 'and I could not rejoice, but just stood there silently, watching the bonfires as they dimmed, glowed red, and went out, one by one, up and down the valley.'

Over the next few days the usual symbols of surrender—sheets, towels, tea cloths, white aprons—were displayed or removed according to the rumours of the moment. One night straggling remnants of the soldiery came down from the woods begging for food and civilian clothing, and left before daybreak in ill-fitting cast-offs. The soldiers told of the annihilation of their unit, trapped in a narrow seven-mile gorge and destroyed by bombardment. That news caused all the white drapery of surrender to be hung next day from every window down the valley. The portrait of Hitler was taken down from the Ratszimmer over the village school and burned on the iron stove. Christabel Bielenberg continued:

We waited for four days in a kind of vacuum, wondering who would get us first. When we heard that enemy soldiers had taken Furtwangen, the nearest town to us to the west, we couldn't restrain our impatience any longer and decided to go off on our bicycles to Furtwangen to see for ourselves. It was like a drunken circus along the road. There were hordes of liberated Russian forced labourers, all dressed in clothes they had looted from all the ransacked shops, roaring with laughter and falling all over the road. And there were soldiers in huge army trucks tearing past all over the road in a crazy kind of way—it was a fantastic scene. At first I thought the soldiers were American because they were driving American trucks and smoking Lucky Strike cigarettes. But they weren't Americans, they were French, dressed up in bits and pieces of British Army uniforms.

When we got to Furtwangen it was in pandemonium. All the radios had been requisitioned from their German owners and put in the windows facing outwards towards the street—and each radio was playing a different programme at full blast. All the freed Russians and Poles were waltzing down the street—it was just like a carnival going through the town. The Germans were walking round in a daze wearing white armbands as a sign of surrender. As for the French, it seemed *La Grande Armée* really hardly existed. The troops were not French but Moroccan—magnificent-looking Spahis who had come in on beautiful Arab ponies. These were the men who occupied our area.

That was when the raping started. The Spahis raped up and down our valley in the first few days. Two people were shot trying to protect their wives. Then they moved out and another lot of French colonial troops moved in—Goums from the Sahara, tall, black, strange people in uniforms like grey dressing-gowns. They were terrifying. First they came into Rohrbach and stole all the chickens and my children's rabbits. A few days later they came at night and surrounded every house in the village and raped every female between 12 and 80. Luckily they didn't trouble us—perhaps because of the little Union Jack which I had painted on a piece of paper and put up in the window of the Adler—but Peter slept with an axe next to the bed just in case. What was so frightening about them was the silent way in which they moved. I remember one day I saw them coming up the village street chasing hens—hens and women were the main things they were after, they'd pounce on a hen and then they'd kill it—and they came up to the door and one of them asked: 'Where's your husband?' I said that he was away and as I was talking to them I suddenly realised that one of them was standing right behind me—he had climbed in through a window and crept right up to me through that creaking wooden Black Forest house without making the slightest sound. It was quite extraordinary how they moved.

The reaction of the simple Black Forest country-folk to being occupied by Spahis and Goums was one of sheer terror. 'By comparison,' Peter Bielenberg recounted, 'the black soldiers of the US Army were tremendously popular with the German people. As a result of being under-dogs in America they were humane and sympathetic towards the defeated, and they were the best-behaved soldiers of the Occupation—they were very gentle, they smiled, they gave children sweets.'

The end of the war and the beginning of Occupation government was not a simultaneous event for all the cities and towns of Germany but a staggered progression which followed the Allied front as it moved from west to east. Thus by the time Berchtesgaden (in the far south-east of Germany) was captured and occupied on 5 May Aachen (in the north-west) had been ruled by American Military Government for six months. To take over the running of a flattened German town in the immediate wake of the fighting was a daunting task. One American Military Government officer calculated that in the course of his duties he had written his signature 540,000 times in a month. Most Military Government officers did not know Germany or speak German. Many of the ruined cities had been cut off from their railway lines, electricity grids, and food distribution.

However, with the aid of a skeleton German local government staff the Military Government detachments achieved miracles of improvisation in restoring essential services and law and order to the areas in their charge. Even though there were towns so shattered by bombing that they had almost ceased to exist. Jülich and Düren, two towns on the Roer river which guarded the Cologne plain, had been obliterated. Jülich seemed absolutely devoid of any kind of living thing, and the Military Government officer who had been assigned there threw up his hands in hopelessness. Later he located twelve inhabitants—ten Russians and two Belgian slave-workers who had run away from their SS guards and holed up in the cellars of this ghost-town. The two Belgians had lived a luxurious life. During the day they stayed in the most comfortable cellar they could find and at night they went out to forage. In two months they consumed 22 large tins of meat, 151 eggs, and 200 bottles of cognac and champagne—one bottle of each per man per day. 'We will never forget Jülich so long as we live,' they told the Americans when they finally emerged from their troglodytic life of ease.

In the captured cities of the Rhineland the Military Government detachments could always fall back on the services of the troops for law and order and essential services. But further into Germany, in the wake of the great swathes cut by the advancing armies as they rolled back the German front, there were few troops to hand. Within forty-eight hours of seizing an objective the tactical units would be moving on, leaving the follow-up Military Government—a staff of some ten officers with twenty other ranks to govern a city of up to half a million inhabitants—high and dry. In the remoter areas this could sometimes prove a frightening situation.

Eastward beyond the annihilated Rhineland towns a series of Military Government outposts had been established. Out there, deep in darkest

Germany, lawless and chaotic conditions prevailed in the hiatus between the end of Nazi rule and the establishment of firm Allied government. The main road taken by the Allied advance, the autobahn out to Hanover, bore testimony of the struggle. The outskirts of every town were ringed with zig-zag slit trenches and pockmarked with white, cordite-rimmed mortar craters. There were bombed houses in every village, a shell hole in every church steeple where Allied artillery had shot out the German observation officer.

The roads were jammed with long columns of American petrol tankers and ammunition lorries racing up to the front bumper to bumper in one direction and endless streams of German prisoners-of-war and French, Dutch and Belgian slave-labourers coming away from it in the other. The German prisoners were grim-faced, dusty, dishevelled. The freed slaves, travelling home on foot, on bicycles, by horse and cart or looted motor-cars, even fire-engines, were deliriously happy, waving wildly at any Allied soldiers that passed by and swarming round any who had stopped, excitedly trading schnapps and loot for cigarettes. These slave workers, 10,000,000 of whom had been brought into the Fatherland from the conquered territories of Europe to do industrial labour, farm work and domestic drudgery for their German masters, presented the Allies with one of their biggest and most intractable problems during the advance into Germany.

In January 1945 the only displaced persons (or DPs) in SHAEF hands had been twenty-nine Poles. The number had then increased in leaps. By the end of March there were 145,000, by the middle of April—when the Germans had run out of space in which to herd them—there were a million, two weeks later there were two million, and the total was still rocketing upwards. Before long there were so many that SHAEF had to divert entire divisions of combat troops (like the 29th US Infantry Division) to handle the flow. The Ninth US Army had to provide 200,000 army rations a day to feed them, the First Army a million a month. The problem was not made easier by the DPs' overriding impulse to get away from where they were by any means. An entire advance was held up by one Russian DP clanking home to the USSR on a steam-roller which blocked the road east. Some DPs took to the back roads and formed themselves into bands of thirty or forty and turned to outright banditry. Others simply ran riot.

For many freed slave workers the thirst for alcohol was almost as urgent as the hunger for revenge. Often they drank almost any fluid that came to hand. At Osnabruck many Russian ex-prisoners died after they drank V-2 rocket fuel which they had found in a goods yard. In the railway sidings at Salzwedel a tank car full of alcohol was found by a group of liberated Serbs. Immediately there was a mad fight at the railway yard by hundreds of former prisoners—Serbs, French, Italians, Russians, Poles, Ukrainians.

19

Stumbling over the rails and sleepers, milling around the tanker car, they wrestled with each other while a group of men struggled to open the valve on top of the car and someone else tried to smash a hole in the side with an axe. When the alcohol first spurted out the mob screamed and kicked, bit and punched as they held hats, shoes, mess tins under the jet, opened their mouths under it, and drank from the spreading puddle beside the railway track, scooping the raw chemical liquor up in their hands, or licking it up like animals at a waterhole. Few paid heed to a Czech boy who ran round shouting: 'It's methyl alcohol I tell you! It's poison!'

The saturnalia in Salzwedel would have raged on all day if a fire had not broken out in the main street. When the Americans saw flames licking up the rooftops they decided to act. From the endless motorised army columns streaming east several vehicles detached themselves and headed for the town. Soon an American Town Major arrived. He stood no nonsense, but drove round the streets in an armoured car, firing shots over the heads of the mob. Anyone who resisted was felled with a blow of his fist. Within an hour he had forced the very prisoners whom his comrades had freed from the horrors of Nazi captivity back behind the barbed wire of the camps from which they had broken out. Armed American soldiers were posted guard over them, a curfew was imposed, and a loudspeaker mounted on an armoured car blared out the news that anyone going back to the town would be shot. To alleviate overcrowding, several hundred men, women and children were later that day driven in trucks to a nearby army camp abandoned by the Germans. Here a vast crowd of ragged humanity was quartered in a noisy and airless gymnasium. In one corner a group of girls with yellow and violet 'P's on their blouses were singing traditional Polish songs. In another corner some of the men who had drunk methyl alcohol in the railway yard now lay writhing in agony as the poison took deadly effect. A number went blind, others vomited or were stricken with diarrhoea and relieved themselves where they were. Over the heads of the sick and dying small boys swarmed up the wall bars and swung on the ropes and trapezes. One fell off and plunged to the floor. Fatally injured, he lay screaming for several minutes until some Italians mercifully wrapped his head in a blanket.

Night fell. The methyl alcohol drinkers groaned more loudly in their agony. A crowd of male ex-prisoners broke in among the Polish and Ukrainian women as they lay sleeping. There were sounds of cursing, laughing, crying, whimpering as men and women grappled with each other in a tangled heap on the gymnasium floor. The noises of copulation mingled with the snores of drunken peasants, the lullabies of crooning mothers, the groaning of the sick begging for water, the death rattles of the dying. At three in the morning one of the Italians had an attack of delirium tremens and crawled over the sleepers miaowing, barking and squeaking and banging his head against the wall.

Dawn revealed a scene like a battlefield. Hundreds of bony bodies lay in one great sweating heap on the floor—men in torn shirts and unbuttoned trousers, women with open mouths and chalk-white faces, children grimacing like monkeys in their sleep, corpses already stiffened in the contorted agony of death. At 6 a.m. the westerners—the French, Dutch, Belgians, Luxembourgians and Czechs—were taken out and sent to better accommodation in the former German officers' quarters. Those left behind—the easterners and Axis nationals—muttered angrily and pounded on the locked doors with iron bars. 'We're Allies too!' the Italians shouted. Like rats in a cage the exhausted remnants in the stinking gym turned on each other. Hysterical fighting broke out. The Poles raised the shout: 'Kill the Ukrainians!' A massacre was forestalled by the sudden booming of a voice over the loudspeaker. In five languages the Americans announced that the gymnasium would shortly be inspected. At 8 a.m. a group of high-ranking officers came in. One glance was enough, and they withdrew in horror. Within minutes the order had been given for the children to be taken out into the fresh air and the Italians to carry the dead and dying to the garage.

The loudspeaker suddenly boomed again. Food was on its way, a voice announced, afterwards everybody would be moved to new quarters.

American soldiers opened the gymnasium doors and the inmates poured out into the courtyard. The soldiers formed the crowd into long queues and issued everyone with a spoon and a metal bowl. Jeeps drove up laden with huge dixies of hot soup and—wonder of wonders!—piles of white bread. A limousine disgorged smiling Red Cross nurses in khaki army trousers and zippered white jackets. A sanitary squad disinfected the corpses and carried the sick off to waiting ambulances. A party of soldiers erected an immense bathhouse on the former German Army *Sportsplatz*. Behind separate screens men and women took off their ragged clothes, were dusted with DDT, given an injection, then put under the hot showers. In the men's area a black GI with a gun hanging from a lanyard round his neck handed each man a clean set of underwear and a new suit as he emerged from the shower. Then a sergeant standing at a table gave every ex-prisoner a food parcel and a card inscribed: '*Allied Expeditionary Force—DP Index Card*'. The ex-prisoners came up to the table as if it were an altar and received the DP card like a communion wafer. The men reverently bowed their heads and the women lowered their eyes and smiled coyly at the American sergeant. Next in the chain of human redemption came a black soldier in shorts who dispensed army beds and fluffy blankets from the back of a truck. The ex-prisoners sat down by the courtyard wall in the sun—and then they smiled at each other. 'Suddenly everything seemed so simple, easy, logical,' Tadeusz Nowakowski observed, 'although only a few hours before it had been beyond the range of human imagining . . . Suffering never unites people, it only separates

21

them; only joy can bring them together. There is no fraternity in defeat, the only fraternity is in victory.'

That afternoon the loudspeaker blared again: 'Today is Sunday! In half an hour trucks with field chapels will arrive.'

On the football ground trucks drove up bearing four army chaplains— an Orthodox priest, a Catholic priest, a Rabbi and a Protestant pastor. The trucks parked in a row and their backs were let down to reveal four field altars. The Jewish women gathered by a truck with a golden star on its side; the Russians by a truck carrying golden icons; the Poles and Italians by a truck with an altar to the Virgin Mary in it. Four services began simultaneously. Hymns were played from records broadcast through an immense loudspeaker, but they were soon drowned by the voices of the four congregations, their voices raised in a multitude of languages till they soared and merged into a single great inarticulate lamentation. Timid German bystanders were waved in by an officer and joined the congregation at the Protestant truck. 'My God ...' boomed the loud-speaker, 'Mon Dieu ... Mein Gott ... Mio Dio ... Boze nasz ... Gospody, pomilui ...' SHAEF had produced a short sermon specially written for liberated prisoners. Now it was read through the loudspeaker. 'Alleluia! The Lord is victorious, and the spirit of unrighteousness has been reduced to dust and ashes! ... All you who have been delivered by the victorious Allied armies now are free to return to your own free countries, that you may build a new and better life on the ruins of tyranny and evil ... O Lord who has so miraculously created the dignity of human nature, grant us faith in reconciliation, assure the triumph of love.'

Up in the sky the bombers droned over. Along the road the trucks moved east in an endless column. The sun was shining, a breeze was blowing, the air was warm and smelled of spring.

Other Military Government detachments performed small miracles in restoring the shattered communities for which they were responsible to some sort of running order. They did so by the use of tact, humanity and common sense—and the help of the Germans themselves. One such was in Hanover.

War correspondent Leonard Mosley was appalled by his first sight of this ravaged city. 'Hanover looked like a wound in the earth rather than a city. I could not recognise anywhere; whole streets had disappeared, and squares and gardens with them, covered over in piles of brick and stone and mortar. Several times, the narrow path the bulldozers had cleared to the centre of the city, there was a signpost still hanging with a street name on it; I followed it because I knew it would lead me to the Rathaus.'

The devastated streets were so crowded with people ferrying their household goods on their backs or wheeling them about in wheelbarrows that Mosley had to hoot his way through. Round the green-domed

Rathaus, which still stood more or less intact, there were perhaps as many as two thousand people, waiting patiently and in good humour to get into the building—children, young women, elderly men, soldiers in Wehrmacht uniform; French, Dutch, Polish, Russian and Greek foreign workers; grimy, bearded British POWs arriving from liberated camps in a steady stream of looted German cars. Though Hanover was an American area under the operational control of US First Army, the Military Government at the Rathaus was British. The Military Governor, Major G. H. Lamb, white-haired, ruddy-faced and in his mid-fifties, was clearly there to get a job done and stood no nonsense from anyone. At lunchtime Mosley was driving with him to his suburban mess when their car was blocked by a huge crowd swarming about in a street of half-destroyed factories:

> Scores of fights were going on; men and women were rolling in the gutters, tearing at each other's hair, and at the packages they clutched to their bosoms. The Major didn't even seem surprised to see it.
>
> 'This is the sort of thing that goes on all day,' he said, as if it were a procession instead of a riot. 'Looting, fighting, rape, murder—what a town!'
>
> He brought the car to a halt, got out and took his revolver from its holster. He fired two quick shots in the air. The effect was immediate; the roar of the crowd died away, the fighting ceased, stolen packages were dropped to the ground. Four or five hundred ugly-looking slave-workers and Germans, half of them drunk from stolen wine, turned and looked at him.
>
> The Major waved his revolver. Then in a terrific roar from such a mild and modestly built man: '*Raus!* Go on there—*raus* the whole lot of you before I start firing lower!'

Silence followed. Then the looters in the crowd nodded their heads, saluted the Major, and helped people to their feet whom they had been kicking a few moments ago. Then quietly and quickly they dispersed.

Four more times the Major had to do the same thing before they reached the mess. Looting fever had gripped Hanover. One milling mass of screaming people had broken into a warehouse and ran out with their arms full—of door knobs. They kicked and scratched at those who had more door-knobs than themselves. Naturally the door-knobs were of no conceivable use to anyone, since in bomb-levelled Hanover there were very few doors.

Not all looting was as pointless as this, nor were looters only foreign DPs. The ancient castle of Cziczewicz near Paderborn, for example, was looted of the wealth of generations not by drunken DPs but by swarms of local German women and children amid scenes like something out of the French Revolution. In Steyerberg, in the Weser valley, Alan Moorehead watched villagers and refugees empty a warehouse of the most beautiful wines he had ever seen. In wheelbarrows and handcarts they made off with Margaux and château-bottled Haut-Brion of 1929 vintage, cases of

Château d'Yquem, Amontillado sherries of 1911. 'Half-demented children were romping among the really great prizes of the place—a Rothschild Chateau Lafite 1891—and this was in the magnum, jeroboam and the rehoboam, which is the most beautiful kind of bottle in the world and on account of its size very easily dropped and smashed.' By morning the place was ankle-deep in a slush of fine wines.

The looting fever was not confined to the undisciplined rabbles of DPs or German civilians. It was also endemic among the advancing Allied armies. The war was still on and it seemed eminently natural and time-hallowed to help oneself to the enemy's goods and chattels, and sometimes his women.

Even the staidest middle-aged English officers caught the bug. They went into German farmhouses and took carpets from floors, pictures from walls, wine from wine cellars, silver from sideboards, cheeses from larders, and chickens from yards.

Among the American spearhead troops, eggs suddenly became an obsession, more highly prized for a while than champagne or schnapps. Infantrymen and stretcher-bearers alike ransacked every new village and country town they came to, breaking into the chicken coops and demanding eggs at gunpoint. Sometimes they took forty or fifty at a time and ate ten or twelve at a sitting. Even in bombed-out cities far from a chicken-run the soldiers pursued their obsession. 'You want jewellery?' a nervous Cologne housewife asked an American soldier who accosted her soon after the city fell. 'Naw, keep it, I ain't no looter,' the GI replied. 'But you got any eggs? I'll take eggs.' The craze seemed catching. American Military Government officer Frank Gabell remembered: 'I was in charge of a small German town when Montgomery's headquarters came and stayed for a week. All orders to German civilians had to be issued by me and not even Montgomery or his staff could do so. One day one of the Field Marshal's staff came to me with a request: 'Would you please have two dozen fresh eggs delivered to the English officers' mess each morning?' And this with the war at its peak, artillery blasting all around. I had studied military government for at least a year and this request floored me. I burst out laughing. But I saw to it that Montgomery's mess had two dozen fresh eggs each morning delivered by a local farmer.' Some soldiers with a sharper eye for business—officers mostly—looted things for the profit they yielded on the black market in Brussels, the biggest in liberated Europe. Some specialised according to demand. One young officer took adding machines and sporting guns. Another had already taken five car loads of ball-bearings from Germany to Brussels, and made several other trips with slaughtered cows in the back of his car. Cars in particular were at a premium. A 50-year old British officer explained how to get hold of one: 'It's no use going to garages. Field security and Military Government usually put a sentry on those. What you do is drive around until you see a house with a garage. Then you get the owner and take the key off him. He's probably hidden the battery and the tyres, but if you show him a little persuasion he'll cough up quick enough.'

In this way most of the officers of the British divisions advancing through Germany, from the divisional commander downwards, had acquired cars, sometimes even two or three cars, for themselves. One division, making a rapid advance in one of the last actions of the war, was found to be twice its normal length because of all the German cars it had picked up, and there were traffic jams throughout the division's area. The divisional commander was obliged to order his military police to stop all unauthorised cars, drive them off the road and fix them so that they would never get back on it again. In the next few hours scores of cars were driven into the fields, where the military police fired tommy-guns into their tyres and cylinder heads, sprinkled them with petrol and set them on fire.

But the most grievous losses suffered by the German populace at this time were not due to private greed or revenge but to official policy arising out of military necessity. When British or American soldiers wanted accommodation, there was no question of taking rooms with a German family. The rule was strict: the Germans were given immediate notice to quit.

Clearly the military units of an invading army could not be expected to share their billets with enemy subjects. But there were times when it seemed exceptionally harsh to push an obviously harmless German family on to the streets with nowhere to go. On such occasions the regulations were ignored, and everyone was happy—the German family was safe from DPs for as long as the soldiers stayed, and the soldiers had someone to do their cooking and their washing for them. For Leonard Mosley, guest of the military governor of the city of Hanover, there could be no such compromise. If he was going to stay in the city it would have to be in a whole house from which the occupants had been evicted. With heavy heart he accompanied the requisitioning officer, a Canadian Captain, to his new quarters—a small modern dwelling in a miraculously undamaged street of modest working-class houses. The Canadian rang the door bell and an attractive teenage girl answered it. 'You speak English?' asked the Captain.

'A little,' the girl replied. 'Please?'

'It is now two o'clock. You will leave your home by three o'clock, for this officer.'

'Please?' the girl said again. '*Ach Gott, was ist?*—Mama! Mama!' She ran back into the house.

The captain turned to the war reporter. 'Can't afford to give them more than an hour,' he said. 'Gives them too much time. They take everything. You got a radio?'

Mosley nodded.

'Guess we'll let them take their radio, then. Sheets? Okay, let them take their sheets. But nothing else. Wonder if they've got any wine?'

By 3.15 the German family had moved out and Mosley and his friend had moved in. The Canadian Captain had come several times for a drink and cast an eye over the contents of the house while he was there.

One day a squad of British soldiers arrived at the house, tore the stove from the wall and carted it off to replace a broken one in the British officers' mess. To the protesting mother a Dutch sergeant summed up the situation with brutal simplicity: '*Meine Frau,* you will not be going back to your house for a long time. It has been requisitioned. It is not your house any longer. You will not need to worry about your stove for a long time. You will not have a house to put one in.'

So the Allied advance continued in one of the speediest and most over-whelming pursuits in the history of war. In a single day the 351st Infantry Division of the Ninth US Army advanced 220 miles and the 10th Armored Division of the Third US Army captured twenty-eight towns. In its enthusiasm and impatience the 329th Infantry Division commandeered German trucks, fire-engines, cement-mixers, horse-wagons and buses to speed up its eastward advance along roads choked with civilians—some fleeing east to escape the Russians, some west to escape the Anglo-Americans. To facilitate the advance, Allied commanders made phone calls from public telephone boxes to the next town in line, ordering the Mayor to surrender or see the town wiped out. Sometimes they dropped special bombs or fired special shells into the towns with messages that spelled out the same alternatives.

By now the cities were a mess of ruins—'Pompeiis petrified by the volcano of modern war', as one British officer put it—but the countryside looked untouched by war. The cattle and horses were sleek, the pigs fat, the chickens abundant. It was a country of gabled hamlets and church spires, fairy-tale woods and valleys filled with wild flowers and trout streams. The tanks raced eastward between orchards in full blossom, through forests redolent of pine gum. But the bucolic innocence of the landscape belied the depth of evil which the German interior had kept hidden from the invaders till now.

2

A Fine Hell

As the Allied advance continued the Third Reich began to spew out its hidden horrors. The existence of the Nazi concentration camps had been known to the world at large since the 1930s. The exact nature of such camps had been fully revealed when the Red Army overran Majdanek and other death camps in Poland late in 1944 and had been known to the inner cabinets of the British and American governments and to the Pope for a good deal longer. But until the last month of the war the soldiers of the British and American armies had had no direct experience of these places and the horrors they contained. Then, as they overran the camps in Germany one by one and saw the bestialities of Nazism with their own eyes, their attitude to Germany and the Germans underwent a violent change. If any of them had ever wondered why they were fighting in this war they were finally given their answer in Buchenwald, Belsen, Dachau and other camps whose names have remained synonymous with the lowest moral point ever reached by civilised man.

On 6 April the Americans reached Ohrdruf-Nord, a satellite work camp for the larger concentration camp at Buchenwald. They found ninety bodies there, including twenty-nine prisoners who had been shot in the back of the neck a few hours before, and an American airman who had died of typhus. It was the first camp to fall to the Allies and was considered sufficiently important for General Eisenhower and his top American commanders, Generals Patton and Bradley, to pay a flying visit. They were physically as well as mentally nauseated—Patton actually vomited—and more angry than they had ever been in the war.

On 11 April the Americans overran Nordhausen concentration camp in the Harz Mountains. By now the scale of horror had begun to escalate: there were 3,000 unburied bodies stacked like logs many feet high at Nordhausen, and 2,000 survivors in the last stages of starvation. Even the most battle-hardened troops were shattered, and one American sergeant admitted: 'It was like stepping into the Dark Ages.' That same day other American units reached Buchenwald, near Weimar. They found 21,000 prisoners who had taken the camp over from their SS guards and gruesome evidence of the sadism of the SS camp system: meat hooks on which to hang prisoners, incinerators in which to cremate them, piles of bones and skulls, and lampshades and bookends decorated with tattooed human skin from some of the 55,000 men who had died there—the hobby, it was alleged of a former commandant's wife, Ilse Koch. But if Buchenwald was to shatter the average American soldier, and Dachau (where the GIs found 33,000 inmates so starved that they were too weak to move) even more so, nothing could match the descent into hell experienced by the British soldiers in their march on Lüneburg a few days later.

The spearhead of the British advance towards Lüneburg and Hamburg had been blocked by an unusual problem at a place called Belsen, a mile or two from a German army command at Bergen. Belsen was a concentration camp: the German Army at Bergen had forewarned the British that a full-blown epidemic of typhus had broken out among the prisoners in the camp and that it would be in the best interests of everybody if they bypassed the place. On 15 April the German Army Commander at Bergen–Belsen concluded a truce with the General commanding the British VIII Corps, under which it was agreed that Belsen was to be treated as a neutral zone by both sides, i.e. no shots were to be fired out of it or into it. A battalion of German infantry and a Hungarian Regiment would remain at the camp to guard the perimeter and prevent a mass break-out of typhus-infested inmates, and fifty SS men, acting in a purely administrative capacity, would be waiting there to hand over the camp to the British holding party while the main body of the British spearhead carried on past the place.

It was the British view that before anything else was done the prisoners in Belsen should be fully informed as to what was happening. The officer in charge of Loudspeaker Unit No. 14 was therefore instructed to drive forward with the leading British tanks, enter the camp and make an announcement by loudspeaker to the prisoners inside. This officer was Captain Derrick Sington, a linguist and journalist in uniform, and his Loud-speaker Unit consisted of a van with a battery of enormous loudspeakers mounted on the top of it, and two NCOs—Sergeant Eric Clyne, a Jewish *émigré* from Berlin, and Lance-Corporal Sidney Roberts, a London cockney.

Sington's Loudspeaker Unit set off at once and soon caught up with the long cavalcade of Sherman tanks, scout-cars and Bren carriers of the 23rd Hussars which was proceeding up the main road north-east to Bergen amid a din of exhausts and clanking tank tracks. The loudspeaker lorry fell into line, drove slowly forward through woods of fragrant fir and eventually arrived at the edge of the Belsen neutral zone, which was clearly marked with white notices: DANGER TYPHUS.

Inside the concentration camp the inmates heard the clanking sound of tanks drawing nearer. Rudolf Kürstermeier, a German socialist and anti-Nazi journalist who had been a political prisoner in prisons and camps since 1933, recalled that morning in Belsen:

> I was awakened suddenly by one of the Russian workers in our block. 'Come on! Come on! Quickly! Quickly! There are tanks on the road!'
> Only a narrow strip of wood separated the camp from the road outside. No shot was to be heard, only the grinding and rattling and roaring of the tanks. But what tanks were they? Some of us noticed the white star on the sides.
> 'That is not the British mark!'
> 'Perhaps they are Canadian?'
> Somebody suggested that they were Russian, another that they were Australian and one man even ventured: 'Chilean!' I ended the speculation by saying: 'They are Allied tanks. Nothing else matters!'
> Unable to stand any longer I went back to bed. In the distance I heard the tanks pass the camp gate and a voice calling from a loud-speaker van. I knew that we were free.

Captain Sington's unit turned a bend in the road and saw ahead the entrance to the Belsen camp—a single pole across the roadway on either side. A group of smartly dressed officers stood waiting in front of it—a bull-like German officer with a red moustache, a Hungarian captain, and a powerfully built SS-Hauptsturmführer with a scar across one cheek. The officers saluted as Sington clambered out. He asked them about the state of the camp.

'They are calm at present,' replied the SS officer, Josef Kramer, the Camp Commandant, a man previously responsible for selecting Jews for the gas chambers at Auschwitz.

'I propose to go in and make a loudspeaker announcement,' Sington told him in German.

'They're calm now. It would be unwise to risk a tumult,' Kramer replied.

'What type of prisoners have you got in here?' Sington asked him.

'Homosexuals and professional criminals, as well as some *Bibel Forscher.*' (Bibel Forscher were members of a pacifist religious sect.)

'And political prisoners?'

'Oh yes, there are the *Häftlinge,*' Kramer said in a friendly confiding way.

'What's the total?'

'Forty thousand in this camp and fifteen thousand more in the overflow camp in the barracks up the road.'

Sington told Kramer to open the gate. He looked taken aback.

'I can't do that without authority from the Wehrmacht commandant,' he protested.

Sington waved to him with his hand to lift the barrier. The barrier went up.

'Stand on the running board,' Sington ordered. Kramer mounted it. 'You have to guide us round the camp, stopping at suitable points to make loudspeaker announcements.'

They drove through the barrier. Two hundred yards further they reached a high wooden gate with criss-cross wiring. It reminded Sington of the entrance to a zoo. Once through the gate this resemblance was strengthened. On the left of the thoroughfare stood row upon row of green wooden huts, and they came into a smell of ordure—like the smell of a monkey-house.

A strange simian throng crowded to the barbed-wire fences surrounding the compounds. They had shaven heads and striped penitentiary suits. Sington had experienced gratitude and welcome from liberated people in France, Belgium and Holland. But this was different.

'The half-credulous cheers of these almost lost men,' Derrick Sington wrote later, 'of these clowns in their terrible motley, who had once been Polish officers, land-workers in the Ukraine, Budapest doctors, and students in France, impelled a stronger emotion, and I had to fight back my tears.'

As they carried on through the camp, crowds of prisoners began to surge through the barbed wire into the main thoroughfare and Kramer leaned forward and said: 'Now the tumult is beginning.'

A German soldier opened fire just over the heads of the prisoners. Sington ran at him with revolver drawn and ordered him to stop.

'He stopped firing,' Sington wrote, 'but suddenly a dozen striped figures jumped into the crowd, hitting again and again with sticks and packing-case strips. No leaps in a ballet could have astonished me as did these kangaroo jumps. They were like prancing zebras, these creatures in broad-striped garments, careering here and there, smiting to left and right, bending double with the impetus of the blows they struck. Half-way across the road I saw a thin creature on his back trying to ward off blow after blow from a thick stick.'

The men were the trusties, block leaders called '*Capos*' who, though prisoners themselves, kept order for the SS in return for various privileges. They were trying to keep back the stampeding mob making for the big camp kitchen. 'I did not yet understand,' Sington wrote later, 'that mortal starvation conditioned all happenings in the camp.' He drove on. French women were crying out to him: 'You must deliver us. It is FRIGHTFUL, this camp.' A wraith-like figure with a crutch threw away his crutch and fell on his knees, clasping his hands in thanksgiving. The truck turned through a barbed-wire gateway, entered one of the two women's camps, halted and began an announcement:

'The Germans have nothing more to do with this camp. The camp is now under the control of the British Army.' At this point a great cheer went up which continued for one or two minutes. Sington recalled: 'In a few seconds the car was surrounded by hundreds of women. They cried and wailed hysterically, uncontrollably, and no word from the loudspeakers could be heard.' The compounds of the camp were planted with young birch trees, and the women plucked sprigs and small branches and hurled them on to the car. They drove back to the main entrance. Kramer jumped off the running board and Sington said to him: 'You've made a fine hell here.'

Captain Sington's Unit was now joined by a few more British officers and NCOs, including the Chief Medical Officer of the Second British Army, Brigadier Glyn Hughes, and Colonel Taylor, commanding the 63rd Anti-Tank Regiment, who had been given the daunting job of British camp commandant at Belsen. Colonel Kramer was told: 'For every inmate of the camp who is shot one SS man will be executed.' Shots were ringing out from the far end of the camp. Prisoners were being killed at the very hour of liberation.

Hundreds of pyjama-clad figures were milling about on the highway. Some of them cried out in English: 'God save the King!' and 'How do you do?' Suddenly Sington heard screaming coming from a potato patch. Lying on the straw was a man in agony. The upper part of his body was jerking up and down. Then he fell still and stopped screaming.

Sington looked at Kramer. 'Pick up that man and take him to the hospital,' he ordered.

The SS commandant flushed, threw back his head and stepped back a pace.

'Pick up that man!' Sington covered Kramer with his revolver. Kramer moved forward and stooped down. Sington pushed the revolver into his back as he slung the body over his shoulder and lumbered off. It was getting dark. The first afternoon of liberation was drawing to an end. Bright-eyed women called to the Tommies: 'Good night, boys!' Sington recalled: 'It was like some fantastic closing-time.'

In those first few unforgettable hours the British had only had time to make a most cursory inventory at Belsen concentration camp. Nor until the next day did the full extent and depth of the horror and human degradation of this dreadful place become fully apparent—and with it the unprecedented magnitude of the medical and logistical challenge confronting the British Army.

Eight hundred inmates died the day the British arrived at Belsen. That left about 40,000 alive or half-alive in the main camp. Of these 25,000 were women, 18,000 of them Jewesses who had been evacuated to Belsen from Auschwitz and the German slave-labour camps as a result of the advance of the Allied armies from east and west. In addition there were 2,000 Russian women forced labourers who had been sent to concentration camps for acts of defiance, together with several thousand women who had been arrested by the Gestapo for their part in the resistance to the German occupation in France and other countries. The 15,000 men in Belsen consisted of Jews, *réfractaires* and political prisoners, some of them German. There was also a handful of British and Americans. Belsen had originally been a Russian prisoner-of-war camp and many thousands of Russians had died there. Towards the end of the war it had become an emergency overflow camp for evacuated inmates of other camps and because the war situation had interrupted supplies there had been no proper food for months, and for the last four days no food or fresh water at all. Then typhus had broken out, followed by typhoid. Over a quarter of the people found alive were to die in this pestilential hole in the following four weeks, mostly of typhus, dysentery, starvation and exhaustion of body and spirit.

One woman, distraught to the point of madness, came to the milk store, and asked for some milk for her baby. The soldier took the baby and saw that it was black in the face and shrivelled up and had been dead for days. The mother continued to beg for milk so he poured some between its dead lips and the mother carried the child off, crooning with joy. But she had only gone a few yards when she stumbled and fell dead to the ground. There were worse scenes inside the overcrowded blocks where women lay overlapping each other on the bare floor amid a stench of sweat and excrement. Many had dysentery, and in each hut compound there were never less than half a dozen women openly defecating amid the litter of old rags, rotting boots and little black turnips like cannon-balls.

Under the birch trees in distant corners of the camp lay tangled heaps of naked corpses. The SS had made great efforts to dispose of the bodies of the 17,000 inmates who had died before the British arrived. They had burned many of them in a gigantic, stinking funeral pyre, and tossed others into a mass grave. But the prisoners died more quickly than they could be buried and when the British arrived there were ten thousand corpses still lying unburied. From some of the corpses the brains, heart and livers had been cut out and eaten by the starving survivors. The SS staff were formed into a burial party to collect the bodies and bury them. The inmates greeted their former guards with howls of execration wherever they went. Some were so tired that they fell exhausted among the corpses. If any of them tried to run away the British soldiers, filled with an implacable anger, shot them to death.

When they were not gathering corpses the SS guards were kept locked up in cells. War correspondent Alan Moorehead was taken to meet them. The women guards, who had been more sadistic than the men, struck him as uniformly ugly and in some cases distinctly cretinous. The SS men were evidently having a rough time. A member of the French underground had been sent specially to interrogate them.

'I'm afraid they are not a pretty sight,' an English captain told Moorehead.

A sergeant unbolted a door and pulled it back with a loud crack. He strode into the cell jabbing a metal spike in front of him.

'Get up!' he shouted. 'Get up; get up, you dirty bastards!'

Some of the SS men had faces and shirts splattered with blood. They had great difficulty in standing up and swayed on their feet or trembled violently. The English captain took Moorehead to see the SS doctor.

'He's a nice specimen,' said the captain. 'He invented some of the tortures here. He had one trick of injecting creosote and petrol into the prisoners' veins. He used to go round the huts and say: 'Too many people in here. Far too many.' Then he used to loose off his revolver round the hut.'

The SS doctor lay in his own blood, a massive figure with a bedraggled beard.

'Why don't you kill me?' he whispered, struggling painfully to his feet and flinging wide his arms. 'Why don't you kill me? I can't stand any more.'

The same phrases, Moorehead recalled, dribbled from his lips repeatedly.

Order began to return to Belsen concentration camp. In the first few hours the prisoners had taken matters into their own hands. They had kicked to death the unpopular *'Capos'*. They had slaughtered Colonel Kramer's pigs. They had stormed and looted the food and clothing store. Some of them had pitched SS tents under the trees and moved into them out of the hell of the huts. The rest was up to the British, who treated Belsen as one of the direst emergencies that ever confronted a British Army.

Men of the Oxfordshire Yeomanry arrived to reinforce the Anti-Tank Regiment. People crowded round them to kiss their hands and feet. The hated Kramer was led off through the camp in manacles. Food, water and medical supplies were rushed in. Field ambulance units, field hygiene units, casualty clearing stations, a mobile bacteriological laboratory, a nutritional team, mobile shower units, medics, hospital teams, Red Cross nurses and 97 British medical students in UNRRA uniforms arrived to care for the sick and dying. Among the inmates were found 50 doctors and 150 trained nurses, though all but a few were too ill or demoralised to help their British colleagues. The blocks were cleaned up, disinfected and deloused, and the inmates were sorted out according to nationality and state of life or death. The typhus cases began to be moved to an improvised hospital outside the camp. Emergency cases were treated in the SS pharmacy and the dysentery cases fed on Bengal famine mixture.

The ghastly job of stripping the inmates and moving them out of the huts fell on the soldiers of No. 11 Light Field Ambulance. The sights and smells inside the huts were so awful that the men could only work in them for ten minutes at a time, and though they wore protective clothing twenty of them went down with typhus. The uninfected were sent in batches to the bath-house, dusted with delousing powder, and taken by lorries, a thousand or so a day, to new accommodation in the large Panzer Training Barracks at Bergen a mile down the road. But with the best will in the world it took time to treat and evacuate 40,000 people caught up in a human calamity beyond anyone's experience. Even the simple logistics were daunting—750 new beds had to be found from somewhere every day, for example, to keep pace with hospital admissions.

Something like 500 people a day continued to die as more became infected with typhus and the dying succumbed to weakness and dysentery. Bulldozers were brought up to shovel the corpses into great pits.

On 24 April the German mayor of Celle and other towns round about were summoned, as representatives of the German people, to view the horrors of Belsen. They were led to the edge of the burial pit, which was half full of corpses and skeletons, and the SS men and women were paraded on the other side of the grave. The Military Government officer in charge of non-medical work in the camp, Colonel Spottiswoode, then read a statement in German which was broadcast across the whole camp through Derrick Sington's loudspeaker car: 'What you will see here is the final and utter condemnation of the Nazi Party. It justifies every measure which the United Nations will take to exterminate that Party. What you will see here is such a disgrace to the German people that their name must be erased from the list of civilised nations. You stand here judged by what you will see in this camp. It is your lot to begin the hard task of restoring the name of the German people to the list of civilised nations. But this cannot be done until you have reared a new generation amongst whom it is impossible to find people prepared to commit such crimes. We will now begin our tour.' One German mayor covered his face with his hand and wept as the Colonel spoke; another was sick.

For months afterwards the problem of treating 12,000 critically ill people and feeding and caring for 15,000 others remained a continuously pressing one for the 3,000 British soldiers who were entrusted with the task. For many of the survivors there remained the struggle to regain mental health and rejoin normal society. For some it was a long climb back; for some, deranged by their experiences in the camps, the loss of loved ones or the after-effects of typhus, it proved impossible. Block 27 of the hospital area at the Panzer Training School had to be made into a lunatic asylum. The woods near the former Wehrmacht Theatre were used as a cemetery where some of the 13,000 prisoners of Belsen who did not survive their liberation were buried.

It was not only the former inmates of Belsen who were condemned to bear the scars of the place for a long time after. Many of their liberators were also profoundly affected by what they had seen there. 'Why? Why? Why?' Alan Moorehead asked himself. 'Why had it happened? With all one's soul one felt: 'This is not war. Nor is it anything to do with here and now, with this one place at this one moment. This is timeless and all mankind is involved in it. This touches me and I am responsible. Why has it happened? How did we let it happen?' Captain Peter Fabian, on special detachment from the 49th West Riding Division, was in Belsen shortly after the British entered the place and stayed there to help for more than a week. He has never got over it:

> I was very near a nervous breakdown. I was paralysed by the whole thing. To me it was completely beyond tears—unless you feel you can cry when humanity dies. To my way of thinking it was humanity itself which had died this inglorious death of degradation and filth in Belsen . . . I remember one day a group of VIPs came to inspect the new hospital accommodation at the Panzer Training Barracks. They were shown the laundry where all the bodies were washed and sorted out. Then they were shown into the hospital wards in the former German Officers' Mess, where the worst cases of starvation were treated. I still remember the magnificent parquet floor, so shiny and spotless you could see your face in it, and now covered with rows and rows of beds all very smart and crisp and clean. The VIPs walked past the beds taking a detached, sympathetic interest in the people who were lying there—most of whom were going to be dead within 48 hours or so— and as they passed one bed a woman jumped out of bed, pulled up her smock and did a crap on the floor right in front of them, on this beautiful parquet floor. She did it with complete lack of concern. To her it was the most natural thing in the world to do. She wanted a shit at that moment so she had a shit at that moment, because that is what she had been doing for years. She was a German, too, from a civilised background—not a gipsy used to living rough.
>
> That was the first shock. The mess was cleared up and half an hour later came another shock. We stopped in front of a woman wriggling violently about in her bed and when we took the bedclothes off there was a live pig in the bed. We took the pig away from her and the woman screamed her head off. It was food to her, you see. Hunger psychosis. Even though they now had enough to eat they still felt hungry, still stole food and hoarded it. Many of them had piles of loaves under their beds, all going mouldy.
>
> We went through a very bad spell afterwards. We were drunk every night for quite a few months. I've never been able to shake off a certain distaste for Germany ever since. But you can't blame the Germans entirely for it. Some of them organised it all but some of the ones who carried it out were not German at all. Even the SS were victims of the situation, were being hardened into being beasts against their will. I'm afraid it could happen again—and probably has in Korea and Algeria and Vietnam and elsewhere. I'm sure it could even have happened here, in England.

Most Germans disclaimed all prior knowledge of the atrocities of the camps. But many Allied soldiers frankly disbelieved them. In Dachau town, for instance, the prisoners of the nearby concentration camp were marched or taken by train right through the middle of the town. The small concentration camp at Thekla, near Leipzig, was directly overlooked by

German houses. Some Germans did admit they knew something dreadful was going on in the camps but claimed there was nothing they could do about it. The farmer who delivered the turnips and carrots which were the only food available to the inmates of Belsen in the last months was careful never to ask what was happening behind the barbed wire, he said, for fear of ending up inside the camp himself. General Eisenhower and his Allied Commanders were so enraged by the atrocities in the camps that they ordered the citizens of local German towns to help bury the dead. At Eisenhower's insistence 1,000 German men of Gardelegen were appointed to bury the 1,000 political prisoners who had been locked in a barn and burned to death near the town. Each German was responsible for burying one prisoner and tending the grave for ever more; the name of the German as well as the victim was inscribed on the headstone.

As for Derrick Sington, the first Allied officer to enter Belsen, he stayed in the camp until August. On his second day he met Gertrude Neumann, a great-niece of Franz Kafka who from behind the wire had watched his arrival the day before. She had arrived in Belsen two weeks previously after surviving three and a half years in Theresienstadt and Auschwitz and forced labour in Hamburg during the air raids. Unlike many who had spent far longer in the camp, she was neither emaciated nor demoralised and she had been made a hut leader. Derrick Sington appointed her his interpreter, then his unofficial secretary. He took to eating his bully-beef sandwiches at lunch-time sitting on the end of one of the bunks in her hut. Finally, after three more years spent in war crimes work and newspaper work in Germany the couple married and left the ruins of the Reich and the memories of Nazi tyranny for the north London suburb of Neasden—a far cry from the theory and practice of hell.

The relief of Belsen began on the same day that the Red Army launched its final assault on Berlin. For the last few weeks of the European war the soldiers of the Allied Expeditionary Force were thus to feel in their hearts the rage and anger their Russian comrades had known for years—and were now to slake in Hitler's embattled capital.

On 11 April the armoured vanguard of Simpson's Ninth US Army reached the Elbe near Magdeburg and secured a bridgehead on the other side after a lightning advance of 57 miles since daybreak. Simpson's forces were now only 53 miles from Berlin and facing only light opposition. If Churchill hoped to persuade Roosevelt to put pressure on Eisenhower to change his mind about Berlin, now was the time. But fate intervened. On the morning of 12 April, while Ninth Army tanks were rumbling across the east bank of the Elbe, Roosevelt collapsed at his home in Warm Springs, and in the afternoon he died. 'At that time,' Bradley reported later, 'we could probably have pushed on to Berlin . . . Zhukov had not yet crossed the Oder, and Berlin lay midway between our forces.' In Simpson's opinion his lead divisions in Ninth Army could drive straight down the autobahn and be in Berlin in twenty-four hours. According to the *Washington Post* American advance patrols had already reached Potsdam and there was nothing between Simpson and Hitler except Eisenhower. On 14 April Eisenhower decided to hold the main line of the Allied advance along the River Elbe and wait for the Russians there. He ordered Simpson back across the river. That same day the Russians captured Vienna. Two days later, while Patton and Patch were racing south in the direction of Hitler's house and the National Redoubt that never was, the Russians opened their last offensive on the Oder and began their great advance on Berlin.

3

Storm

Spring in Berlin, 1945. Through the fire-blackened ruins the scent of lilac rose in waves out of derelict gardens whose owners had fled or died. Crocuses struggled out of the rubble. The stumps of trees amputated by the bombing were bursting with green leaf. Only the birds were missing. There were no sparrows in the eaves, no thrushes singing in the Tiergarten. The birds had heard the rumble of the guns growing hourly nearer: a rumble which steadily grew into a roar.

The war was rolling towards Berlin from the east like a storm. Nobody mentioned the word 'Russian' any more: 'they', the unmentionable, would be at the city gates soon enough. Not that there was any hard news from the front. The radio had been dead for days. The taps ran dry, the gas spluttered a dying flame. A cold wind from Silesia knifed through the glassless windows of the bombed-out apartment blocks, rattling the blackout blinds. In backyards and waste lots the women and children filled handkerchiefs and hats with nettles and dandelion leaves for the pot. Down in the streets the barricades were guarded by elderly Volksturm (Home Guard) men in patched uniforms and by children wearing coal-scuttle steel helmets. German soldiers, weary to death, trudged through the streets to the front, out of step and dragging their feet. In the east the sky was the colour of fire.

On 21 April central Berlin came under direct Russian artillery fire for the first time. In ironic salute for Hitler's birthday several Red Army salvoes were hurled into Hermannplatz, killing a number of people queuing outside Karstadt's department store. Hitler was shocked to hear shells exploding near the Reich Chancellery.

The Russians were nearer than he had dared believe. One spearhead was on the Havel river, only fifteen miles north of the city. Another was at Baruth, twenty miles to the south. By 21 April Russian tanks were pouring into the suburbs of the capital and there was no power on earth—certainly not the remnants of the German Army or any fanatical appeal to resistance by Adolf Hitler—that could stop them. The battle for Berlin had reached a crucial stage—and it was clear that it would be fought inside the city itself.

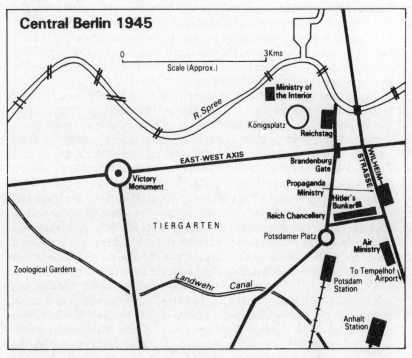

Central Berlin 1945

The great Soviet offensive had begun five days previously. On 16 April the Russians had let loose a huge artillery bombardment of the German front along the Oder and Neisse rivers, fifty miles to the east of the capital. Nearly 17,000 guns, mortars and Katyusha multiple rocket-launchers (called 'Stalin Organs' by the Germans) had opened fire at dawn in a volley so devastating that it could be heard all the way to Berlin. Three Russian Army Groups, called Fronts, were ranged along the east banks of the Oder and Neisse, supported by three Red Air Armies with nearly 6,700 planes. In the centre, on the middle Oder directly facing Berlin, was Marshal Georgy Zhukov's 1st Belorussian Front—eleven armies (with General Vasily Chuikov's crack Eighth Army Guards as spearhead), totalling 768,000 men and nearly 1,800 tanks. On Zhukov's left, on the Neisse to the south, was Marshal Ivan Konev's 1st Ukrainian Front—seven armies totalling over 500,000 men and 1,400 tanks. Still assembling on Zhukov's right, along the lower Oder, were the three armies of Marshal Konstantin Rokossovky's 2nd Belorussian Front—314,000 men and over 640 tanks.

Zhukov's and Konev's forces were committed to the attack on Berlin itself, Rokossovky's to the protection of Zhukov's northern flank and the conquest of the north German plain. Over 3,800 tanks and one and a half million Soviet soldiers were thus poised to invade the Reich from the east—one and a quarter million of them bound for the capital. Behind them were a million more troops of the support units, and another 2,300 tanks, making a grand total of 2,500,000 men and 6,250 tanks ultimately committed to the battle for Berlin—then the third largest city in the world and the biggest ever to be stormed by force of arms.

Against the formidable weight of the Red Army the Wehrmacht could muster only two exhausted, under-strength armies from Army Group Vistula under General Gotthard Heinrici (the Third Panzer Army under General Hasso von Manteuffel and the Ninth Army under General Theodor Busse, comprising some 400,000 men in all) and the Fourth Panzer Army (the most northerly formation of Field Marshal Ferdinand Schörner's Army Group Centre in Czechoslovakia). The Germans were outnumbered by a ratio of 5 to 1 in men, 5 to 1 in tanks, 3 to 1 in planes, and 15 to 1 in guns. But though the odds against the Germans were next to hopeless Hitler was determined that Berlin should be defended fanatically shell-hole by shell-hole to the last man and the last bullet—a decision which would ensure the final destruction of the city and the slaughter of countless thousands of civilians caught up in the holocaust.

To most of Hitler's generals, the idea of fighting inside the city was anathema. This was partly because the battle for Berlin would be decided outside the city and fighting in the streets could only delay the inevitable outcome by a few days; and partly because Berlin was not defensible anyway. Not until the month preceding the Soviet assault was work started on erecting defences against a ground attack. Trenches were dug and roadblocks thrown up in the streets and parks. A three-ring defence system was organised: an outer ring which followed the line of the autobahn ring road at a radius of twenty miles from the city centre; a second ring which followed the elevated commuter railway line known as the S-Bahn at a distance of ten miles from the centre; and an inner ring which followed the perimeter of the city centre round the government quarter and the park known as the Tiergarten—an area designated as the Citadel.

Hitler had declared Berlin a fortress—the last of a long line of fortresses. But the fortifications earned the derision of the Berliners who were to be defended by them. 'It will take the Russians two hours and five minutes to get past a road block in Berlin,' they scoffed. 'Two hours laughing at it and five minutes pushing it aside.' There were few trained troops to hold the city, few tanks, little artillery and no planes. Many of the rifles were foreign ones for which no compatible ammunition could be found; when ammunition could be found it was limited to an average of five rounds per rifle. The principal weapon was the Panzerfaust, a primitive but deadly anti-tank bazooka—a one-shot device which after firing left the soldier who fired it the option of running away from the Russian tanks or throwing stones at them.

When SS General Gustav Krukenberg arrived to take command of the SS 'Nordland' Division—one of several SS formations of foreign volunteers in Berlin—he was able to drive through the west part of the city 'without encountering soldiers or defence installations of any kind'—even though the Russians were by then on the banks of the Havel near Spandau, less than eight miles from Hitler's bunker. He also found that the 'Nordland' Division was only at battalion strength, that his command headquarters in the city centre consisted of an underground carriage with broken windows and no phone or lights, and that the defences of the central sector of the city existed on paper only.

When General Helmuch Weidling, a rough old monocled daredevil, was put in command of the defence of Berlin, his first reaction was to declare: 'It would be much better to have me shot.' Hitler's plans for the relief of the capital struck Weidling as fantasy. Could anyone really believe that the huge Russian forces could be driven back just like that? 'The Führer has ordered the defence of Berlin,' he was reassured by Hitler's Chief of Staff, 'because he is positive the war will be over once it falls.' But the men, munitions and gasoline required for the defence of Berlin had already been expended on the defence of the Oder, and Berlin's last great ammunition dump had just been blown up by retreating troops.

Not surprisingly the morale of soldiers and civilians in Berlin was at a low ebb—particularly as British and American heavy bombers continued to pound the city into rubble in round-the-clock saturation bombing raids right up to the moment the Russians set foot inside the city. More than 1,500,000 Berliners had been evacuated, and many thousands continued to pour out westwards in the hope of avoiding the coming storm; but 1,750,000 remained, and their numbers were augmented daily by thousands of refugees pouring into the city from the east, out of the path of the Red Army. One way or another it was inevitable that when the battle came a multitude of women, children, the sick and elderly would inhabit a front line on to which every weapon of modern war would be turned. Many Berliners made their wills, and looked about for means of suicide, mostly by poison and guns; and when Hitler's mistress Eva Braun took up permanent residence in the Führerbunker, the other residents guessed the end was near and dubbed her the 'Angel of Death'.

Stalin's ambition was to capture Berlin by May Day. This gave his forces on the Oder and Neisse just fifteen days in which to break through the German front line, encircle the capital and fight their way through the streets to the two most important objectives in the city—Target 105, the Reichstag, and Target 106, the Reich Chancellery. Stalin failed by one day.

Though initial resistance by the German forces opposing the Russians along the two rivers was in the main courageous and determined, it was soon swept aside by the overwhelming weight of the Red Army offensive. By the second day Konev was not only across the Neisse but across the Spree, Berlin's last natural barrier to the east, as well. By the third day his tanks were covering a lot of ground against light resistance. On 19 April they advanced thirty miles. On 20 April they advanced nearly forty miles, to a position only twenty-two miles south of Berlin. Zhukov was also closing rapidly on the capital. By 20 April he had captured Bernau, only ten miles away, and was beginning to encircle the city to the north. This was also the day that Rokossovsky joined the offensive and began his breakout on the lower Oder in support of Zhukov's flank—and the day that Adolf Hitler celebrated his 56th birthday in the Bunker below Target 106.

Hitler's birthday was the occasion for the last meeting of the top leaders of the Third Reich. Himmler, Goering, Speer and Dönitz all came to the Berlin bunker to pay their respects, then went their separate ways—Goering to his house in the Bavarian Alps, Himmler to Lübeck on the Baltic, where he had arranged secret talks with the Swedish diplomat Count Folke Bernadotte to discuss the surrender of Germany to the British and the Americans—an act of blatant treachery which was to have serious consequences. Among the top Nazis only Goebbels stayed in Berlin. On 20 April Hitler invited him to move into the bunker with his wife and children. At the same time he ordained that in the event of Germany being cut in two by an American-Russian link-up Admiral Dönitz, the C-in-C of the Navy, was to become commander of all territories in the north and Field Marshal Keitel of all territories in the south. The stage was thus set for the final dénouement.

With the capital of the Reich now visible to the Russians on the horizon, and with Russian shells now ranging on to the city centre, Hitler pinned his hopes on the German armies outside the city—General Busse's Ninth Army to the south; Marshal Schörner's 4th Panzer Army 120 miles to the south-east; and SS General Steiner's battle group to the north. But Hitler had been incarcerated in the bunker for over three months and his grasp on reality was fading fast. Schörner's army was too far away from Berlin to affect the issue; Busse's army was about to be encircled and destroyed; and Steiner's was made up of scratch, hotch-potch units still in the process of grouping. When Hitler learned on 22 April that Steiner had not carried out his order to cut through Zhukov's forces now encircling Berlin to the north, he broke down in an outburst the like of which none had seen before in the bunker. 'The war is lost!' he screamed. The Third Reich was finished; there was nothing left for him to do but die. The others could leave for Berchtesgaden and continue the war from there; but he would stay in Berlin and meet his fate when it came. 'I shall defend the city to the end,' he told his generals. 'Either I win this battle for the Reich's capital or I shall fall as a symbol of the Reich.' When Goering learnt of the Führer's breakdown he sent him a telegram offering to take over control of the Reich in his place. For his pains he was placed under arrest by the SS in Berchtesgaden and deprived of all his offices.

By now Zhukov had already outflanked Berlin and was swinging south to meet up with Konev, only five miles from the capital. Within that tightening Russian ring every man and woman in Berlin, from Adolf Hitler and Eva Braun down to the humblest citizen, was now confronted with nemesis. But even in the ensuing atmosphere of panic and dread, hope flickered fitfully. On 23 April Eva Braun wrote a letter to her sister Gretl, enclosing gifts of coffee, tobacco and canned food for 'Papa', 'Mutti' and other members of her family, together with instructions for the disposal of her gold watch, her diamond watch, her private correspondence, photograph albums, unpaid bills and the Führer's love letters. Of the situation in Berlin she wrote:

> My darling little sister,
> Each day and each hour may be our last. The Führer himself has lost all hope for a happy conclusion. Everyone here, including me, will continue to hope as long as life is in us. Please keep your head high and do not doubt. There is still hope ... At the moment the word is that things are improved, and General Burgdorf, who gave us only a 10% chance yesterday, today thinks it has risen to 50%. Well! Perhaps things will go right after all.
> P.S. I just spoke to the Führer. I think he is also more optimistic about the future than he was yesterday.

But on 23 April the final stage of the encirclement of the capital began and Busse's Ninth Army—some 200,000 desperate and determined men, muddled up with tens of thousands of civilian refugees in the woods to the south-east of the city—was virtually surrounded and cut off. By 24 April eight Russian armies, four of them tank armies, were closing in on Berlin to complete the great ring of steel and fire around the city. To the north and east they reached the S-Bahn defence ring, the second of Berlin's three defensive perimeters, which ran along the city's ring railway. In the south-west Russian tanks were on the outskirts of Potsdam, and in the north-west almost at Spandau. In the south-east the 1st Belorussian and 1st Ukrainian Fronts had met and completed the encirclement of that part of the capital. By 25 April—the day Russian and American troops met on the Elbe—the troops of Zhukov and Konev had linked up, thus completing the lock on Berlin. On 26 April the Russians captured the Zehlendorf and Dahlem districts in South Berlin, and on the next day Spandau, Neukölln and

Gatow airfield fell. By then the telephone lines to Berlin were dead and the only way the High Command headquarters could communicate with Hitler's bunker was by short-wave radio transmitted from a tethered balloon.

There was very little that Hitler or his High Command could do about anything. The war and the battle for Berlin was clearly lost. To continue to fight and sacrifice countless lives was senseless. Yet the palsied, enfeebled, prematurely aged old man in a soup-stained uniform living deep under the ground of the Reich Chancellery gardens continued to demand absolute obedience and fanatical resistance, continued to shriek nonsensical orders to non-existent or half-exterminated armies, continued to dream of driving the Red Army from Berlin and back across the Oder, and to exhort his shrunken, battered forces to 'decide the battle for the capital victoriously' and bring about 'the decisive turning-point of the war'. On 27 April Keitel transmitted a postscript to Hitler's message to the armies: 'History and the German people will despise everyone who does not do his utmost to save the situation and the Führer.'

In vain the undermanned, underarmed German armies outside Berlin were ordered to the relief of the encircled city. One after the other they were stopped short of their objectives by vastly superior forces, suffering such heavy losses that their own survival became their paramount priority. In the many battles that raged around Berlin whole formations vanished, only to re-emerge days later as shadows of their former selves. Late in the afternoon of 27 April Manteuffel's 3rd Panzer Army—all that remained of Heinrici's ravaged Army Group Vistula to the north of Berlin—appeared to break completely under the massed weight of Rokossovsky's 2nd Belorussian Front on the Lower Oder. Manteuffel reported that half his infantry divisions and his entire Flak artillery—some hundred thousand men—had stopped fighting and were fleeing west. The soldiers had 'spoken', he said. 'The war was over'. Jodl ought to come out and see for himself what a waste of time it was to talk about relieving Berlin. The best, the only thing, was to negotiate with the Anglo-Americans and extricate the remnants of the army from the Russian front as quickly as possible. Counter-attack was useless; the roads were clogged with refugees and retreating troops. An enraged Jodl threatened both Manteuffel and Heinrici, the senior army commander, with the 'ultimate consequences' for treason if they did not stand and counter-attack. But the troops would not stand, nor would the generals order them to—for it was Heinrici, determined to salvage what was left of his Army Group, who had authorised Manteuffel to withdraw the 3rd Panzer Army in the first place, against every express order of the Führer, in order to forestall its complete encirclement and destruction by the Russians north of Berlin. As Heinrici observed, they were 'marching home in columns', and nothing would make them fight.

When Keitel drove out to inspect the situation for himself, he was appalled to find that the front was now twenty miles further west than he had expected and that the troops were being pulled back in a well-organised retreat. When Heinrici ordered further withdrawals, Keitel relieved him of his command. Manteuffel, meanwhile, continued to shepherd his troops away from Berlin towards the sanctuary of the British lines in the west. Thus the Berlin defences in the north were left wide open to the Red Army.

Nothing now could make any difference to the outcome. Worse was to follow next day, 28 April, when Busse's Ninth Army, trying to break out of the Russian encirclement and join up with Wenck to the west, was cut to pieces on the march in some of the worst fighting of the war. Konstantin Simonov, a Russian novelist who was attached to the Red Army as war correspondent, described the scene in the aftermath of the carnage at the Berlin–Dresden autobahn:

> Shortly before we reached the Berlin ring road we came across a dreadful spectacle. The autobahn cut through a dense forest divided by a long clearing that disappeared into the far distance. The German troops had tried to break through to the autobahn along this clearing, and at the intersection of the two they had suffered a devastating defeat—evidently before daybreak. This was the picture we saw: in front of us lay Berlin, and to our right a forest clearing, now a chaos of jumbled tanks, cars, armoured cars, trucks, special vehicles and ambulances. They had uprooted hundreds of trees, probably in an attempt to turn around and escape. In this black, charred confusion of steel, timber, guns, cases and papers, a bloody mass of mutilated corpses lay strewn along the clearing as far as the eye could see . . .
> Then I noticed a host of wounded men lying on greatcoats and blankets or leaning against tree trunks; some of them bandaged and others covered in blood, with no-one to tend to them . . . The broad concrete ribbon of the autobahn ran straight past this grisly scene. For two hundred yards it was pitted with craters of various size, looking like so many pockmarks, and vehicles on their way to Berlin had to weave in and out between them.

The Ninth Army was doomed. In a death march to the west that lasted another week only 20,000 to 25,000 soldiers out of the original 200,000 succeeded in extricating themselves from the Russian ring and giving themselves up to the Americans. Berlin could not be relieved; nor could it be properly defended by the ill-assorted collection of anti-aircraft troops, U-boat crews, SS guards, armed policemen, elderly Volksturm men and Hitler Youth, stiffened with a sprinkling of veteran survivors from the 56th Panzers. By the evening of 27 April the defenders of Berlin had been pushed into a pocket measuring nine and a half miles long from east to west and one to three miles wide from north to south, and Russian spearheads had reached the edge of the government quarter in the centre of the city.

Shells and rockets—nearly two million of them, some 36,000 tons of metal—poured ceaselessly into streets and squares strewn with dead and wounded, burning tanks and vehicles, twisted metal and piles of rubble. The dust from the bombardment hung over the streets like a fog and visibility on the ground was reduced to a few hundred yards. Flame-throwers were used to burn out last-ditch resisters in cellars and sewers, incinerating soldiers and civilians alike. Soviet gunners fired point blank into office and apartment blocks, burying German snipers and machine-gunners in the ruins. To outflank German street barricades the Russians advanced straight through courtyards, basements and buildings, blasting doors and walls with bazookas: in this way Zhukov's troops were able to clear as many as 600 city blocks in the course of a single day.

Two main Red Army thrusts were aimed in the direction of the Tiergarten, the location of Berlin's famous Zoo. In one of the monstrous 130-foot flak towers which dominated the Zoo up to 30,000 soldiers and civilians, many of them dying or demented, some already dead, were packed cheek by jowl, while Russian shells detonated against the concrete walls and shrapnel rattled like hail against the steel shutters of the windows. In the Zoo itself the bitter fighting sent the caged animals and birds into frenzy. A Russian war correspondent entered the Zoo after the fighting had moved on. He found a single starving elephant (an Indian one called Siam) trumpeting in the ruins of the elephant house. In the hippo pool a surviving hippopotamus by the name of Knaut circled round its mate, Rosa, who floated dead in the water with the fin of an unexploded shell sticking out of its carcass. In the ape house a very large chimpanzee and a huge gorilla with two stab wounds in its chest lay dead on a concrete platform, against which was propped an SS machine-gunner, also dead, with his weapon still on his knees.

As the battle drew nearer the heart of the city—to the Reichstag building and the Chancellery bunker—every gun was brought to bear, the air was filled with the steady howling and screeching of katyushas and the drone of squadrons of Russian fighter-bombers scouring the roof-tops for targets and prey or dropping leaflets into the carnage below:

'BERLINERS! FURTHER RESISTANCE IS USELESS. YOU HAVE NOTHING TO FEAR FROM THE RED ARMY. YOU CAN STILL SAVE WHAT IS LEFT TO BE SAVED.'

The streets between the buildings of the government quarter were filled with the muzzle-flash of guns, the yellow puff of bomb-bursts, the red glow of fires, the stench of phosphorus, the staccato rattle of machine-guns, the avalanche-rumble of collapsing houses, the screams of the women and the wounded. Casualties soared and the hospitals overflowed; morphine and anaesthetics soon ran out and amputated limbs and excised organs and intestines, which could only be buried during lulls in the shelling, piled up in dustbins.

In the primitive emergency casualty station in the large cellars under the New Reich Chancellery one of Hitler's doctors, Professor Schenk, worked night and day to carry out 370 major operations in seven days on the appallingly wounded men and boys dragged down from the battle in the streets. To make matters worse, Schenk was not a surgeon at all but an internist, and had to be advised on trickier incisions in the head, spine and stomach by another of Hitler's doctors, Professor Werner Haase, who was himself dying of TB and gave his instructions lying on a bunk bed panting for breath. So Berlin sank into barbarism.

Not surprisingly, few eye-witnesses of this Armageddon kept any record of their experiences. An exception was an officer of the Müncheberg Division—a Panzer formation which had suffered heavy losses even before the battle for Berlin began, and was to go on dying until by the very end it had ceased to exist—who kept a war diary through the thick of battle. Written in the clipped style of a soldier constantly on the move, the diary vividly evokes horror of war in a capital city. The Münchebergs are being driven back block by block towards the Führer-bunker by Chuikov's Eighth Guards Army advancing from the south:

April 25: 5.30 a.m. New, massive tank attack. We are forced to retreat. Heavy street fighting—many civilian casualties. Dying animals. Women fleeing from cellar to cellar. We retreat again, under heavy Russian air attacks. Deserters, hanged or shot. What we see on this march is unforgettable. Heavy fighting in the business district, inside the Stock Exchange. The first skirmishes in the subway tunnels, through which the Russians are trying to get behind our lines. The tunnels are packed with civilians.
April 26: The night sky is fiery red. Heavy shelling. Otherwise a terrible silence. About 5.30 a.m. another ghastly artillery barrage. The Russians attack. We have to retreat again, fighting for street after street . . .

The Münchebergs moved to a new command post in the subway tunnels under Anhalt railway station, just south of the Reich Chancellery. Occasional trains rolled slowly through, going noboby knew where. The diary continued:

The station looks like an armed camp. Women and children huddling in niches and corners and listening for the sounds of battle. Shells hit the roof, cement crumbles from the ceiling. Powder smell and smoke in the tunnels. Suddenly water splashes into our command post. Screams, cries, curses in the tunnel. People are fighting round the ladders that run through air shafts up to the street. Water comes rushing through the tunnels. The crowds get panicky, stumble and fall over rails and sleepers. Children and wounded are deserted, people are trampled to death. The water covers them. It rises three feet or more, then it slowly goes down. The panic lasts for hours. Many are drowned. Reason: somewhere, on somebody's command, engineers have blasted the locks of one of the canals to flood the tunnels against the Russians who are trying to get through them . . . A terrible sight at the entrance of the subway station, one flight below street level: a heavy shell has pierced the roof, and men, women, soldiers, children are literally squashed against the walls.

April 27: Continuous attack throughout the night. Increasing signs of dissolution. Hardly any communications among troops. Telephone cables shot to pieces. Physical conditions are indescribable. No rest, no relief. No regular food, hardly any bread. We get water from the tunnels and filter it. Nervous breakdowns. The wounded that are not torn apart are hardly taken in anywhere. The civilians in their cellars are afraid of them. Too many of them have been hanged as deserters. And the flying courts-martial drive the civilians out of cellars where they pick up deserters because they are accessories to the crime . . .

During the afternoon of the 27th the Münchebergs were forced to retreat to the Potsdamer Platz, barely three hundred yards from Hitler's bunker.

The whole expanse of Potsdamer Platz is a waste of ruins. Masses of damaged vehicles, half-smashed trailers of the ambulances with the wounded still in them. Dead people are everywhere, many of them appallingly cut up by tanks and trucks.

We cannot hold our present position. At four o'clock in the morning we retreat through the subway tunnels. In the tunnels next to ours the Russians march in the opposite direction to the positions we have lost.

The civilians of Berlin were as much in the front line of the battle as the soldiers who were fighting it—helpless in a dying city. The great majority of them were women, children and old men. Like their Führer, the Berliners shunned the light of day and sat out the battle as best they could under the ground. Crowded together in squalid basements, air-raid bunkers and subway tunnels eerily lit by flickering candles, these so-called 'cellar tribes' presented a pitiful vision of life in a civilisation at the end of its tether. The normal services that supported urban life had broken down. There were no newspapers, no transport, no deliveries. The only meat to be had was from the dead horses killed by the gunfire; they were quickly carved up where they lay, though there was no gas on which to cook the flesh, and to use electricity for cooking (if there was any) was punishable by death.

The cellar tribes crept and crawled about the ruins whenever the fighting allowed, looking for a better hole, coming up for air. The women braved the fighting and scuttled from their shelters with buckets and saucepans to fetch whatever water there was from the standpipes in the streets. Many were caught in the open by the shelling and spattered over the walls or dismembered. The dead lay where they fell, or were pulled into passageways or packed into cupboards. The city was out of control. Those who could find it took to drink. In the well-stocked cellars in Kleiststrasse people filled their buckets with gigantic cocktails of mixed spirits and fought each other for unbroken bottles, standing ankle-deep in spilt alcohol. Others sought escape in sex or suicide. Many desperate German women fled from their apartments to the Reich Chancellery and the bunker complex beneath it, where they abandoned themselves in the arms of the German soldiery to saturnalian orgies. In a banqueting room in the city centre a group of dignitaries and their wives sat down to their last supper in their finest evening clothes, jewellery and decorations, then toasted each other with poisoned chalices and collapsed round the table amongst the cut glass and the silver.

4

End-Game

Ever since the Red Army crossed the frontiers of the Reich and swept across East Prussia and the eastern provinces, terrifying stories of Russian excesses against the civilian population, of murder, rape and plunder on a prodigious scale had reached the ears of the fearful Berliners daily and by the hour. They were therefore somewhat relieved at the behaviour of the first Russian front-line troops they encountered in the city—well turned-out, clean-shaven young men more concerned with rounding up German soldiers and suspected Nazis than butchering civilians or molesting women. These were the men of the 'quality' regiments, like the Red Guards.

Some districts (notably the old working-class district of Wedding) welcomed their Russian conquerors with red flags—Nazi flags with the swastika torn off. Some Red Army units brought with them an ebullient whiff of footlights and circus. An American prisoner of war liberated by some of Rokossovsky's tank men thought they looked more like Mexican revolutionaries, wild men with banjos and concertinas strapped to their backs, firing their rifles and tommy-guns in every direction. Another unit plundered the costume department of the UFA film studios and went back into battle wearing Spanish doublets and Napoleonic uniforms, dancing wildly through the streets to the music of accordions and firing their guns in the air.

The first some Germans knew of the Red Army's arrival was the sound of their beautiful and melancholy singing as they marched down the streets to the front. For other Berliners it was the smell of cowpat and horse dung: the Red Army was an army of peasant farmers. Berliners found it an extraordinary spectacle to see horses, saddled, bridled and tethered, in the middle of an invading army; and soldiers sprawled in the straw in the backs of carts with lambs, goats and pigs—for the Russians brought their livestock with them on the hoof and so were independent of supply-lines. One woman recorded her first glimpse of the enemy in the streets:

> Crouched down, I creep to the window. An endless supply column is pulling up outside: well-fed mares with foals between their legs, a cow mooing to be milked. In the garage opposite they are already setting up a field kitchen. For the first time we're able to distinguish individual types: broad round-cropped heads, well-nourished, unperturbed. Not a civilian in sight. For the moment the Russians have the streets to themselves. But one senses a whispering and trembling under all the houses. If only someone could paint a proper picture of this fearful, hidden underworld of the great city.
>
> In the middle of the street several Russians are riding stolen bikes. They teach each other how to ride, sit stiff on the saddles like chimpanzees bicycling in the zoo, crash into trees and giggle happily . . .

The Russian soldiery struck the Germans as very simple-minded and odd. Even in ruins Berlin was a sophisticated city by Russian standards and Soviet soldiers were endlessly fascinated and bemused by things that westerners took for granted—cigarette lighters; flush toilets, in which they peeled potatoes and washed their faces; electric light-bulbs, which they unscrewed to take home in the belief that the light was trapped inside the bulb and would glow anywhere; feather eiderdowns, which they slit open and crawled inside. The Russians were obsessively covetous of wrist-watches, which they called *uri* (from the German *Uhr*, watch). Day and night the Berliners were bombarded with the pidgin cry: '*Uri! Uri!*' Some Russians wore looted watches on both wrists and all the way up both arms, and were endlessly preoccupied in winding, comparing and correcting them.

Naturally there were not many Allied eyewitnesses of the fate that befell Berlin, but there were a few. Len Carpenter was a 26-year-old Yorkshire-man who had been captured by the Germans during the retreat to Dunkirk in 1940. Near the end of the war he had graduated to a kind of prison without bars near Berlin and when the guards vanished he wandered off and moved into an empty flat in the western end of the city, where he supported himself on a weekly Red Cross parcel. During the air raids he took shelter in the cellar, always being careful not to reveal his nationality when the Germans cursed 'those English swine up there', and when the Russians invaded the city he took up almost permanent residence in the cellar. Looking back, he recalled,

> I think I must have got through the battle in a kind of coma. I remember going out and queuing up for some salt pork in the middle of the fighting and the queue being strafed by a Russian plane, and I remember joining in when the Germans started looting the shops and getting a big tin of jam and a typewriter, of all useless things. I remember the Hitler Youth boys singing

as they marched past after driving the Russians out of Herrenstrasse railway station, and I remember the first Russians to arrive—they were Russians who had been fighting on the German side and when they took shelter in the cellar with us I thought, 'Just my luck to be caught by the Red Army with this lot in tow.'

One day I did an unbelievably foolhardy thing. I went into the Foreign Office building to get my records out of the files. The building had been abandoned by the Germans but if anyone had caught me then I'd have been shot out of hand. I found my records and went back to the cellar, and when all the guns and shouting had died down I emerged into the streets. From quite a distance away I could hear the shrieks of young girls. A local cobbler who was a communist went forward to meet the Russians and show them his Party card but all they did was pinch the leather jacket off his back . . . I had a chit printed in four languages which said I was a British subject, but they weren't interested, they couldn't read, they just dropped it on the ground. Then I went off with them on a plundering foray. We broke into a shoe shop with a lovely stock of shoes in it, and we broke into the wine and spirit shops, all sorts of places. I thought it would have been a case of honour among thieves but they weren't very pally at all.

Most Berliners agreed that the first Russians were friendly enough, sharing their food and candy with the local children, politely greeting the civilians as they searched the cellars for soldiers and guns. But as a Soviet lieutenant warned the Mother Superior of an orphanage and maternity hospital in the southern suburbs: 'These are good, disciplined and decent soldiers. But I must tell you—the ones coming up behind are pigs.'

For after the 'quality' troops of the forward fighting units in the first echelon came the 'quantity' troops of the support units in the second echelon—drunken thugs, bent on loot and rape. Many of this second wave of soldiers were from Asiatic Russia and brought with them a view of the rights of conquest inherited from Genghis Khan and Tamerlane the Great. Others were members of penal battalions or were ex-prisoners from the German slave camps who had been liberated by the Red Army, given a weapon, put in the ranks and sent up to the front. Such men were the scourge of Berlin. All of them, whether from 'quality' or 'quantity' outfits, were inflamed by front-line propaganda which reminded them—if they needed reminding—that they were at last in 'the City of the Devil', 'the lair of the Fascist beast'. And most of them at one time or another were turned wild by alcohol, large stores of which they found intact in sealed warehouses inside the city. It was then that every German woman learned to dread a Russian when he grunted the all-too familiar words: '*Frau, komm!*' An anonymous woman diarist, who spoke a little Russian, described her cellar's first encounter with a specimen of the Red Army second wave: 'Everyone seems paralysed; no one moves; no one utters a word. All one can hear is the occasional sound of breathing. Now the beam of light falls and remains on the eighteen-year-old who, with the white shimmering bandage around her head, is lying in a deck chair. Pointing at the girl the Russian asks in German in a threatening noice: 'How many years?' No one answers. The girl lies there as though turned to stone. Once more the Russian bellows furiously: 'How many years?' I quickly answer in Russian: 'This is a student; she's eighteen . . . Head *kaputt*, from bombing.'

A little later another Russian broke into the cellar, 'a bull of a man', the woman diarist noted, 'dead drunk, brandishing a revolver.' His chosen victim was the distiller's wife, the fattest woman in the cellar. He chased her across the cellar and was struggling with her in the doorway when his revolver suddenly went off accidentally. In the ensuing panic the Russian ran off, but shortly afterwards three more soldiers burst into the cellar. This time it was the turn of the baker's wife, who was also very fat. By the flickering light of an oil wick in a saucer they tried to prise her reluctant frame out of her deck-chair, one pulling her arm, another pushing her back, but they were frustrated by the arrival of an officer, and left. Then it was the woman diarist's turn. She was seized and raped by two soldiers in the corridor outside the cellar. She sought refuge in a flat on the first floor but was raped again by a giant Siberian—'broad as a wardrobe, with paws like a lumberjack'—who at least was gentleman enough to take off his boots and unbuckle his gun. The next day, 28 April, was even worse. Two Russian soldiers forced their way into the apartment after kicking the door in. While one stood guard the other pushed the woman into a room, barricaded the door with an armchair, and threw her on to the bed. Afterwards she relived the horror in her diary:

> Shut your eyes, clench your teeth, don't utter a sound. Only when the underwear is ripped apart with a tearing sound, the teeth grind involuntarily. The last underwear.
> I feel the fingers at my mouth, smell the reek of horses and tobacco. I open my eyes. Adroitly the fingers force my jaws apart. Eye looks into eye. Then the man above me slowly let his spittle dribble into my mouth . . .
> Paralysis. Not disgust, just utter coldness. The spine seems to be frozen, icy dizziness encircles the back of the head. I find myself gliding and sinking deep down through the pillows, through the floor . . .
> Before leaving he fishes something out of his pocket, throws it without a word on the night table, pushes the chair away and slams the door behind him. What he has left behind turns out to be a crumpled packet of cigarettes. The fee.

Russian soldiers raped women and girls of all sorts and all ages, from children of ten to old ladies of eighty, at all sorts of times and in all sorts of circumstances, many of them most unpropitious—in public, for example, or in turn in a queue or a gang, and (usually) in uniform, boots and army hat, with pistol in hand or rifle on back. 'One couldn't help marvelling at the way in which the Russians were in the mood for the act at all times,' noted Friedrich Luft, an eyewitness to these impromptu displays of Soviet virility. 'I was surprised to see how quickly, abruptly, and without the least preparation they invariably set about it.' Some women were kept for the collective pleasure of an entire unit and were raped ceaselessly.

Out of a total female population of 1,400,000 (including children) some 90,000 subsequently sought medical assistance as a consequence of rape, and presumably the total number of rape victims was substantially higher than this. About 80 per cent of all rapes took place in the ten-day period between 24 April and 3 May, at the climax of the battle for Berlin. For some women the experience was so traumatic that they went mad or killed themselves—over two hundred committed suicide in the district of Pankow alone. Others were able to shrug it off philosophically or somehow bury their individual suffering in the collective catastrophe. 'Better a Russian on the belly', they would say, comparing the Russian rape with the American bombing, 'than an American on the head.'

Resourceful women avoided rape by a variety of means. Some put on repulsive disguises. Some feigned infectious diseases—scarlet fever was particularly dreaded by the Red Army men. Others used psychological ploys: they faked amorous or wanton advances towards their aggressors, which often shocked or nonplussed them, or pretended to be wrong in the head—like the woman who played toy trains on the floor when six Russians broke into her flat.

Afterwards a myth grew up that two entire Soviet Army Groups had systematically forced themselves on the women of Berlin on the orders of a Jewish writer in Moscow (Ilya Ehrenburg) as an act of revenge against the German race. In fact, the majority of Russians probably raped the women of Berlin because they had not had leave or a woman for a long time; because they were inflamed with alcohol; and because they looked on rape as a part of their booty. Not all of them got away with it. Some were summarily shot by the more responsible officers among them; a few were sent for court-martial and long prison sentences back home.

As the Germans soon found, the Russians were bafflingly contradictory and capricious people who lurched unpredictably between the extremes of ferocity and brutality on the one hand and generosity and sentimentality on the other. Sometimes the rapists were seized by a sudden affection or compassion for their victims and showered them with gifts of bread and fish. A fifty-year old admirer of a woman whose nephew he had helped to shoot took to serenading her with a mouth-organ at six o'clock every morning. A Russian who raped a young German mother fell in love with her, brought milk for her eight-week old baby and fed it to the child himself.

The woman diarist eventually found a protector—a kindly and romantic Red Army major who defended her against the excesses of his men. For she could not look to support from German menfolk—the young bloods, the flower of the nation, were dead, dying, or defeated. The great majority of those who were left were cowed, cringing—even downright cowardly. This is hardly surprising. If they showed themselves in the streets they might be drafted into the Volkssturm and killed in the fighting. If they tried to prevent Russian soldiers raping their wives and daughters they would almost certainly be shot. So they hid themselves away and did nothing. Among the Germans it was the women who were the heroes of Berlin. It was they who braved the artillery fire to forage for food and water in the streets. It was they who fed the men, cleared up the mess, looked after the sick, hid the young girls, bore the brunt of the Russians' brutishness. The women of Berlin began to look down on their men as the weaker sex and felt disappointed in them and even sorry for them. The anonymous Berlin diarist perceived this too, and noted prophetically: 'The man-dominated Nazi world glorifying the strong man is tottering and with it the myth "man". In former times and wars men could boast that the privilege of killing and being killed for the Fatherland was theirs. Today we women have a share in it. This changes us, makes us rebellious. At the end of this war there will emerge, apart from many other defeats, the defeat of man as a sex.'

By 28 April, the day this remarkable woman was raped by the fourth man in twenty-four hours, a more obvious and imminent defeat was facing Germany's manhood. Chuikov's troops had reached the Landwehr canal, which formed the southern perimeter of the government quarter in the city centre. Kuznetsov's Third Shock Army stood on the Spree River, which formed the northern perimeter of the government quarter, and his 150th Division was preparing to attack the SS Ministry of the Interior ('Himmler's House') and beyond it the much-prized target of the Reichstag building. The battle for the Tiergarten, the public park whose eastern end fringed the Reich Chancellery, had reached a climactic stage with some of the bitterest fighting since Stalingrad. Savage fighting between the Russians and the Münchebergers was also in progress in the Potsdamer Platz, just round the corner from Hitler's bunker.

By now the Chancellery itself was under continuous shellfire. Explosions shook the cement membrane of the bunker, and the sulphurous reek of cordite was sucked down into that underground warren by the bunker's ventilation system. Communications between the Führer and what was left of his domain in the world above had almost ceased to exist. The airfields had already been captured and the last usable landing strip—the improvised runway along the grand boulevard known as the east–west Axis—was under heavy Russian fire.

The progress of the battle in Berlin could only be followed by calling random numbers on the telephone, but often Russian voices answered the calls, and increasingly the lines were dead. Enemy radio bulletins were Hitler's main source of information. These reported that Mussolini had been captured alive by communist partisans in Italy, and that Bavarian separatists had begun an uprising and seized the Munich broadcasting station. But what did it matter? Hitler paced up and down the bunker corridors, clutching a Berlin petrol-station street-map that was falling apart in his clammy hands. His power was now so shrunken that it covered no more than a few square yards of disputed city street. His main preoccupation was his own fate; he was obsessed with the fear that he would be captured alive by the Russians, 'squeezed until the pips squeak and then displayed in a Moscow Zoo.'

Still Hitler clung to hope and life; still he cherished the fantasy that Wenck's Army would fight its way through to Berlin and throw the Russians back. It was clear to all but a faithful few in the bunker that the Führer must die. It required a new development to persuade Hitler to think so too. At 9 p.m. on 28 April the BBC broadcast a version of a Reuter's despatch to the effect that a guarantee of unconditional German surrender had been made to the British and American governments by Heinrich Himmler. The news stunned the Führer more than anyone else. He was seized with another fit of fury. Himmler was beyond the reach of his vengeance but there was a perfect substitute on hand, for Himmler's liaison officer at the bunker, SS Brigadeführer Hermann Fegelein, who had married Eva Braun's sister and was therefore Hitler's prospective brother-in-law, was already under arrest on suspicion of desertion in the face of the enemy.

Fegelein had not been seen in the bunker for two days and Hitler had begun to suspect that he was planning to decamp. His adjutant had last seen him in civilian clothes in his apartment off the Kurfürstendamm, and during the course of the day he telephoned his sister-in-law and told her: 'Eva, you must abandon the Führer if you can't persuade him to leave Berlin. Don't be stupid, it's a matter of life and death.' Fegelein was eventually apprehended in his apartment in the company of his latest mistress and brought back under guard, roaring drunk, to the Reich Chancellery.

Fegelein's fate was soon sealed. Papers relating to Himmler's treachery were found among his personal effects, together with two money belts of gold sovereigns and other enemy currencies. To make matters worse General Burgdorf, Hitler's ADC, who was now drunk, ran through the bunker spreading the rumour that Himmler had promised to forward Hitler's body to Eisenhower as a pledge of his serious intent—and that Fegelein was the man who would actually deliver the Führer's corpse to SHAEF after his death. Hitler ordered Fegelein to be executed at once, and the luckless general was led out into the Chancellery grounds and shot by a firing-squad.

Hitler then ordered the new Chief of the Luftwaffe, Field Marshal von Greim, to leave Berlin on a special mission: he was to arrest the traitor

Himmler. Greim succeeded in taking off from the east–west Axis in a training plane under heavy Russian gunfire—the last plane out of Berlin. But Himmler was to live a little longer and meet a different kind of end.

Hitler now abandoned all hope. Himmler's treachery and the failure of the relieving armies to break through had destroyed his will to live. He ordered the glass cyanide capsules supplied by his SS doctor to be tested on his favourite Alsatian dog: when the dog was seen to die Hitler handed out capsules to his staff in the bunker. The mood of the inmates of that fetid cavern was now growing hysterical.

Then, in the early hours of the morning of 29 April, he married Eva Braun. After a champagne wedding breakfast attended by ten or so intimates, he retired to another room to dictate his personal will and political testament. He blamed the Jews for the war and the British for the invasion of Poland. He expelled Himmler and Goering from the Party and Speer from the Cabinet, and he appointed Dönitz as his successor as President of the Reich and Supreme Commander of the Armed Forces, with Goebbels as Chancellor, Bormann as Party Minister and Schörner as Supreme Commander of the Army. He called on the nation to continue the fight against international Jewry, 'the poisoner of all nations.' Then he signed. It was four o'clock in the morning.

In an hour or so the Russians were stirring again after the nightly lull in the fighting. At seven o'clock their guns let fly a ten-minute barrage at 'Himmler's House'. At noon two Soviet regiments broke into the burning building and began a room-to-room battle which was to last all that day and most of the coming night. Elsewhere, as savage fighting continued to rage around the Zoo, the Anhalt station and other strongpoints of German resistance, more Red Army reinforcements poured into Berlin.

At the last war conference in the bunker the Commandant of Berlin, General Weidling, presented a bleak report: there was no ammunition, no air drops could be expected: hope was at an end. The Russians had reached the Adlon Hotel in Wilhelmstrasse, only four blocks away. They had occupied most of the Tiergarten and encircled the German positions in the Potsdamer Platz, only three hundred yards from the bunker. The fighting in Berlin could go on for another twenty-four hours at most, but by 1 May 'the Russians will be able to spit in our windows.' He proposed assembling a strike force for a break-out, but Hitler told him that the capitulation of the city was out of the question. He himself would remain in Berlin. He did not want to have to wait for the end 'somewhere under the open sky or in a farmhouse,' he told Weidling. He was not prepared to be caught wandering about the woods like a common criminal. He would end his life here. After midnight Keitel confirmed from High Command HQ that the Ninth Army had been surrounded and the Twelfth Army had been stopped.

'If we are to go under,' Goebbels had declared, 'then the whole German nation will go under with us so gloriously that even in a thousand years time the heroic apocalypse of the Germans will have pride of place in the history of the world.'

When Adolf Hitler woke at sunrise on 30 April, the last day of his life, the apocalypse above his bunker was less than heroic. At times Berlin seemed to have regressed to a primordial jungle state: an escaped lion had been seen loping past the Gestapo headquarters in Albrechtstrasse and rumour had it that a zebra had been grazing in one of the city's cemeteries. At other times the city resembled a vision of hell by Hieronymous Bosch: shell-holes exposed corpses lying several layers deep in the subways; the screams of women raped by groups of Russians, children burned by napalm, and German soldiers undergoing amputation without anaesthetic counterpointed the monstrous noise of the guns; on iron bedsteads in the burned-out ruins of the Elisabeth Hospital lay the charred bodies of Russian soldiers and the German nurses they were in the act of raping when the building went up in flames.

At 8.30 a.m. Russian artillery opened up a ninety-minute barrage on the Reichstag, the huge fire-gutted shell of the former German Parliament, a quarter of a mile to the north of Hitler's bunker. For the Soviets the Reichstag was the symbol of the Third Reich and its capture a symbol of victory. An entire Red Army Division, the 150th Rifle Division of Kuznetsov's Third Shock Army, was assigned to the assault of this building, which was defended by 6,000 to 7,000 German troops, most of them SS. A second Russian division was allocated to the assault for the purposes of mopping up, and four special task-groups of four men each were assigned to the task of planting the Red Victory Banner on the Reichstag.

At 10 a.m. the first infantry wave began the assault, but ran into fierce German resistance. At 1 p.m. every available gun was brought to bear in another tremendous barrage on the Reichstag building. Then, flying the Red Flag, the lead assault group stormed up to the Reichstag steps and raced up the central staircase inside. Germans holding the cellars and upper storeys of the Reichstag prevented the Soviets from rushing the whole building. It was 2.30 p.m. before they won control of the second storey after prolonged hand-to-hand combat in burning corridors and rooms filled with smoke; it was 6 p.m. before they launched their attack on the upper levels; and it was nearly 11 p.m. before two veteran scouts, Sgt. Mikhail Yegorov and Sgt. Meliton Kantariya, succeeded in raising the flag of victory—Red Banner no. 5 of the Third Shock Army, an enormous Hammer and Sickle—among the copper statuary on the Reichstag roof, where, illuminated by the glare of the burning city, it was hailed by a vast cheer from the Russian troops below. By which time the cadavers of Adolf and Eva Hitler, incinerated almost beyond recognition, lay side by side in a shell crater in the Chancellery building site covered in a thin layer of sand, rubble and old planks.

The Führer and his wife had bade a formal farewell to the people still remaining in the bunker at 3 p.m. Afterwards a bleary-eyed Hitler, informed his adjutant, Günsche, that he and his wife were going to commit suicide and wanted their bodies reduced to ashes. 'After my death', he told Günsche, 'I don't want to be put on exhibition in a Russian waxworks'. The couple then entered Hitler's private apartment and closed the steel fire-proof, gas-proof and sound-proof door behind them. No one present ever saw them alive again.

At 3.40 p.m. Bormann, Goebbels, Günsche and Hitler's valet, Linge, entered the room, which was filled with a choking mixture of toxic cordite and cyanide fumes. Eva Hitler was sitting dead at one end of a blue and white sofa. She had bitten a cyanide capsule; her nostrils were discoloured and her mouth shut tight. Hitler was sitting two feet apart, slumped over the other end of the sofa, with blood dripping steadily from his right temple. He had shot himself with a 7.65 Walther pistol, and bitten a cyanide capsule at the moment he pulled the trigger. His mother's photograph was on a table beside him. A painting of Frederick the Great glowered down at him from the wall.

For several minutes everyone was too shocked to speak. Hitler's valet automatically picked up a Dresden vase of spring tulips and daffodils which Hitler had knocked over when he slumped forward, examined the vase for cracks, refilled it with the flowers and set it back on the table. Then the bodies were wrapped in brown army blankets and carried up the four flights of concrete stairs to the waste lot by the bunker's emergency exit in the Chancellery ground.

The bodies were laid in a foundation trench by a cement mixer near the exit and fifty gallons of petrol were poured over them. Then Martin Bormann tossed a flaming brand into the trench and with a burst of blue flame and a black puff of smoke the corpses caught fire and began to burn. Standing inside the doorway of the bunker exit, sheltering from the flying shrapnel and debris of another katyusha rocket barrage, nine prominent members of the bunker, including Bormann and Goebbels, stood to rigid attention with raised arms in a final Nazi salute of farewell. Then they turned and descended again into the nether world.

As the bodies sputtered and bubbled in the fire in the Chancellery garden, Eva Hitler's rose up into an equestrian posture, as if she were riding in a saddle, with her hands stretched out as if holding imaginary reins. Later some SS men tossed the bodies into a shell hole and filled it in with dirt and rubble.

Though Hitler was dead the German state remained. Two matters urgently needed to be resolved in order to ensure its continuity. The first was that of the succession. Bormann's immediate act on his return to the lower bunker was to send a telegram to Admiral Dönitz informing him that he had been appointed Hitler's successor as Head of State and was 'empowered immediately to take all of the measures required of the current situation.' The second matter was that of negotiating an end to the fighting. It was decided to send an emissary from the bunker to parley with the Russians and arrange a ceasefire so that Dönitz and his German government could assemble in Berlin and discuss the terms of the surrender. Hitler's Chief of Staff in the bunker, General Hans Krebs, who had learnt Russian as a military attaché in Moscow before the war, was chosen for this delicate task.

In the early hours of 1 May Krebs went through the lines under a white flag and was taken to the headquarters of General Chuikov—the only senior Soviet army general with a command post inside the city. Chuikov was having supper with his political staff and some Soviet war correspondents, including a poet and a composer looking for inspiration for a symphony commemorating the Berlin victory, when Krebs arrived. The composer, the only Russian not in uniform, was bundled into a cupboard; the war correspondents were passed off as members of Chuikov's war council.

The discussions were protracted.Chuikov telephoned Zhukov and then Stalin to tell them the news that Hitler was dead and that Goebbels was asking for a ceasefire. Stalin had just gone to bed in the Kremlin but got up to take the call from Berlin. 'So—that's the end of the bastard,' he commented when he heard of Hitler's suicide. 'Too bad we didn't manage to take him alive.' There could be no negotiations with Krebs or any other Hitlerites, Stalin told Chuikov—only unconditional surrender. Then Stalin went back to bed to rest for the great May Day parade in Red Square.

Chuikov turned to Krebs. 'We can hold talks with you only in the event of complete capitulation to the USSR, the USA and England,' he told the German. Krebs could only offer a truce. For hours the wrangling continued. The Russians were disappointed that Krebs had not come to negotiate a general surrender. They would allow a provisional German government to be formed, they told him, but only after capitulation. At 10.15 a.m., six and a half hours after Krebs's arrival at Chuikov's headquarters, Moscow signalled an ultimatum: capitulation or the resumption of the full artillery bombardment of Berlin. By this time, as it happened, the Russian composer in the cupboard was running very short of air, and as poor Krebs sat wringing his hands, the composer suddenly passed out, fell through the cupboard door and lay senseless at Krebs's feet—to the German's total consternation.

Krebs's adjutant now made a dangerous journey back to the bunker to present to Goebbels a personal account of the Russian demands for an unconditional surrender. Goebbels grew very agitated when he heard it.

'To that I shall never, never agree!' he shouted. The talks were broken off. Krebs was ordered back to the bunker. A heavy Soviet artillery bombardment was let loose on the Reich Chancellery which created panic among the occupants of the bunker. The end had come, it was clear, and now was the time to get out—either by escape or suicide.

Goebbels and his wife had turned a deaf ear to all plans to spirit their five children, aged five to twelve, out of Berlin. As long ago as March, Goebbels had confided to an aide: 'Neither my wife nor a single one of my offspring will be among the survivors of the coming débâcle.' In the early evening of 1 May, as the Goebbels children were getting ready for bed, Magda Goebbels gave them each a chocolate containing a soporific drug, and when they were asleep she crushed a cyanide capsule inside their mouths and killed them. Afterwards, ashen-faced and red-eyed, she sipped champagne and chain-smoked cigarettes until 8.30 p.m., when she accompanied her husband up the bunker stairs to the garden for the final act. There, standing in the dark under a sky glowing with the fires of Berlin, she bit a cyanide capsule while her husband fired a pistol into the back of her head. Immediately afterwards Goebbels simultaneously bit into a capsule and put a bullet into his right temple as his Führer had done. Two SS officers then emptied six cans of petrol over the bodies and after setting them alight retreated to the safety of the bunker. The two bodies burned all through the night.

The rest of the bunker occupants, apart from Krebs and Burgsdorf, who also killed themselves, chose to escape. At 11 p.m. the first of the break-out groups made its departure. There were ten such groups made up of the occupants of the bunker, among whom some twenty of Hitler's inner circle remained, and the 800 unwounded troops still holding out around the Reich Chancellery. Their plan was to strike north through the city's subway system and surface in the north of the city beyond the Russian ring; then cut cross-country to the headquarters of Dönitz, the new Reich President, at Plön on the Baltic. To give the escapers a headstart it had been agreed that General Weidling, the Commandant of Berlin, would not sign any capitulation agreement with the Russians until dawn the next day.

All through the hours of darkness the break-out groups stumbled and scuttled through the darkened streets and tunnels of Berlin. All but a hundred or so survived. Most were taken prisoner by the Russians. Among the few who got clear away to the west were Hitler's secretaries, his chauffeur Erik Kempka, the Hitler Youth Leader, Artur Axmann, and Goebbels's aide, Dr Werner Naumann. Of Martin Bormann there was no sign. For years it was assumed he had succeeded in escaping—perhaps as far as South America. In fact he had taken cyanide when he found his escape route cut off near the Lehrter railway station and twenty-seven years later his remains and those of one of the bunker medics, Dr Stumpfegger, were discovered during site clearance works at the spot where they had died.

Only one man was eventually left in the bunker. This was Johannes Hentschel, who was in charge of the machinery that powered the ventilation system and the water-pump, both for the bunker and for the Chancellery cellars where many hundreds of wounded soldiers still lay in the emergency casualty station. At dawn, at about the same time that General Weidling, the Commandant of Berlin, was setting out for General Chuikov's headquarters to offer the surrender of the city, Hentschel went up into the Chancellery garden for a breath of air. What he saw was Berlin covered in a thick, low-level layer of cloud that shimmered orange and lemon like a Saharan dust-storm. The air was full of ashes and cinders that made his eyes sore. In the distance he could hear rifle-fire and the occasional mortar or rocket. In the garden eight or nine corpses lay sprawled about, some with their heads severed and limbs scattered around. Goebbels's body had been roasted rather than burned, Hentschel noted, and his face was a deep purple. Flocks of mallard ducks flew over in triple formations, 'like Messerschmitts', heading for their spring nesting-sites in the Tiergarten. The perfume of jasmine and hyacinth wafted across from Hitler's glassless greenhouse. Hentschel went and picked a bunch of tulips to cheer up his post in the abandoned bunker, then returned to the catacomb below.

At about nine he heard voices approaching and saw a dozen giggling Red Army women medics or interns approaching him. 'Where is Gitler's Frau?' they asked him in Russian gutturals. Hentschel led them to Eva Hitler's boudoir. Half an hour later they emerged and ran off down the tunnel loaded with souvenirs of all kinds—helmets, gas masks, Hitler's monogrammed silver, crystal glass, an accordion, a telephone, and a dozen black satin brassières trimmed with lace. More Red Army officers found their way down into the bunker depths. Some stared in horror at the dead bodies of the Goebbels children, stacked two by two on three bunks. Others struck the neck of a champagne bottle with a bayonet and danced round Hentschel as if he were King of the May, singing Russian drinking songs as they danced. Meanwhile, an anguished General Weidling had arrived at Chuikov's headquarters at five o'clock that morning. His negotiations did not last long. He wrote a proclamation calling on the German troops in Berlin to surrender and then made a recording of it to be broadcast by Soviet loudspeaker vans. These vans were driven out into every part of the city and blared out Weidling's message into the ruins: 'Further resistance is useless. My orders are: cease resistance forthwith.'

At 3 p.m. on the afternoon of 2 May the guns fell silent in Berlin—one day later than Stalin had planned. The city was enveloped in uncanny quiet. The sky was still yellow from the many fires that burned throughout the city, but there were no more shells—only the cheers of the Russian soldiers hugging each other among the ruins. The women of Berlin stood in the water queues in the cold, pouring rain, regaled by Russians playing accordions and singing songs. 'Gitler *kaputt!*' they yelled. 'Goebbels *kaputt! Voyna kaputt!*'—The war's over!

In the windowless, candlelit rooms of their German women-friends that night Red Army men played frenzied tunes on their mouth-organs and danced the dances of their homelands—of the Ukraine, Uzbekistan, the open Steppes. In Chuikov's mess high-ranking German officers captured in the break-out were entertained to a Russian victory supper of vodka, caviar, chicken, fish and tea and congratulated on the valour of their troops in the battle for Berlin. Inside the Reichstag the Russian soldiers scrawled their names on the walls in paints of every conceivable colour: within a week the walls were covered in names to the height of a man; within two weeks to the height of a man standing on another man's shoulders. *Voyna kaputt.*

Order was already returning to the ruins. The living were being dug out of the rubble. The dead were being collected and piled up in heaps ready for burning. Little red memorial columns surmounted by a white star sprouted over the graves of the hastily buried Russian dead. Allotment gardens were being dug; bread, potatoes and goulash doled out from Russian soup kitchens; proclamations from the new Soviet military administration posted on walls and trees: weapons must be handed in, looted goods must be returned, municipal employees must report back to work. At Berlin airport German women were clearing the runway with their bare hands. Huge columns of exhausted blank-faced German prisoners filed eastwards along gutted streets towards a future that was unthinkable. Exhausted Russian infantry sat on the kerb covered in dust. In the districts away from the centre lay empty and silent, the houses boarded up and deserted.

Soviet tanks patrolled the forlorn expanses of the shattered capital and scores of little red victory flags flickered amongst the wreckage. An endless horse-drawn caravanserai of Asiatic Russian supply units moved into the vacuum, their wagons piled high with carpets, beds, toilets, bicycles, umbrellas and other booty, as well as cages full of live chickens, ducks and geese, and gipsy-like women from beyond the Urals. The Occupation had begun.

Though Berlin had been surrendered to the Russians, fighting of the most appalling savagery continued to rage in the outlying districts and countryside outside, where surviving German formations fought desperately to break out of the Russian trap. On the day of the surrender a column of 30,000 German troops fought its way through Red Army lines westward from Spandau. That same day a well-armed column of 17,000 German troops, including the remnants of the Müncheberg Division, struck out across the Havel river to the west of the city in a running battle that lasted four days. The bridge over the Havel, which had been kept open throughout the battle by a very determined group of Hitler Youth, was under intense Soviet fire and clogged with refugees fleeing from the city. In the panic to escape, the Münchebergs' tanks rolled straight over the lines of refugees on the bridge, and when the infantry went over after them the bridge was thick with blood. Once across, the German column broke into scattered groups and took to the woods and swamps—no longer soldiers but fugitives in hiding.

To the south of the city, meanwhile, pathetic remnants of Busse's Ninth Army, with only two tanks left and many utterly exhausted soldiers crawling on their hands and knees, finally broke through to join up with Wenck's Twelfth Army after a nightmare fighting retreat along a route strewn with tens of thousands of dead and dying men. Next day both armies, totalling 110,000 to 125,000 men, began to surrender to the Americans. To the north Rokossovsky's 2nd Belorussian Front, racing to cut off Manteuffel's Third Panzer Army before it could give itself up to the British, reached the Baltic coast and the demarcation line with the British along the Elbe—the end of the line. Between 100,000 and 120,000 German soldiers of the 3rd Panzer Army and Army Group Steiner had by then succeeded in surrendering to the British and Americans.

The great push which had taken the Red Army from the Oder to the Elbe and captured the capital of the Nazi Reich had taken just eighteen days. During that short time the Russians destroyed no less than ninety-three German divisions (including twelve Panzer divisions), and took 480,000 German officers and men prisoner, many of whom were to die in captivity later. During the course of the battle 125,000 German civilians lost their lives—including 6,400 from suicide and 22,000 from heart attacks—together with an undetermined number of German soldiers. The three Soviet Fronts lost 305,000 dead, wounded and missing, along with 2,156 tanks and 527 planes. Between half a million and a million human beings thus lost their lives, their well-being, their sanity or their freedom as a result of this terrible and unnecessary final battle.

5

Victory

With Germany overrun and German forces in a state of collapse, it was clear to all that victory in Europe, VE-Day—an abbreviation coined by the Director of the United States Office of War Mobilisation for the target-date from which American industry could start returning to peacetime production—was now only a matter of days away. On 1 May a million Germans had laid down their arms in Italy. Berlin had fallen to the Russians on the 2nd; Hamburg to the British on the 3rd; and Hitler's house at Berchtesgaden to the Americans on the 4th. The Czechs were up in arms against the German occupation in Prague and the Danish resistance had taken over in Copenhagen. Hitler's suicide removed the last administrative and psychological obstacle to the unconditional German surrender demanded by the Allies.

Rumours of imminent peace now swept through allied capitals. The Supreme Commander, General Eisenhower, began to turn his thoughts to his troops' future, to the Pacific War and demobilisation—and to his broadcast and newsreel speech for VE-Day. The end of the war now depended not so much on the military efforts of the Allied Armies as on the administrative activities of the remaining fragments of the Nazi government. The succession of Grand Admiral Dönitz as the new Reich Chancellor and Commander-in-Chief of the German Armed Forces had provided at a single stroke a leader to whom the German forces could transfer their allegiance and with whom the Allies could treat.

For a few more days Dönitz, at his headquarters in Flensburg, in Schleswig–Holstein, kept up the fight, maintaining the front in the East so that as many German soldiers and civilians as possible could escape to the west and surrender to the Anglo-Americans rather than fall into Russian hands. But on 4 May, once British and American columns had sealed off Schleswig–Holstein and the Danish peninsula from penetration by the advancing Red Army, Dönitz authorised the surrender of all German forces in north-west Germany, Holland and Denmark. That day an armistice was signed at Field Marshal Montgomery's tented headquarters on Lüneberg Heath: all hostilities in these areas were to cease at 8 a.m. on 5 May. Two and a half million German soldiers on the northern flank of the Allied battlefront were now in British hands.

Dönitz's headquarters at Flensburg lay within the surrender area, so a general surrender of all the remaining German forces in Europe in the very near future seemed inevitable. But it was to prove a cumbersome thing to arrange. A surrender delegation from Dönitz's headquarters, headed by Admiral Hans-Georg von Friedeburg, was delayed by bad weather and did not arrive at Eisenhower's tactical SHAEF headquarters—a three-storey red brick schoolhouse at Reims, 88 miles north-east of Paris—until late afternoon on 5 May. Then it turned out that they were not empowered to sign a surrender, only talk terms. When Friedeburg, who seemed on the verge of a nervous collapse, was told to contact Dönitz with a view to sending Commanders-in-Chief with the necessary authority to surrender, it was found that there was no direct way of communicating with him, and a message had to be sent in code to the British Second Army and carried from there by courier to Dönitz in Flensburg.

It was not until 5 p.m. on Sunday 6 May that the German Chief-of-Staff, General Alfred August Jodl arrived at Reims to negotiate the end of hostilities, accompanied by his aide Major Wilhelm Oxenius, and escorted by Montgomery's Chief-of-Staff, General de Guingand. Like von Friedeburg, Jodl was at the end of his tether, and had had hardly any sleep for the last three nights. But he strode from his car as alert and smartly turned out as ever, and shortly after his arrival at the schoolhouse his aide emerged from his office to ask for coffee and 'a map of Europe'.

The people at SHAEF had been led to believe by von Friedeburg that Jodl would sign the surrender document straight away, but it soon became clear that Jodl had no such intention. His object was to play for time to enable countless thousands of Germans on the Eastern Front the chance to withdraw westwards and thus evade captivity and death at the hands of the Russians. A total of 1,850,000 German soldiers were still fighting their way out of Russian encirclement—including 600,000 men of Army Group Centre in Czechoslovakia, 430,000 men of Army Group South in Austria, and 180,000 of Army Group South-East in Yugoslavia. In Latvia and East Prussia 300,000 German troops were too far behind the Russian lines to be rescued. 'He told us frankly and with deep conviction', Major-General Kenneth Strong, Eisenhower's British Chief of Intelligence, who was acting as interpreter at the discussions, reported later, 'that we would soon find ourselves fighting Russia and that if Germany were given time to evacuate as many troops and civilians as possible to the west there would be large resources available to help the Allies in the struggle against the Russians.'

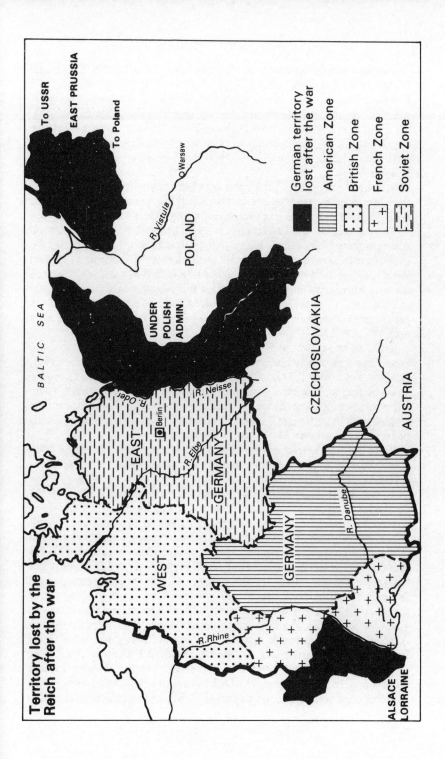

Territory lost by the Reich after the war

To USSR

EAST PRUSSIA

To Poland

BALTIC SEA

R. Vistula

○ Warsaw

POLAND

UNDER POLISH ADMIN.

R. Oder

R. Neisse

Berlin

EAST GERMANY

R. Elbe

CZECHOSLOVAKIA

WEST GERMANY

R. Danube

GERMANY

AUSTRIA

R. Rhine

ALSACE LORRAINE

German territory lost after the war

American Zone

British Zone

French Zone

Soviet Zone

Jodl was firmly informed by Eisenhower's Chief of Staff, General Walter Bedell Smith, who was in charge of the negotiations, that Eisenhower insisted on the surrender document being signed at once. 'If you decline, the discussions will be considered closed,' Smith told him. 'You will have to deal with the Russians alone. Our Air Force will resume operations. Our lines will be closed even to individual German soldiers and civilians. I don't understand why you don't want to surrender to our Russian Allies.'

Jodl, aware as perhaps Smith was not of the brutality meted out against the German population by the invading Russians, retorted: 'Even if you are right, I should not be able to convince a single German that you are.'

The discussions dragged on into the night and still the war went on and still men were being killed. When Jodl again asked for more time, on the grounds that breakdown of communications made it difficult to contact some German Army units, Eisenhower finally lost all patience. 'You tell them,' he ordered General Strong, 'that forty-eight hours from midnight tonight, I will close my lines on the Western Front so no more Germans can get through. Whether they sign or not—no matter how much time they take.'

Jodl had won two days' grace. He radioed Dönitz proposing the immediate westward withdrawal of German troops on the Eastern Front, and as a result some 1,500,000 of them were saved from Russian captivity. Then he sent an historic signal: 'General Eisenhower insists that we sign today . . . I see no alternative—chaos or signature. I ask you to confirm immediately by radio that I have full powers to sign capitulation. Hostilities will then cease on 9 May, 0001 hours our time.'

From the Nazi headquarters at Flensburg a reply came through at 0040 hours the next morning: Admiral Dönitz authorises signature of surrender under conditions stated.—Keitel.'

In the early hours of 7 May 1945, the first formal signing of the surrender agreement took place. The venue was Eisenhower's L-shaped war room—once the students' recreation room in the little red schoolhouse. Its pale blue walls were covered in battle-maps, casualty charts and prisoner counts, and its cramped 30-foot square area was packed with war reporters, microphones and a Hollywood-style battery of film lights and newsreel cameras. The representatives of the Allied powers were assembled on one side of a large table, which had been pushed to one end of the room to make space for the press. Then there were Major-General François Sevez, the French representative; General Frederick Morgan, Admiral Harold Burrough and Air Marshal Sir James Robb for Great Britain; General Carl Spaatz, Commander of the US Strategic Air Forces in Europe, and Major General Ivan Suslaparov, the Russian Liaison Officer at SHAEF. Suslaparov had still not received official authority from Moscow empowering him to sign for the USSR, but had already decided to go ahead and do so on his own initiative. Jodl, von Friedeburg and Oxenius bowed stiffly before taking their seats on the opposite side of the table. Four copies of the surrender documents, bound in plain grey paper covers, lay on the table. Eisenhower, refusing to treat directly with the German officers, was not present in the room but waited in his office down the corridor, pacing up and down impatiently.

Under the watchful gaze of the seventeen accredited press correspondents and the glare of their lights, General Beddell Smith asked Jodl if all the points in the documents were clear and whether he was prepared to sign. Jodl gave a slight nod of assent. Two special fountain pens were produced, one solid gold and the other gold-plated, both of them the personal property of General Eisenhower. The gold-plated one was handed to the blanched but impassive General Jodl who was the first to sign the surrender agreement. Beddell Smith then signed the document with the solid gold pen, followed by General Suslaparov and General Sevez. The official time on the document was given as 2.41 a.m. British Double Summer Time. The time set for the complete cessation of hostilities in Europe was given as 23.01 Central European time, 8 May (or one minute after midnight, 9 May, British Time).

When the signing was over Jodl stood up and said in English to Beddell Smith: 'I want to say a word.' He picked up the microphone on the table and lapsed into German, which General Strong translated. 'General!' Jodl, on the verge of tears, exclaimed. 'With this signature the German people and the German armed forces are, for better or worse, delivered into the victor's hands. In this war, which has lasted more than five years, both have achieved and suffered more than perhaps any other people in the world. In this hour I can only express the hope that the victor will treat them with generosity.'

Complete silence greeted this plea from Jodl. No written translation was made of it. Smith simply nodded and Jodl's head dropped. It was noticed that his hands were trembling violently. He saluted, turned on his heels and left the room, led out by Strong and followed by the rest of the German delegation. Outside in the hall, Lt. Kay Summersby, Eisenhower's English WAC secretary and confidante, heard the heavy tramp of German boots and saw Jodl, Friedeburg and Oxenius march past her into Eisenhower's office, looking (she recalled later) like 'the exact prototypes of film-land Nazis, sour-faced, glum, erect and despicable.' They clicked their heels and smartly saluted the Supreme Allied Commander, who had drawn himself up to his full height and looked more military than Kay Summersby had ever seen him before.

'Do you understand all the provisions of the document of surrender you have signed?' Eisenhower demanded.

'*Ja*' Jodl replied.

'You will' Eisenhower continued, 'officially and personally, be held responsible if the terms of this surrender are violated, including its provisions for German commanders to appear in Berlin at the moment set by the Russian High Command to accomplish formal surrender to that government. That is all.'

The Germans marched out. When they had gone Eisenhower broke into an immense grin, posed for the cameras, recorded a short statement for the radio, and sent a formal cable to the Combined Chiefs-of-Staff in Washington: 'The mission of this Allied Force was fulfilled at 02.41 local time, May 7, 1945.'

Eisenhower then telephoned General Omar Bradley, the Twelfth US Army Group Commander, at his headquarters in the Fürstenhof Hotel in Bad Wildungen. 'Brad, it's all over,' Ike told him. Bradley in turn rang General Patton, commanding the Third US Army, who was asleep in his trailer at Regensburg. 'Ike just called me, George,' Bradley told him. 'The Germans have surrendered. It takes effect at midnight. We are to hold in place everywhere up and down the line. There's no sense in taking any more casualties now.' Bradley opened his map case and wrote D+335 on it, then went to the window and tore open the black-out curtains and let the lights of his room shine out into the darkness of Germany. The war in Europe was over: or so it seemed.

Bradley knew it, the Allied High Command knew it, the Germans knew it, but nobody else was going to be allowed to know it for many confusing hours and even days. All the Allied and liberated countries in the West were seething with rumour and speculation about the imminence of VE-Day. But Churchill and Truman had promised Stalin that news of the Reims surrender would be held back until the formal Russian ratification had taken place in Berlin, and Eisenhower therefore refused to allow the reporters at Reims to file their stories for another day and a half, that is until 1 p.m. GMT Tuesday 8 May. It should have been obvious that any attempt to suppress a news story of such magnitude was doomed to failure. In the event, 7 May, VE-1, was to prove to be the day of the biggest muddle in the history of mass communication.

In Moscow, where news of the signing had not yet been received, Colonel General Alexei Antonov, the Soviet Deputy Chief of Staff, had already learnt that the text of the Reims surrender differed from that approved by the Big Three and refused to accept its validity. In Reims, Eisenhower's political adviser, Robert Murphy, had discovered the same fact and was deeply perturbed. The surrender document was not the one which had been drawn up by the experts of the European Advisory Commission with the approval of the American, British and Russian governments, and which Murphy had handed over to General Smith in March. It was instead a document drawn up by General Smith himself. 'I discovered that a strange document—that is, strange to me—had been used,' Murphy wrote later. 'General Smith, exhausted, had gone to bed, but I telephoned him and asked what had happened to the EAC-approved text. At first he could not recall having received any surrender papers from me. But don't you remember that big blue folder which I told you were the terms approved by everybody? I asked. The Chief of Staff, now thoroughly awakened, jumped into his uniform and raced back to head-quarters. We found the big blue folder exactly where he had filed it in his personal top-secret cabinet.' Moments later an urgent telegram arrived from Washington saying that Moscow was protesting that the surrender terms which had just been signed were not the EAC agreement which had been endorsed by the Russians. Murphy attributed this ridiculous state of affairs to 'a rare lapse of memory' on Smith's part.

For Eisenhower meanwhile the day had begun quietly enough in bed with an early morning read of a western called *Cartridge Carnival*. But by nine SHAEF was already in turmoil—'The worst day I ever put in at the Supreme Commander's office,' Kay Summersby recalled.

> Everything was in a muddle. One message stated the Germans in Czechoslovakia refused to surrender to the Russians. A second message noted that the German Radio announced the Nazis had made a separate peace with the Western Allies, not with the Russians. The latter not only complained bitterly at this report, but advised SHAEF they no longer felt that General Suslaparov had been an acceptable representative at the Reims ceremony.
>
> Around three, the final blow fell. Beetle (Beddell Smith) roared into the office like a madman: Ed Kennedy of Associated Press had smuggled into America a story about the Reims surrender. The 'scoop' already hummed over AP wires into the United States, leaving a pack of angry correspondents in France, a group of very upset gentlemen in the Kremlin, 10 Downing Street and the White House—and a very irate Supreme Commander.

The cause of the trouble was a respected foreign correspondent from New York, Edward Kennedy, Chief of the Paris Bureau of the Associated Press agency. Returning to Paris from Reims, Kennedy broke the rules by phoning the story of the surrender through to London by military phone that afternoon. He justified his action on the grounds that the BBC had just broadcast an English translation of a speech that Count Schwerin von Krosigk, the German Foreign Minister, had delivered on Radio Flensburg, announcing the unconditional surrender of German forces. To Kennedy's way of thinking it was simply inconceivable that the German would have made the broadcast without the permission of SHAEF, so he felt perfectly justified in breaking the story, thereby dishonouring the agreements of the leaders of the Grand Alliance and SHAEF and scooping the entire Allied Press Corps. At 3.36 p.m. London time, teleprinters all over America suddenly spelt out the dramatic message: 'GERMANY

SURRENDERED UNCONDITIONALLY TO THE WESTERN ALLIES AND RUSSIA 2.41 AM FRENCH TIME TODAY.'

On the west coast of America any premature celebrations were soon officially damped down but New York erupted uncontrollably as if VE-1 was really VE-Day itself. The news swept through the city, according to the *New York Times*, with gale velocity. People in the streets and office-workers up in the skyscrapers screamed it aloud. 'Rivercraft east and west took it up and fed the din with siren and whistle blasts. Cabbies pounded it out on their horns. Women ran down 23rd Street and Eighth Avenue excitedly shouting, "It's over! The war's over!"' From a hundred thousand windows paper of every kind cascaded down—ledgers, scrap, playing cards, streamers, pages torn from telephone directories, ticker-tape. From the windows of dress manufacturers workers threw bale after bale of rayon, silk, woollens, prints and foulards which shimmered and rippled in the morning sunlight. 'Within the hour', continued the *Times*, 'Sixth, Seventh and Eighth Avenues were eight to ten inches deep in multi-coloured fabrics.' By lunchtime Times Square was packed with vast crowds that stopped the traffic as far as the eye could see. An entire cinema queue was on its knees in prayers of thanksgiving. Outside a Broadway Hotel a line of American, Canadian and British servicemen were receiving the kisses of an endless queue of New York girls. By 5 p.m. the city authorities estimated that a million or more New Yorkers had danced in the streets.

In several capitals of Europe, too, the end of the war was celebrated before the ceasefire took official effect. The streets of Paris were full of crowds and fireworks. In Rome, the bells of St Peter's and a hundred other churches rang in jubilation. In Stockholm confetti showered down in the streets and the Swedish government, hitherto neutral, at last broke off diplomatic relations with Germany. In London, deprived of news for most of the day, great crowds gathered in the late evening in blacked-out Piccadilly Circus and Trafalgar Square. 'VE-Day may be tomorrow', reported the *Daily Mail*, 'but the war is over tonight.'

In Dublin, however, anti-British, pro-Nazi sentiments still prevailed. The Irish Republic was one of the few nations to send a telegram of condolence to Germany on the death of Hitler and scuffles broke out when the Union Jack and flags of the other Allied nations were hoisted above Trinity College. And in Moscow there were no celebrations of any kind, for no news had been given to the people, and Stalin was already in the process of repudiating the Reims surrender.

Early on the morning of 7 May, the Soviet High Command despatched a message to Eisenhower at Reims demanding that the signing of the 'Act of Military Surrender' should take place in Berlin with Marshal Zhukov, the Commander in Chief of the Russian Western Front and conqueror of Berlin, representing the Soviet government. This message crossed with one from Eisenhower informing the Russians that the signing had already taken place at Reims, with General Suslaparov signing for the Soviets. This news incensed Stalin and roused his deepest suspicions. The Reims surrender was seen not only as an Anglo-American attempt to rob the Russians of their full glory in the victory against the Germans but even as a perfidious manoeuvre to conclude a separate peace with the Germans and make a common front against the Soviets.

According to the Russians, radio intercepts indicated that large elements of the German Army were refusing to surrender to the Red Army after the Reims signing. Chief Marshal of Artillery Voronov recalled receiving a phone call that day from Stalin, who furiously demanded: 'For what is Suslaparov famous?' (Suslaparov was an Artillery General). Voronov replied that he had not particularly distinguished himself in any way. Whereupon Stalin exploded: 'Then how dare he sign a document of such tremendous importance?' Suslaparov, Stalin insisted, should be severely punished. The Reims signing would be relegated to the status of a mere 'protocol of surrender', a humble Anglo-American preliminary to a great full-dress Soviet finale of the 'General Act of Surrender' in Berlin on the following day, to be conducted by Marshal Zhukov. Only after that would the Russians acknowledge the end of the war in Europe. In the meantime the Russian people would be left in ignorance of events—and the war, technically, would still go on.

All of which emphasised a fact which had been all too easily obscured under the umbrella of the term 'Grand Alliance'—namely that there had not only been two separate fronts in Europe but two separate wars, the Russian one against Germany in the east and the Anglo-American one against Germany in the west, and these two separate wars required two separate surrenders by the two-times loser, Germany.

Captain George Bailey, a US Army SHAEF interpreter in German and Russian at the Reims surrender negotiations, first heard of the Soviet repudiation at 5.30 p.m. on 7 May. General Bedell Smith asked him if he could provide a Russian translation of the Articles of Surrender in seventeen typewritten fair copies by 8 a.m. the next morning so that they could be taken to Berlin for the Soviet surrender ceremony later that day. The problem was the typewriting. The only Russian typewriters that Bailey knew of were at the Liaison School in Paris. Conscious of the urgency of the situation, Bedell Smith promptly gave Bailey his car and his driver and dispatched him to Paris with a block of foolscap paper.

It took Bailey only two hours to reach Paris but all of three hours to cross it. 'We encountered human roadblocks every foot of the way,' he recounted later. 'The good people of Paris were already celebrating VE-Day. Every last street was full of jubilant, jostling, dancing crowds through which we could only thread our way at a speed of three or four miles an hour.' In vain Bailey pleaded with the crowds to let him through.

The war was not yet over, he tried to explain, feeling like a fool as he did so. Indeed, if he did not get his Russian typewriter, and the Soviets did not get their Russian translations, he was not sure when the war would be over.

'We arrived at the Liaison School billets around 11 at night. Of course we found them empty. Like everyone else, the officers and men of the school were out celebrating. It took me almost three hours of frantic scurrying from bar to bistro to boudoir to track down five of them.' Alas, two of the five were drunk, and none of the others could type. It was already nearly two in the morning of 8 May, VE-Day. 'In the next three hours, in a sequence of seek-it-and-sock-it pandemonium, we used up some 200 sheets of typing paper but managed to produce the 17 fair copies.'

George Bailey had been forty-six hours without sleep but his ordeal was not yet over. He still had to get the Russian document back to General Smith before the Anglo-American delegates flew off to the Soviet surrender ceremony in Berlin. He left Paris at 5 a.m., fell asleep, and woke to find the driver had missed the Reims turn and was way off course. They doubled back at high speed and arrived at SHAEF headquarters just in time to make the plane. One last obstacle barred the fulfilment of Captain Bailey's bizarre but historic mission. His garrison cap had been whisked off his head and carried away as a trophy by a French girl in the mêlée in Paris. Now an RAF Wing Commander barred his path and immediately called him to account for being improperly dressed. 'I sought to impress him with the importance of my mission,' Bailey wrote later, 'so that he would stop nattering and let me pass: I announced that I was carrying 17 fair copies of the Articles of Surrender in Russian. "You are?" he said. "Well you're not a very fair copy of an officer are you?" The he made way. My rejoinder was in Russian.'

At 8.25 p.m. two US Air Force C-47s took off from Reims and headed east for Berlin. In the first plane was George Bailey's Russian translation of the surrender documents, intended to serve as a basis for the final agreed version of the Act of Military Surrender in Berlin. Among those on board was Air Chief Marshal Tedder, the Deputy Supreme Commander, representing Eisenhower, who had declined to take part in the Berlin ceremony of surrender on the grounds that it might detract from the importance of the Reims ceremony and lower his own prestige; and the unfortunate Major-General Suslaparov. Behind them flew another C-47 carrying the German delegation that had signed the Reims surrender. An RAF C-47 joined them en route carrying the head German representative, Field Marshal Wilhelm Keitel, and other high-ranking German officers—all of them, particularly Keitel, 'aloof, coldly and militarily correct'. Another plane bringing the French representative, General de Lattre de Tassigny, joined the formation later.

Escorted over Soviet-occupied Germany by a Russian fighter escort, the planes landed at Tempelhof airfield at 11 a.m. Zhukov's entire staff headed by Marshal Vasili Sokolovsky, was there to greet them, the first representatives of the Western Allies to enter Berlin, at the head of a battalion-strong guard of honour, the massed Allied flags and a band playing 'God Save the King', 'The Star-Spangled Banner' and the Russian National Anthem. For General Suslaparov there was a different kind of reception party. After disembarking from the plane, the man who had prematurely signed for Russia at Reims was led away and never seen again by his Anglo-American colleagues. All subsequent enquiries by SHAEF about his whereabouts were met with silence or incomprehension on the part of the Soviet authorities. (In fact, Suslaparov was not shot, but he came very near to it.)

The combined parties were driven off in a caravan of captured German vehicles through the still-smoking ruins of the devastated German capital to Zhukov's headquarters, housed in a German Army Engineering College at Karlshorst, a suburb in the north-east of the city. Here they were quartered in a street of modest little workers' houses, where shiny-faced Russian women soldiers served them with a lunch of thick white bread, black and red caviar, ham, fish, good Rhine wine and cognac.

The Western representatives had expected to be back in Reims by evening, but the afternoon ebbed away as the Anglo-American, French and Russian interpreters argued over details of the surrender document, and it became clear that they would have to spend the night in Berlin. As darkness fell over the ruins the power failed and Eisenhower's chief stenographer had to type out the final version of the surrender document in the light of a candle held over the typewriter by high ranking officers of the SHAEF delegation. Then at 10.30 p.m. they were summoned to the Surrender Hall for the long-awaited drama of the final Nazi surrender.

The room was large, measuring some 60 by 40 feet, two storeys in height and with a balcony at one end. If the Reims war room had looked like Hollywood, Captain Butcher noted, 'we were now looking at something that was super-Hollywood.' The room was brilliantly lit with banks of movie lights and festooned with a spider-web of microphone leads and power-cables. A hundred members of the Russian Press Corps swarmed all over the place in shouting confusion. Across one end of the room ran a long table for the principals on the Allies' side. Three more tables extended at right angles from it—one for the Press, another for American, British and Soviet officers, the third, as yet empty, for the Germans.

The short and stern Marshal Zhukov took his place at the centre of the top table. Eisenhower's representative Tedder sat at his right, the American Air Force General Spaatz at his left. On Tedder's right sat Stalin's political representative from the Kremlin, Andrei Vyshinsky, the Soviet Deputy Commissar for Foreign Affairs, a man to whom even Zhukov was forced to defer.

Marshal Zhukov called the meeting to order and gave the command for the guards to bring in the German delegation. 'As a door opened behind the empty table,' Kay Summersby recalled, 'a silence smothered the babble. Every pair of eyes in the room focused on a tall German officer in smart blue-grey Field Marshal's uniform, his chest covered with decorations and medals, his head held high. He stepped stiffly to the table, jerked up his silver-headed baton in a curt salute and sat down.' Keitel, noted Butcher, was still arrogant and defiant and seemed to survey the room like he might the terrain of a battlefield. 'Ah, the French are here too!' Vyshinsky heard him mutter when he set eyes on General de Lattre. 'That's all we need!' By contrast Friedeburg looked morose and had deep black rings round his eyes. (Two weeks later he was to commit suicide.)

Tedder now rose and in a high, thin, suitably harsh voice, asked the Germans if they accepted the terms of surrender. Keitel nodded and the Germans then walked across to the top table opposite Zhukov where several copies of the surrender document were laid in front of them. Keitel disdainfully pulled off one grey glove before taking the pen and peered with contempt at the Russian newsmen who were jostling around him. Then Keitel signed. It was 23.30 Central European Time. The ceasefire had been in force for half an hour. Flash-bulbs popped; photographers and reporters climbed on to the tables to get a better view—one newsreel cameraman was punched on the jaw as he shoved others out of the way and promptly replied in kind. While Zhukov and Tedder signed for the Allies, with Spaatz and de Lattre de Tessigny as witnesses, Keitel became involved in a heated argument with his American interpreter, angrily claiming that more time was needed to transmit the final surrender orders to all sections of the German front. But it was too late. He had already signed the surrender agreement. Amid the undignified farce and acrimony of that noisy room in Soviet suburban Berlin, the war in Europe was at last ended.

A short while later in the same room, at the same tables now covered with tablecloths made of torn-up linen bedsheets and covered with a forest of vodka and champagne bottles, the Russian victory banquet got under way. This was a VE-Day party to end all VE-Day parties, and lasted four and a half hours till six in the morning. A Russian orchestra played in the balcony and the vodka flowed—the American contingent believed it to be Lend-Lease alcohol with a flavour like vodka and an effect like TNT. 'Zhukov, Tedder, Spaatz and de Lattre de Tassigny seemed to be popping up like jacks-in-the-box offering toast after toast, barely giving me time to sit down and fill my glass and repeat,' lamented Harry Butcher. There were something around twenty-five individual toasts—to Stalin, to Eisenhower, to Churchill, Roosevelt, Truman, victory, peace and British–American–Soviet friendship—each one accompanied by a loud musical chord from the orchestra in the balcony and a final deadly *do dna* ('bottoms up') in wine or vodka from the assembled exalted company of marshals, generals and commissars. By five most of the banquet guests were good and drunk. Some of the Russians were under the table and three generals had to be carried out. Ike's naval aide crept off to his cottage to sleep it off and woke fighting drunk when a search-party came to find him. Everyone was singing—in four different languages—and the orchestra was growing increasingly atonal as more vodka found its way up to their balcony. In their small villa nearby, Keitel and his German delegation were being fed a roast dinner, rounded off with strawberries and Russian champagne. It was a *very* strange night.

By the time Marshal of the Royal Air Force Tedder and his party were en route to Paris, the nations in the west had already finished celebrating VE-Day and the USSR had not yet even begun.

Churchill had at last felt free to announce the end of the war to the British people in a broadcast from the Cabinet Room at 10 Downing Street at 3 p.m. London time on 8 May. 'Advance Britannia!' he had concluded rousingly. 'Long live the cause of freedom! God save the King!' That afternoon Britain's war leader made a triumphant entry into a packed House of Commons; later he appeared with the Royal Family on the balcony of Buckingham Palace and treated a similar multitude to an impromptu speech in Whitehall. 'This is your victory,' he told the throng. 'It is the victory of the cause of freedom in every land. In all our long history we have never seen a greater day than this . . . God bless you all.'

For six years the entire land had endured total blackout after sunset. Now all the great public buildings of the British capital were brilliantly illumined in a dazzling blaze of floodlights, the glare of thousands of bonfires cast an orange-red glow in the sky over the city, like the glows of the fires in the blitz a few years before. All across the country huge beacons burst into flame one after the other, stretching mile after mile until it seemed the very hills were on fire.

In Germany the reaction to VE-Day was muted, among Germans and Allied soldiers alike. Though the shooting war had stopped, many British and American units had more pressing tasks to perform than celebration of the ceasefire, and for many of the combat troops their first emotion was to mourn their fallen comrades who could not see this day. Lester Atwell, a private in the US Army, recalled: 'We sat in silence. I searched for some feeling, waited for it to develop. There was hardly any sensation at all. A moment later I was aware of an inward caving in, followed by a sore-throat feeling when I thought of those who had been forced to give up their lives for this moment.' There were no celebrations and that night Atwell and his fellow-GIs had to report back on duty. The only thing different about

VE-Day was a plane that flew over with its lights on—the first he had seen in Europe.

The day after VE-Day, Captain Saul Padover, who had followed the battle-front through Germany as an officer of the Psychological Warfare Division, wrote to his wife in America:

> In Germany there was death, there was fear, there was inner despair. The Germans showed no awareness of, or even surface interest in, the peace . . . It was startling to cross from Germany into France. On one side death and destruction and hopelessness and total greyness; on the other side gay flags, cheering, happiness. The Germans had massacred millions of innocent people; they had inflicted unhappiness on hundreds of millions by killings, by enslavement, and by separation of families. And now the wheels of justice had turned, and the world celebrated the crushing of the Nazi monster. By this act of defeat, the Germans were more cut off from the rest of the world than ever before. They were no longer members of the community of peoples but a race apart, cursed and feared as no race has ever been in recorded history. Only the coming generation of Germans can redeem their country. One must hope and pray that they will not fail.

In POW camps in England a sombre gloom descended on the German inmates: they stopped singing all their patriotic songs and went about bowed down in a state of shock. A teenage radar technician, Private Erich Leverkus, sailing to the USA on an American POW ship, wrote a laconic entry in his diary on 8 May: 'Unconditional surrender of Germany = end of the war. First bowel motion since being captured five weeks ago.' A 21-year-old U-boat First Officer, Herbert Schnitt, wrote in a journal after the surrender of his submarine in the Irish Sea on 9 May: 'Our mood is indescribable: depressed and dejected, expectant and curious, completely insecure yet defiant. Already while at sea it had begun: self-examination, self-tormenting questions about "why" and "wherefore". Was it really all lies our Führer told us, everything criminal that they ordered us to do? Were they fools, cowards, criminals, or only men who have submitted to superior force? Were they traitors—or were we—for capitulating?'

While Churchill was broadcasting the news of the German surrender on the afternoon of 8 May, the Russian radio was broadcasting a little story about two rabbits and a bird on its daily programme for younger listeners. Not until the early hours of 9 May were the Russian people told that the war in which one-ninth of their population had been slaughtered was over. In the Soviet Union, Victory Day was therefore celebrated one day later than in the west—a difference ominous of the far greater differences which would soon leave the Grand Alliance in ruins.

But May 9 proved an unforgettable day in Moscow. There was no mistaking the spontaneous friendliness of the two or three million Russians who thronged Red Square and Gorky Street and the Moscow River embankments towards their British and American allies. Crowds thousands strong gathered outside the American Embassy shouting 'Long live America!' Pretty Russian factory girls danced on the pavement with American GIs. Outside the British Embassy a throng of Russians gathered after a victory service attended by Churchill's wife and the Dean of Canterbury Cathedral, the Reverend Dr Hewlett Johnson, both on official visits to the USSR. 'A dense crowd, enthusiastic and genial, released at last from the long strain of war, blocked our road and engulfed us, cheering every Englishman or American,' the Dean of Canterbury reported later. 'They seized General Younger, a British officer in full uniform and, tossing him in the air, caught him as gently as if he were a babe. My turn came next, and I saw a Moscow crowd from a considerable altitude.'

That evening Stalin broadcast to the nation: 'Fascist Germany has been forced to her knees by the Red Army and the troops of our Allies . . . the Great Patriotic War has ended with our complete victory. Glory to our heroic Red Army . . . Glory to our great people . . . eternal glory to the heroes who fell in the struggle.' A thousand guns lined wheel to wheel along the river bank let loose an artillery salute of thirty salvoes. Red Air Force planes swooped and circled over the city and after dark a hundred orchestras and bands struck up in all the squares and parks. An immense victory firework-display—the biggest anyone could remember—flashed and fizzled over the city, and coloured searchlight beams played on the sky and on a gigantic red banner suspended a thousand feet overhead from a barrage balloon. Through the grille of his cell window in Lubyanka Prison, a former Red Army artillery captain, Alexander Solzhenitsyn, heard the noise of the guns and saw the lights over the city. 'From all the windows of all the Moscow prisons,' he was to recall, 'we, too, former prisoners of war and former front-line soldiers, watched the Moscow heavens, patterned with fireworks and crisscrossed by the beams of searchlights . . . that victory was not for us.'

The rhetoric of peace and hope was misleading. Whole populations had celebrated the end of tyranny and bloodshed and the dawning of a new era—but in the weeks and months that followed millions of people would continue to die.

APPENDIX

Almost 40 million human beings from twenty-one different countries had lost their lives in the war that had just ended in Europe—half of them civilians. This was more than twice the total of dead in the war against Japan and more than twice the total of dead on all fronts in World War One.

The worst casualties had been incurred in Eastern Europe. Poland lost nearly 5.5 million of its people—more than one-sixth of the pre-war population. Yugoslavia lost nearly 2 million—more than a tenth of its population. The Soviet Union lost a horrendous 20 million people—more than a tenth of its population, including over 6 million civilians. Germany, too, paid a fearful price for Hitler's war. Six per cent of the pre-war population, totalling over 7 million, died as a consequence of the war—3,760,000 military, 3,810,000 civilians (over 170,000 German Jews included). Of all Germans born in 1924 25 per cent were dead by the end of the war, and 31 per cent wounded—a casualty rate of more than one in two. The worst casualty ratios were among ethnic groups who fell victim to the Nazi racial extermination programme. Nearly 6 million Jews perished out of the estimated 10 million living in Europe before the war—most of them from Poland and the Soviet Union. The gypsies of Eastern Europe, totalling some half million, were virtually exterminated.

By comparison with this horrific tally of dead, the Western Allies suffered relatively light casualties in proportion to their populations. France (520,000 military and civilian dead), Britain (390,000 dead, including 60,000 civilians), the United States (170,000 dead, all military) and Canada (40,000 dead) lost 1 per cent or less of their populations, as did Italy, Germany's principal ally (400,000 dead, including 70,000 civilians).

These figures ignore the no less horrendous totals of wounded—2 million in Germany alone—and the tens of millions of people uprooted from their homes by the war and its aftermath: a displacement of peoples on a scale without precedent in the history of the human race. The sheer size of this disaster was due to a number of causes: the immense geographical extent of the war front, involving almost every country in Europe; sophisticated and lethal weaponry, especially in the air; Nazi savagery, especially towards the Jews and the Slavs; and the concept of total war and the moral acceptance of civilian casualties as a means of achieving a strategic military objective, as in the area bombing of German cities, or achieving political goals, as in the Germans' use of terror against subject populations.

The material damage caused by the war was as cataclysmic as the human slaughter. Air raids, artillery bombardment, street battles and scorched-earth tactics had partly destroyed cities as far apart as Coventry, Rotterdam, Lyons, Naples, Cracow, Leningrad and Kiev, and severely damaged capitals like London, Vienna, Budapest and Belgrade. Warsaw and Berlin had been almost obliterated. Countless smaller towns and villages had been razed to the ground or turned into ghost towns—like Wiener Neustadt in Austria, which emerged from the air raids and the street-fighting with only 18 houses intact and its population reduced from 45,000 to 860. In Russia 6 million houses had been destroyed, leaving 25 million people homeless. In Düsseldorf 93 per cent of the houses were left uninhabitable. The basic economic infrastructure of Europe had ceased to exist and industrial production had fallen by two-thirds or more. In Russia 3,000 oil wells and 1,000 coalpits had been destroyed and nearly 70 million head of livestock taken by the Germans. Yugoslavia had lost two-thirds of its industrial resources, Poland and France a half. In the whole of the continent only two ports, Antwerp and Bordeaux, were working normally—the rest were blocked with dynamited jetties and sunken ships. More than half the railway stock of France and Germany had been destroyed, and half of Britain's mercantile fleet had been sent to the bottom. The financial system had been destroyed and international trade completely disrupted. Some currencies collapsed completely and inflation got out of hand in many countries: in Hungary one American dollar was worth 11,000,000,000,000,000,000,000 pengoes. Britain was bankrupted by the cost of the war: her exports had declined by nearly 70 per cent, her foreign debts had increased by 600 per cent, largely on account of her borrowings from the USA. Only the United States came out of the war a good deal better off than she went into it. Her war production had grown to enormous size and her domestic economy had been maintained at a high level; her exports alone had risen by 300 per cent during the course of the war.

Such was the balance-sheet of the war in Europe at close of business on VE-Day.

6

Last Rites

With the war officially over, the task remained of mopping up remnants of the German Army still at large. Some 50 per cent of the German forces on the Eastern Front had been extricated by the end of the war leaving over 1,500,000 men still trapped behind Russian lines. It took two months to complete the complex surrender of the huge German armies and their auxiliaries. Some German units were still trying to fight their way out of Russian encirclement, and find asylum in the West; others held out for a day or two because of the pig-headed Nazism of their commanders; most were isolated garrisons with no one to surrender to. In Amsterdam the German garrison fought on until VE-Day itself. On the Atlantic coast of France the fortified U-boat ports of La Rochelle, La Palisse, St-Nazaire and Lorient did not surrender until 9 May. That same day the Channel Islands, the only part of Great Britain occupied by the Nazis in the war, were liberated by British forces.

Though the war was over the Red Army continued its westward advance, rounding up the last German bridgeheads in the Gulf of Danzig and pursuing retreating German troops in Czechoslovakia. On 10 May, the Red Army liberated the last Nazi concentration camp, at Theresienstadt, and the next day met up with the most easterly spearheads of the American Army in Czechoslovakia, Saxony and Austria. The German forces in the Greek islands of the Dodecanese and the Aegean, including the garrisons on the islands of Crete, Rhodes, Leros, Milos and Kos, did not surrender until three days after VE-Day. On 12 May troops of the once-powerful Army Group Courland, in Latvia, began to surrender to the Red Army, though the round-up was not completed until eleven days later, when some 180,000 German prisoners were marched to camps in the Valdai Hills.

The Red Army offensive in Europe did not come to a halt until 13 May, when the last pockets of German resistance in Czechoslovakia were finally eradicated. In Yugoslavia the war went on even longer. Milovan Djilas, one of the closest aides of the Yugoslav communist partisan leader, Marshal Tito, recalled: 'The world celebrated peace and victory while we were still waging war on a grand scale. Not even the Germans dared to surrender to us, to say nothing of the Chetniks, the Ustashi, and other bitter mortal enemies. Joylessness and bitterness overcame most of the leading comrades. Tito was obstinate: for several years Yugoslavia did not celebrate 9 May as its Victory Day but 15 May, when our enemies laid down their arms.' Having finally recognized the partisans as an official Allied Army, the surviving German forces—over 175,000 men—gave themselves up and passed into the less than merciful hands of their Yugoslav captors. Some twenty to thirty thousand Yugoslav collaborators were slaughtered where they stood in a frenzy of retribution.

By 17 May, eight million Germans were reported to be prisoners in the west and many millions more were toiling in captivity in the east. Apart from groups of fugitives from the Army Group Courland, who were to roam for years behind the Soviet lines in the Baltic States in support of local anti-Soviet guerilla bands, the only German combatants still on the loose were fugitive U-boats at sea.

One boat, U-977, under Lt.-Cdr Heinz Schaeffer, slipped out of a Norwegian fjord in early May and remained submerged for 66 days until she was well past the British Naval base at Gibraltar and approaching the Cape Verde Islands. After 104 days at sea, U-977 reached journey's end in the harbour-mouth of Rio de la Plata in Argentina, where her crew expected to receive asylum. But their hopes were soon dashed. U-530, another missing U-boat, had already preceded her into the same port. Wild rumours were circulating to the effect that Hitler was still alive, having been smuggled out of Germany by submarine and landed in the Antarctic, where he was already establishing the nucleus of a new Nazi Reich at New Berchtesgaden. The U-boat crews were interned and dispatched to Washington for interrogation. When it was proved that they had made these long voyages in order to evade captivity, they were repatriated.

In Germany, meanwhile, the Third Reich in the form of the so-called Dönitz government continued in Flensburg. In the last stages of the war this beleaguered outpost of Nazi rule had served a highly useful function for the Allies and the Germans alike. Dönitz was resolved to bring the war to an end and his authority over the German armed forces enabled this to be done as efficiently as the chaotic circumstances allowed. At the same time he was responsible for one of the greatest rescue operations of all time—the withdrawal to the west by sea of over two million German soldiers and refugees from Baltic territories overrun by the Soviets, and the further evacuation after VE-Day of a further 120,000 soldiers and refugees. After the war, however, the Dönitz government largely ceased to serve any useful function, and in Allied eyes was seen first as an anomaly and then as an embarrassment to their plans for Germany's future.

In their tiny enclave surrounded entirely by British troops, the last rulers of the Third Reich busied themselves with their meaningless comic opera administration. Every day Dönitz was driven all of five hundred yards to the government's headquarters in the Naval School at nearby Mürwik in one of Hitler's Mercedes limousines. Albert Speer commuted daily through the British lines from the Duke of Holstein's castle at Glücksburg, where he and his family were now accommodated. Every morning a cabinet meeting was held in one of the schoolrooms. An old radio set formed the basis of the Government's information service. Armed German soldiers stood sentry outside the door and the Reich war flag fluttered from the flagstaff.

The Germans at Flensburg saw themselves as a vital link between the German people and the Western Allies. They hoped that their expert services would soon be called upon to begin the reconstruction of a new Germany and never dreamed that Germany could be run without them. Dönitz hoped to preserve the continuity of the Third Reich, while making his government more acceptable to the Allies by keeping the more extreme Nazis out of office and banning the wearing of SS uniforms.

Some of the Western Allied leaders, notably Churchill, thought the Flensburg government should be tolerated, at least for a while, on the grounds that it might be useful in certain contingencies to have a central German authority in Germany. But the regime soon exceeded itself. A storm of public indignation greeted an arrogant pronouncement over Radio Flensburg by Field Marshal Busch that he was assuming full command of Schleswig-Holstein. The Allied press grew increasingly hostile. 'Recognition of Busch's authority would confirm Dönitz's leadership,' the *New York Times* reported on 13 May. 'This would imply that the German Reich was still in existence and Dönitz was its head of state.' Dönitz should be arrested as a war criminal, the papers urged, and his fake government broken up. The Russians accused the Western Allies of plotting to support fascist states 'as a means of thwarting the democratic aspirations of all freedom-loving people.' When Dönitz began to preach the need for the Anglo-Americans to ally themselves with the Germans against the threatened Bolshevisation of Europe, Eisenhower finally gave the order for the arrest of the Dönitz government and the remains of German High Command.

When Dönitz, Jodl and von Friedeburg arrived at the quarters of the SHAEF liaison group on board the requisitioned liner *Patria* at 9.45 on the morning of 23 May, there was no one to greet them at the gangway, no officer present, no sentries presenting arms. Instead there was a large crowd of Allied pressmen on the deck. Dönitz and his companions were informed by the American Major-General Lowell R. Rooks, head of the SHAEF Control Party at Flensburg, that on General Eisenhower's instructions they were now prisoners of war and their government dissolved. They must pack and be ready to leave by plane at 1.30 that afternoon for an unspecified destination.

At about the same time a party of British infantrymen from 21st Army Group rushed up the steps of the Government HQ at Mürwik armed with grenades, sten-guns and fixed bayonets, charged past the armed German sentries at the door, who sheepishly looked away, and burst into the Foreign Minister's daily conference. The startled Germans were lined up against the wall in the corridor outside and then subjected to a body-search—presumably for poisoned capsules. In various rooms male officers and female secretaries were together subjected to the same humiliation. Dönitz, Jodl and von Friedeburg, who had been taken to Flensburg police headquarters, were also searched.

At Glücksburg, where Speer was arrested, anti-tank guns were trained on the castle, and three battalions of infantry and an armoured regiment surrounded the Flensburg enclave as the round-up intensified. All the prisoners were marched with their hands above their heads to the square of the Mürwik barracks and there they were photographed by the press while their quarters were searched and looted by the soldiers. Dönitz's marshal's baton and several other private possessions were stolen from him in this way. Then the leading members of the Flensburg government, Dönitz, Jodl and Speer, were singled out from the rest and led into a small courtyard where numerous machine-guns were trained on them from first-floor windows and newspaper photographers and newsreel cameramen recorded their indignity for posterity. The arrest of the Dönitz government had been a deliberately humiliating spectacle designed to deprive the German leaders of all dignity and respect—so successfully that both von Friedeburg and Dönitz's secretary killed themselves shortly afterwards.

That evening Dönitz and all the leading members of his entourage were driven under an escort of forty armoured vehicles to Flensburg airfield, where they were loaded on to an American DC4. Later than night they landed in Luxembourg and were driven swiftly through the streets, past the jeering crowds, out into the country towards the river Moselle. At the Palast Hotel in the little riverside resort of Bad Mondorf they stopped. This was 'Camp Ashcan', the processing centre for Hitler's topmost surviving ministers, state secretaries and generals on their long road to trial and retribution. 'From outside we had been able to see Goering and other former members of the leadership of the Third Reich pacing back and forth,' Speer wrote later. 'It was a ghostly experience to find all those who at the end had scattered like chaff in the wind reassembled there.'

'After the arrest of Grand Admiral Dönitz and his associates,' Robert

Murphy, Eisenhower's political adviser, remarked afterwards, 'not even a
remnant remained of any German government. The conquerors of the
Nazis were in complete control and the administration of Germany was
their responsibility.'

Two events underlined the decisiveness of the situation. The first was the
great Victory Parade in Moscow on 24 June. In a ceremonial apotheosis to
the Soviet victory over German fascism, an endless stream of tanks, guns
and katyushas rumbled across the cobblestones of Red Square, marshals
and generals and regiment after regiment of men tramped past Stalin on
the podium above Lenin's mausoleum and past the Deputy Supreme
Commander, Marshal Zhukov, seated astride a white charger. But the
great moment was to come. A Russian air-force general who was present,
A. S. Iakoviev, described the moving finale when the captured Nazi war
banners, each one the flag and emblem of a German fighting unit, were
ritually consigned to infamy: 'The huge orchestra suddenly stopped
playing. Red Square was immersed in silence. Then a menacing staccato
beat of hundreds of drums could be heard. Marching in precise formation
and beating out an iron cadence, a column of Soviet soldiers drew nigh: 200
soldiers carrying 200 Nazi banners. Upon reaching the Mausoleum, the
soldiers did a right turn and flung the captured enemy banners and
standards with the black swastikas at the base of the Mausoleum. There
was a downpour of rain. It was impossible to tear one's eyes from the dirty
banners that had been cast down on to the wet granite.'

The second event was the formal entry of the Anglo-American
forces into the erstwhile capital of the Third Reich—a doubly
portentous occasion which not only affirmed the totality of the German
defeat in war but presaged the imminent break up of the Grand Alliance.
War-time agreements between the Allied leaders had provided for a
joint British–American–Russian occupation of Berlin, and at the last
minute the French were also allowed a section of the city. But it was
the Russians who captured the German capital, and the subsequent entry
of the Western armies after the end of hostilities was to prove a far
from triumphant one, for they were baulked and harassed by the Russians
at every turn.

The first American army recce party set off across the Elbe for the
hundred-mile drive across Soviet-held German territory on 17 June but
were confronted with such hostile obstruction by the Red Army authorities
along the route that only a fraction of the party got through—and even then
only to the outskirts of the city. Between 1 July and 4 July 25,000 American
troops and 25,000 British troops made their official entry into the German
capital. They did not have an easy passage. 'On July 1, 1945, the road to
Berlin was the highroad to Bedlam,' recalled Colonel Frank Howley,
commanding the Berlin detachment of American Military Government.

It was jam packed with tanks, trucks and other vehicles, Military Government people and troops, all hurrying towards the previously forbidden city. Russian officers, in captured ramshackle cars and trucks, raced up and down our columns to see that we weren't escaping with plunder. The road to Berlin was paved with drunks. Some wanted only to exchange toasts in vodka; others behaved like little commissars. When one particularly obstreperous Red Army officer tried to halt a column at a bridge, an American general jumped from his car and personally deposited the struggling Russian in the ditch to allow our column to pass.

A disagreeable summer rain was pelting down when we finally straggled into Berlin late in the afternoon. The Russians had not allowed us to look over our sector before coming in, and none of us knew exactly where to go once we arrived. As it was, hundreds of officers and men milled around, looking for places to stay in the ruins, and most of them, in Class A uniforms, wound up sleeping on the muddy ground in the rain.

So the Anglo-Americans crawled into the German capital, past huge street portraits of Stalin, Zhukov and other Soviet leaders, and conciliatory posters proclaiming: 'The lessons of history show that Hitlers come and go but the German people and the German state remain.'

Colonel Howley's Military Government detachment moved into the Grünewald, a large forested park in the south-west of the city, and under the dripping trees pulled all their vehicles into a protective circle and posted guards, as in the old covered-wagon days of the American West. 'I had managed to avoid pup tents throughout World War Two,' one of Howley's aides, Col. John J. Maginnis, recalled, 'and here I was, with the war over and making a triumphal entry into Berlin, established in that dreaded form of shelter under most dreary and uncomfortable conditions. This was undoubtedly history's most unimpressive entry into the capital of a defeated nation by a conquering power.'

When the British 7th Armoured Division took over Spandau barracks from the Russians they found them inches deep in rotting potatoes and human excreta. 'To open a cupboard was an adventure in itself,' one junior officer recalled of those early days in Berlin. 'It began to seem as if the barracks were part of a bad dream.'

Two weeks after the British and American forces joined the Red Army in the German capital, their national leaders arrived to take part in the last great conference arising out of the war. The Conference of Berlin, better known as the Potsdam Conference, was held at the Cecilienhof Palace at Potsdam, a suburb to the south-east of the city in the Soviet zone, between 17 July and 3 August 1945. It was the first peacetime meeting of the Big Three, and also their last. Convened to tidy up the loose ends left by World War Two, the conference was destined to be, by virtue of the duplicity and default of its members, not so much the finale to a past conflict as the overture to a future one—the worldwide tremor of the Cold War, whose epicentre was destined once again to be Germany.

The Big Three, with their Foreign Ministers and numerous advisers, arrived in Berlin on 15 July, two days before the start of the conference. Josef Stalin who had promoted himself from Marshal to Generalissimo at the end of the war, arrived from Moscow on the former Tsar's imperial train. The American president, Harry Truman flew in by plane from Belgium after an uneventful Atlantic crossing. Winston Churchill had just finished fighting the General Election in Britain and was still waiting for the result. He was fretful and exhausted when he arrived with his party at Gatow airport. 'The sun blazed down,' his personal physician Lord Moran recalled.

> There were Russian soldiers everywhere, lining the road, behind bushes, knee deep in corn. We drove to where a substantial stone house, which was said to have belonged to Schacht, the banker, had been reserved for the Prime Minister. I followed him through two bleak rooms with great chandeliers to the opposite side of the empty house, where French windows that had not been cleaned for a long time opened upon a balcony, and there, without removing his hat, Winston flopped into a garden chair, flanked by two great tubs of hydrangeas. He appeared too weary to move. Presently he looked up. He turned to Tommy Thompson (his personal assistant): 'Get me a whisky.'

For a long time the Prime Minister sat in silence, looking over a lake, where a Russian sentry lurked in a wood and fired his gun at nightfall.

The newly arrived heads of state and their retinues were housed at Babelsberg, a leafy but mosquito-infested suburb next to Potsdam along Lake Griebnitz. War had left Babelsberg unscathed and its comfortable lakeside villas, once the summer retreats of film-stars from the studios in Berlin, were requisitioned to house the newcomers. The British took fifty of them and furnished each one with a Steinway or Bechstein grand piano. The logistics of the conference were on a similar scale. The British Army, for example, was indented for such diverse items as 2,000 conference passes, 100 transfer Union Jacks to stick on staff cars, 60 dustpans, brushes, brooms and mops, 200 fly swats, 250 corkscrews and 150 alarm-clocks. From Babelsberg to the Cecilienhof in Potsdam was only a short drive. The ivy-clad Cecilienhof, built in 1917 for the Crown Prince in English mock-Tudor style, was described as Europe's last grand palace. The main conference room was on the ground floor, a wood-panelled room, with a large round table in the middle where up to fifteen people would be seated at a session. In this gloomy chamber, heavily furnished in an old-fashioned style, the Big Three was meant to decide the fate of nations.

Before the first meeting, Truman and Churchill independently drove out to see the ruins of Berlin. Half-way between Potsdam and the city centre Truman came on the entire American 2nd Armoured Division, at that time the largest armoured division in the world, deployed along one side of the autobahn for his inspection. 'Men and tanks were arrayed down the highway in front of me as far as the eye could see,' Truman wrote later, 'The line was so long, it took twenty-two minutes to ride from the beginning to the end of it.'

To the people in the street Churchill's was the better-known face. At the Reichstag, where a crowd of German and Russian soldiers were bartering on the black market, Churchill got out of the car and slowly climbed up the steps through the crowd, his unmistakable cigar firmly clenched between his teeth. It was an extraordinary moment. Many of the Germans looked away: others stared at him with blank faces. At Hitler's Chancellery the crowd following Churchill's progress swelled to a mob. The Chancellery was smashed to smithereens. The floor was strewn with broken glass and chandeliers, a litter of papers, ribbons and Iron Crosses. Hitler's map of the world he had hoped to conquer hung in tatters and his desk had been turned upside down and its marble-top broken into hundreds of pieces. Some of the pieces, a few Iron Crosses and a piece of the map were quickly pocketed as souvenirs by Churchill's advisers.

A guide led Churchill out across the Chancellery garden to the bunker where his mortal enemy had killed himself. Three flights down the water was rising in the lowest rooms. In Eva Braun's room they noticed a vase containing some twigs—the remains of what less than three months before had been a spray of spring blooms. Churchill could not bear to go any further. Back at the top the guide pointed out the spot where the bodies of Hitler and his wife had been seen burning. Churchill looked for a moment and then turned away in disgust and walked back to his car in silence. He was to write later that with the end of the war all hatred of his former enemies had drained from him. Later, in the Kurfürstendamm, a group of Germans stood and applauded the British Prime Minister. Embarrassed, he half raised his hand in greeting, then lowered it. It was not what he had been led to expect in the Nazi capital.

The Potsdam Conference began in the late afternoon of 17 July 1945. From the very start the Big Three displayed distinct differences of personal and national style—differences that were to grow even deeper when it came to matters of ideology and self-interest. Churchill arrived at the Cecilienhof modestly accompanied by a single plain-clothes detective; Stalin arrived in a bullet-proof car driven along a road lined with a corridor of armed guards; Truman arrived amid the screaming of sirens in a convoy preceded by motor-cycle outriders and armoured jeeps and followed by a truck full of armed men who leapt to the ground and fanned out with guns at the ready as the President's car, festooned with detectives on the running boards, drew up at the Palace.

At Stalin's suggestion Truman agreed to serve as chairman. The principals sat round the green baize-covered table and in an outer room behind them sat their advisers. And so, amid a fug of smoke from Stalin's cigarettes and Churchill's cigars, the discussions began. They were to go on for over two weeks—two weeks in which the leaders of the wartime Grand Alliance bargained, cajoled, bullied, deceived and horse-traded in a kind of poker-game whose stakes were the peace and security of Europe and the world. Most of the talking was done by Churchill, who as the exhausted leader of an exhausted and bankrupt nation had no aces up his sleeve and least power to barter or persuade. Stalin spoke little, only grunting now and then, and fixed the others round the table with a steady, apparently humorous gaze from his steel-blue eyes. His ace was his Army, which already occupied the territories which were the subject of the keenest discussion at the conference—eastern Germany and eastern Europe. Truman was a man of few words, all of them plain and direct. His trump was the atomic bomb, which had been successfully test-fired for the first time in New Mexico on the day before the conference began, and which he intended to brandish before Stalin when the talking got tough.

Even on their evenings off the three leaders tried to use food and music as weapons to advance national prestige or a tactical alliance. When Truman entertained Churchill and Stalin to dinner in his villa one evening he brought in a violinist and a pianist to entertain them. When Stalin's time came to entertain Truman and Churchill in his villa, he was unstinting in his lavishness and doubled the number of musicians.

'Stalin gave his state dinner,' Truman wrote home to his mother and sister, 'and it was a wow. Started with caviar and vodka and wound up with water melon and champagne, with smoked fish, fresh fish, venison, chicken, duck and all sorts of vegetables in between. There was a toast every five minutes until at least twenty-five had been drunk. Stalin sent to Moscow and brought on his two best pianists and two feminine violinists. They were excellent. They played Chopin, Liszt, Tchaikovsky. They had dirty faces though and the gals were rather fat.' Churchill did not share Truman's enjoyment. The Prime Minister resented having to listen to music all evening when he could have had the President and the Generalissimo listening to him. When the party at last broke up he muttered that he would 'get even' with the other two for all that music. Three nights later he took his revenge. For the return party at his own villa Churchill had ordered up the whole of the RAF band who played continuously and at full blast throughout the dinner—*Irish Reel, Skye Boat Song, Ay ay ay ay* and *Songs of the Soviet*—until Stalin was forced to enquire whether they could play anything 'lighter'.

Two events intruded into the daily round of conference business at Potsdam. On 24 July, after Truman had received news of the successful firing of the first atomic bomb, he decided to give Stalin an oblique hint, in effect a veiled threat, concerning the awesome weapon which America now possessed. At the end of the day's session he left his seat and strolled round to where Stalin was sitting. 'I was perhaps five yards away,' Churchill wrote afterwards, 'and I watched with the closest attention the momentous talk. I knew what the President was going to do. What was vital was to watch its effect on Stalin.' Truman recalled: 'I casually mentioned to Stalin that we had a new weapon of unusually destructive force. The Russian Premier showed no special interest. All he said was that he was glad to hear of it and hoped we would "make good use of it against the Japanese".' Both Churchill and Truman were convinced that Stalin had no idea of the significance of the new American weapon, not so much for its effect on Japan as its effect on the Russians. But Marshal Zhukov knew differently. 'On returning to my quarters, Stalin in my presence, told Molotov about his conversation with Truman,' Zhukov remembered. 'The latter reacted immediately: "Let them. We'll have to talk it out with Kurchatov and get him to speed things up". I realised they were talking about research on the atomic bomb.'

The next day, Churchill left Potsdam for England to learn the results of the British General Election—his departure seemed to symbolise the imminent departure of Great Britain from the front rank of power. He never returned. In his place came the victorious Labour prime minister Clement Attlee, who struck virtually everyone at Potsdam, including his own delegation, as a dreary substitute for the old bulldog he had replaced. From that moment the British played little further significant part in the Potsdam conference. The Americans distrusted the new Prime Minister because he was a socialist, the Russians—who were upset over Churchill's defeat—because he was a new face and an unknown quantity. Between them Truman and Stalin continued to carve out their spheres of influence and a new strategic division of the world. The Big Three had been reduced to the Big Two. And behind closed doors and off the record the Big Two settled the fate of Germany.

On 1 August 1945, the heads of state posed for photographers for the last time. Stalin, according to one of the British delegation, was 'dressed like the Emperor of Austria in a bad musical comedy: cream jacket with gold braided collar, blue trousers with a red stripe.' The next day they departed—Truman to oversee the final countdown to the first dropping of an atomic bomb on a human target, Stalin to mastermind a fresh purge of his long-suffering compatriots, Attlee to preside over the dismantling of the British Empire and the reduction of his country to a second-class state. They were never to meet again. At Potsdam Churchill had reiterated à propos of Stalin: 'I like that man.' It was a sentiment Roosevelt had often expressed in the war years. But when Truman was asked what he thought of Stalin, he replied in his usual uncomplicated way: 'I think he's a son of a bitch.' And then he added: 'I guess he thinks I'm one, too.'

It has often been said that the Potsdam Conference was a failure. In the first place, the West failed to prevent the Soviet domination of eastern Europe (above all, the Soviet domination of Poland, on whose behalf the Second World War had started) which was to lead to the division of Europe and the start of the Cold War. In the second place, the big powers failed to remedy the *de facto* division of Germany into two separate halves. Nowhere in the Potsdam Declaration of 2 August 1945, was it explicitly stated that Germany should be divided. But that was the effect and it may be that it was inevitable. That apart, the Potsdam Conference's most important achievement was to produce a set of guidelines for the treatment of defeated Germany by the victorious allies: the amount of reparation to be exacted; the level of industrial production; the minimum material needs of the populace; the re-drawing of the borders with Poland. The Soviet delegation proved tough and obdurate negotiators. 'Stalin and his group either obtained the settlements they sought or swept the ticklish questions under the rug,' observed Truman's adviser on German affairs, Robert Murphy. As a result, many of the agreements at Potsdam were either ignored or countermanded and the Occupation powers went their own way in the running of a prostrate and increasingly divided Germany.

For the German people, the communique issued after Potsdam constituted the first official news received of the Allies' plans for their country. German territory east of the Oder and Neisse rivers—including Pomerania, Silesia, East Brandenburg and East Prussia—was to be ceded to Poland and the millions of Germans who lived in these areas were to be deported to German territory west of the two rivers (with consequences described in Chapter 9). German factories would be dismantled for reparations and the German standard of living was limited to the average of continental western Europe. The outlook was bleak but not entirely hopeless, for at least the plan was that Germany should not be dismembered, but administered by the Allies as a single economic unit.* In the event, these hopes were not fulfilled.

---

* It should be added that although Austria was also occupied by the Allies, the nature and purpose of her Occupation was quite different from that of Germany. The Allies regarded the German annexation of Austria in 1938 as null and void and treated Austria as a liberated country totally independent of Germany. The purpose of the Allied Occupation of Austria under Four-Power Control was to re-establish a free and independent Austria at the earliest opportunity.

7

Hour Zero

The war had not been over for more than a week when SHAEF sent one of their officers on a fact-finding mission to find out how things stood in defeated Germany. US Army Colonel Joe Starnes, the officer selected for this task, travelled two thousand miles across occupied Germany, talking with spearhead Military Government units as far east as the Elbe, and by the time he finally returned to headquarters he had seen more of Germany than any other Allied observer so far. His report to SHAEF was forthright and blunt: 'More than 20 million Germans are homeless or without adequate shelter. The average basic ration is less than 1,000 calories. The ability to wage war in this generation has been destroyed.'

At about the same time that Colonel Starnes was reporting his findings, another report was being prepared by another Allied mission, the Potter–Hyndley Mission, which had been looking at the whole of Europe from the point of view of the coal situation at the end of the war. This mission came to an even bleaker conclusion than Colonel Starnes. 'Unless drastic steps are taken,' its report ran, 'there will occur in Northwest Europe and the Mediterranean next winter a coal famine of such severity as to destroy all semblance of law and order, and thus delay any chance of reasonable security.'

The prospect of violent insurrection throughout Europe was a chilling one. How could it be prevented? There were only three places the desperately needed coal could come from: one was Poland. But Poland was under Soviet Occupation and in a ruined state, so the chances of obtaining Polish coal were virtually nil. Another was the United States. But to get coal from across the Atlantic in the quantities needed would require four hundred 16,000-ton cargo ships in permanent commission, which was impossible.

That left only Germany. The Germans were dependent on coal for heating, electricity, running water, food-processing and railways. Too bad, the report decided. The coal should be taken from Germany 'without any regard for the consequences to Germany.' It was preferable that the Germans should suffer than the rest of Europe. And even though the Allies had only just stopped shooting Germans, they might have to start shooting them again before long. If the coal famine was going to lead to acute unrest in Europe, the Potter–Hyndley Mission would rather it was confined to Germany. 'Should it become necessary to preserve order by shooting,' the report concluded, 'it would surely be better for this to occur in Germany than elsewhere.'

There could be no more crushing demonstration of Germany's abject condition after VE-Day than this. It was, as the Germans themselves called it, *die Stunde Null*, hour zero: the moment of hiatus when the people of a nation that had ceased to exist touched rock-bottom, when the hands of the stop-watch were reset to zero and began to tick towards an unthinkable future. The German nation was now quartered into zones, each occupied, seemingly indefinitely, by one of four victorious foreign armies—the Americans in the south, the British in the north-west, the French in the south-west, the Russians in the east. The capital of the former Reich was similarly divided, the four Occupation sectors governed by a joint command of the victorious powers. Four-power rule in Germany by decree was absolute and undisputed. In a Proclamation to the German People in June, General Eisenhower ordered the populace to obey the Occupation authorities 'immediately and without question'. The Allies had the power of life and death over the Germans. They could shoot to kill. Habeas corpus was suspended and Germans could be imprisoned at will. The Germans had no rights or authority of any kind. Their country was like a gigantic concentration camp in which they lived in enforced isolation from the world. Non-fraternisation laws at first forbade them to converse with British or American soldiers except in the course of duty. They could not travel, send letters, or receive newspapers or books from abroad. They were subject to curfew. They could not use the telephone or travel more than six kilometres from their homes. Their bank accounts were frozen. They could be searched or seized and their property requisitioned at a moment's notice. Meetings of more than five people were prohibited. Males between 14 and 65 and females between 15 and 50 were liable to compulsory labour. They were defeated, disillusioned, demoralised. They were saddled with a history of which they were ashamed and treated as barbarians whether they had been Nazis or not.

Long before hour zero, Hitler had declared: 'We may be destroyed, but if we are, we shall drag a world with us—a world in flames.' Now that vision had become reality. 'Give me five years,' Hitler had told his people before the outbreak of the war, 'and you will not recognise Germany again.' Now the survivors chalked their derision on the walls of the ruined cities: '*Das verdanken wir Hitler*.' For this we thank Hitler.

Not one of the country's great cities had escaped the destruction brought about by the air-bombing and the land-fighting. Hamburg alone had sustained more damage in the war than all the bombed cities of Britain (where half a million homes had been destroyed and four million damaged). In Düsseldorf 93 per cent of the houses were uninhabitable; in Frankfurt, 75 per cent; in Cologne, 66 per cent. In Hanover only 1 per cent of the buildings were undamaged. American foreign correspondent, William Shirer, revisiting Nuremberg after the end of the fighting, recorded in his diary the shock at what he saw: 'It is gone! The lovely medieval town behind the moat is utterly destroyed. It is a vast heap of rubble, beyond description, and beyond hope of re-building. As the prosaic US army puts it, Nuremberg is "91 per cent dead". The old town, I should say, the old Nuremberg of Dürer and Hans Sachs and the Meistersingers, is 99 per cent "dead".'

William Peters, a linguist from the British Army Interpreters Pool, tried to find pre-war friends in Cologne in August 1945. He wrote in his notebook: 'Not a soul was in sight and there was not a sound to be heard. Vegetation covered the street and the ruins. Small bushes grow out of the bomb craters. The cathedral rises high out of the sea of ruins around it. There is a silence over everything. People talk in low voices as if they are afraid to wake the dead below the debris. This is a cemetery and one does not make any noise in a cemetery. Boards on top of some of the ruins state: "US Property. Looting forbidden". What could one loot here but debris?' In Kassel, where the rubble still covered the rotting remains of many of the town's citizens, some streets were labelled 'GRUESOME'. Footpaths wound over the rubble like mountain tracks; main streets meandered like rivers between high banks of debris. In Frankfurt, where streets not completely buried were covered in a rosebay willow herb, the ruins were so vast that Army-issue street-maps served merely as rough compass directories. A visiting British boffin, D. A. Spencer, after passing through Darmstadt in the summer of 1945, noted in his diary: 'Darmstadt is a city of the dead—literally and figuratively. Not a soul in its alleyways between red rubble that were once streets. Long vistas of gaunt ruins—most only shoulder high. And overpowering silence everywhere.' Out of a total of 16 million houses in 'Potsdam' Germany, 2.34 million had been completely destroyed and 4 million had sustained 25 per cent (or more) damage. Out of the total of 5.5 million houses in the British zone, 3.5 million had been destroyed or severely damaged. In western Germany as a whole 20 million people were homeless.

* Various calculations were made at the time to help impart the extent of Germany's ruination. For example, it was worked out that it would take sixteen years to clear the rubble of Berlin, using ten trains a day, each train pulling fifty wagons. It was also calculated that the devastated areas of Germany were covered in 400 million cubic metres of rubble. If that figure is correct it is equivalent to a country the size of Great Britain completely covered in rubble to a height of several feet.

Public buildings, too, had suffered proportionately. In Cologne 92 per cent of the schools were totally wrecked or seriously damaged, and fourteen of the country's twenty-three universities had suffered severe structural damage. Communications had suffered comparable damage. In the British zone 1,000 km of the 13,000 km of railway track was operable, but only in discontinuous sections. Less than half the locomotives in Germany were in working order and only a third of the coaches were reparable.

No waterways were open; all twenty-two of the rail bridges over the Rhine were down, as well as most of the bridges over most of the other rivers in Germany. There was total chaos in the ports. Kiel harbour was blocked with the wrecks of 243 ships. In Hamburg 50 sunken merchant ships and 19 floating docks had been sunk in the harbour. Half the trunk telephone switchboards in the British zone had been destroyed. The interruption in communications seemed to have brought civilised life itself to a halt. Germany had reverted to the Bicycle Age.

Ironically the main target of the air-bombing—the factories and installations of German industry—had escaped relatively lightly. The destruction looked a great deal worse than it really was. In Germany as a whole only 15 to 20 per cent of industrial plant had been totally wiped out in the air raids, and in the case of the mines and steel industry only 10 per cent. Even the Ruhr, the principal target of air bombing, lost only 30 per cent of its plant and machinery, in spite of repeated attacks over a period of years. On average German factories were found to have better stocks of materials at the end of the war than British factories.

It was individual human beings who had suffered most. It was calculated that 3.7 million Germans had been killed in the armed services. Half a million civilians were killed in the air raids, 100,000 in the land fighting, 200,000 in the concentration camps, over a million fleeing the Red Army and 400,000 from related causes. There were two million cripples in west Germany, an uncounted number in east Germany. In the months and years to follow, as millions more German soldiers died in Soviet prison camps and a million more German civilians succumbed to exhaustion and maltreatment in the course of their forcible expulsion from eastern Europe, the total figure was to soar.

For the large majority of those who survived, life was a matter of squalor, penury and hunger. Daily existence was barely supportable. In the first summer a hideous stench of charred remains and putrefying bodies hung above the ruins. Crowded together in improvised quarters in the basements and bunkers beneath the rubble, the living accommodated themselves as best they could; many had fashioned precarious caves for themselves in the debris, where they eked out an almost Stone Age existence. Some lived high up in the bombed apartment blocks in flats which hung precariously like bookshelves, and could only be reached by rope ladder. In Germany as a whole ten people now lived where six had lived before. The average dwelling space in the British zone was equivalent to a space about 9 feet by 6 feet.

An English visitor to the British Zone in 1946, the publisher Victor Gollancz, a devout and remarkable man who had organised the National Committee for Rescue from Nazi Terror in the early days of the war, was appalled by the way ordinary Germans were forced to live and wrote home to his wife of the cellars in Hamburg:

In one room were living a soldier, his wife (who is expecting a baby in a fortnight) and his seventy-two year-old mother. They live, eat, cook, work, and sleep in the one room. There is one bed; a table; two chairs; a very small side-table; and a little cooking stove. The amount of space, apart from that taken up by this furniture, is about 32 square feet.

The old mother sleeps in the bed; *on the floor*, on a filthy rug but no mattress, sleep the husband and wife. The wife's clothes were wretched, and she was barefoot. She has no baby clothes or cradle—nothing. People like this have literally *nothing*. Their chief concern is to get a basket or something to put the baby in. I asked the old mother whether she had enough to eat, and she replied with a smile, '*Nein, nein, ich bin immer hungrig*'—as if that were the fault of her appetite.

This was all pretty shaking, but it was heaven—I really mean this—in comparison with the next place. The next place was like a deliberately vile Daumier cartoon. I doubt whether there could be more hopeless misery, or a more sordid caricature of humanity. Then I try to restore my sense of proportion by remembering that Belsen and Auschwitz were far, almost infinitely, wickeder.

The place was a cellar under rubble in one of the huge devastated areas. For light and air there was one tiny window. On a table was a sort of open lamp with a naked flame. There was one bed in which the husband and wife were sleeping; on a sort of couch was the son, crippled in the war; and on the floor, on an indescribably filthy 'mattress' which was all broken open with the sawdust spilling out, was the daughter. She looked fifty but I suspect she was about twenty-five. This was an extraordinary creature, with a huge nose, a bony, emaciated face, and several front teeth missing. She also appeared to be pretty crippled, and her hand was shaking terribly, I suppose from hunger. There was no free space in the cellar at all and again they lived, ate, and slept here. Nobody could work—the young man could not because he was crippled, and the father because he was too weak. They lived on the father's tobacco card: it brought them in 120 marks [$12 or £3] every six weeks to supplement their wretched dole—40 cigarettes at three marks apiece. The black market here *keeps people alive*. The air was so thick that I could hardly keep my glasses free enough from steam to see. The woman cried when the Salvation Army people gave her some money—and we all hurriedly unloaded our cigarettes with a sort of personal shame.

Oh my dear, get copies of this made and send them to John [Strachey, Minister of Food in London] and Attlee. They are both decent and kind-hearted men; and if only they could send parcels of food to these poor and

97

dear people—I call them dear, because their suffering and often their bravery, make one love them: or is it that loving them is the only way to save one's own self-respect as a human being?

You know I went to Belsen on Tuesday; I don't for a single second forget the other side of the picture. But these are people in an agony of suffering . . .

Nowhere was the scale of the disaster more apparent than in Berlin. Four foreign armies occupied the capital. From the top of the Siegesaüle, the Victory Column, fluttered a French tricoleur. Near the Brandenburg Gate rose an imposing monument to the Red Soldier, which the Berliners, with their usual ironic wit, dubbed 'the Monument to the Unknown Looter'. The city, the third largest in the world, with a population larger than all the towns of the Ruhr put together, had once been the economic centre of the Reich as well as the political capital. Until the end of the war it had been the main transport centre of central Europe and the greatest processing centre on the continent, employing one-fifteenth of all the factory workers in the Greater Reich. But now, in the words of the popular German song, *'Es geht alles vorüber, es geht alles vorbei!'* Everything passes, everything fades away. Berlin was a metropolitan desert. From the air it looked grey, dead and utterly fantastical—a wasteland of empty matchboxes. 'As far as you can see in all directions from a plane above the city,' noted William Shirer, 'a great wilderness of debris, dotted with roofless, burnt-out buildings that look like mousetraps with the low sun shining through the spaces where windows had been.' At night all that could be heard was the gnawing of rats and the trumpeting of the only elephant that had survived the fighting at the zoo. The buildings stood like fossils in the moonlight, as though they had fallen into decay during millenniums.

The British and Americans had dropped 75,000 tons of high explosive on the city and over a million Russians had blasted their way through it from every direction. Before the war there had been 1,600,000 houses, apartments and hotel rooms, now there were only 400,000 left intact—for a population that still numbered in the region of 3,000,000 and was increasing by 25,000 to 30,000 a day as refugees continued to tramp in on their westward flight from the Russians.

Famous buildings, like the State Opera House, were destroyed. The Air Ministry, the War Ministry and the Reich Chancellery were beyond repair. Unexploded Soviet mortar and rocket bombs were still embedded in the asphalt of the Chancellery courtyard. The heavy chandeliers in Hitler's office still hung from the ceilings, but the Führer's personal gold-edged writing-paper and invitation cards were strewn over the floor and the carpets and furnishings had been bayoneted and ripped apart by Russian troops. The Reichsbank had sustained twenty-one direct hits in a single raid the previous February and the Russians had made off with over three million dollars worth of gold from its vaults. Most of the city's famous hotels—the Adlon, the Bristol, the Eden, the Esplanade, the Kaiserhof, where Goebbels kept a suite—were no more, though in the ruins of the Adlon a notice bravely announced that 'Five o'clock Tea' was being served—in the cellar, where the old waiters still went about their business in frock coats and starched collars. The smart café-restaurants like Kempinskis and Kranzlers, famous for its partridge and red kraut, had also gone, though the little pub run by Hitler's half-brother, Alois, survived under new management, and with the name on the signboard, 'A. Hitler' painted out.

The Russians had dismantled and hauled away 80 per cent of Berlin's industrial machinery before the Western Allies reached the city. Brigadier Frank Howley, commanding the first detachment of American military government to enter Berlin in July, recounted: 'They had dismantled the refrigeration plant at the abattoir, torn stoves and pipes out of restaurant kitchens, stripped machinery from mills and factories and were completing the theft of the American Singer Sewing Machine plant when we arrived. Over in the British sector, they had taken out generating equipment from the only modern plant in the city. Much of the looted equipment was of dubious use or had been wrecked through ignorance.'

What the Russians did not take was either buried under the rubble, or rendered useless by the lack of coal and electricity to power it. In the early days the only signs of industry in the city were the gangs of *Trümmerfrauen*, the 'rubble women' who toiled endlessly at salvaging bricks and other materials from the debris in the streets and bombed-out buildings. The only firm to start up before the autumn was one which sharpened used razor blades.

There were something like three thousand breaks in the water mains still waiting to be repaired. The sewage pipes were fractured and leaked raw sewage into the drinking water system, spreading typhoid fever, diphtheria and dysentry. The death-rate of the very young and the very old reached a level not seen since the Thirty Years War nearly three hundred years before: in August, four thousand people died each day, compared with one hundred and fifty before the war. There were no motor ambulances, so the sick and the dead had to be transported by wooden carts or handstretchers, wrapped in rags or paper, as there were no coffins. There were few doctors left in the city and no drugs—not even anaesthetics. In the British zone only one of the 44 hospitals was undamaged. Only one person in ten was under thirty, but there were still 53,000 orphans living like wild animals in holes in the ground, some of them one-eyed or one-legged veterans of seven or so, many so deranged by the bombing and the Russian attack that they screamed at the sight of any uniform, even a Salvation Army one.

There were soldiers everywhere, many of them German, and still in Wehrmacht uniform for want of anything else to wear. They were a terrible sight, these remnants of the great army that had set out to conquer the world and now was buried between the Volga and the Spree. William Shirer recorded in his diary for 2 November:

> The most sorry-looking folk on the street are the demobilised German soldiers. They hobble along in their rags, footsore from walking in worn-out shoes stuffed with newspaper, their uniforms tattered and filthy. They make an impressive picture of defeat and desolation. On a street in Wedding we stopped to talk to a group of them scraping along. God! Were these the crack soldiers who goose-stepped so arrogantly through Poland, France, Russia? These the *Herrenvolk*? They are certainly not arrogant now. They are bent, dirty, tired and hungry.
>
> 'Where do you come from?' I asked them.
>
> 'From Stalingrad,' they said. '*Alles kaputt*.' They grinned and you could see that few of them, though they were young men, had any teeth left. They begged for cigarettes and we passed a pack around. Then they shuffled and hobbled away.

Then there were the Russians. They were a capricious people. If they wanted to get off a train at a place where it was not due to stop, they simply pulled the communication cord. If they wanted a locomotive they simply uncoupled one from a German train and attached it to an eastbound Russian one. An American observer of Russian descent, Nicolas Nabokov, encapsulated the Russian presence in a vignette of a group in the Unter den Linden one summer day three months after the war: 'The entire avenue is clogged with debris. In front of the Adlon stand two trucks. The first one contains a mountain of brass: tubas, trumpets and trombones covered by heavy Bokhara rugs. On top of the rugs sit three sullen-looking Mongolian soldiers. Their uniforms are tattered. They are eating bread. The second truck stands half-cocked on three wheels, blocking the traffic. It contains thousands of naked typewriters, and standing in their midst, a cow moos. Two youngish Russian officers have taken off the fourth wheel of the truck and, watched by a silent crowd of ragged kids, are testing the inner tube in a basin of muddy water.'

Such was Berlin in the first months of defeat and Occupation. It was, as the American Deputy Military Governor, General Clay, described it in a memo that first October, 'the world's largest boarding house, with all the population on relief.' 'Relief' was hardly the right word for the starvation rations doled out to the Berliners in the early days of the Occupation of the city. But Berlin was not alone in going hungry, nor was Germany in general. There was a worldwide food shortage as a consequence of the war and the situation throughout Europe, where production of grain was down by 70 per cent and food in general by half, was calamitous. There was soon to be serious famine in parts of Russia and Rumania and in Greece thousands would starve to death. Even in Britain bread was to be rationed for the first time in the nation's history. In the widespread shortage the Germans came near to the end of the queue. The Allies were reluctant to spare food from their own depleted stocks in order to feed their vanquished enemy. The best they could do was to try and keep the Germans alive, but even that was hard. The number of head of livestock had fallen by 35 per cent since 1944. There were no fertilisers, seed was scarce, farm machinery worn out, labour almost non-existent—the foreign farm-workers had left, the Germans they had replaced were either dead or prisoners-of-war. The first post-war harvest was sown late and there were fears it might fail. To make matters worse, the Russians broke their promise to send grain shipments from the Eastern zone, which in normal times produced most of Germany's cereal crops. General Clay summarised the situation very clearly: 'We had to have food. West Germany had never been self-supporting. Even Germany as a whole could not raise enough to sustain its people. Now their principal producing farmlands located in North, Central and Eastern Germany were much smaller because of the severed Eastern territory. Moreover the produce was not available to the Western zones. Yet the population of these zones had increased by about 4,000,000 and was to increase still more.'

In the British zone nearly half a million German POWs were released on the land by the British Army Military Government in order to bring in the all-important first post-war harvest. This was 'Operation Barleycorn'— the biggest task of civil administration ever undertaken by a military organisation. But the harvest was nearly ruined by three weeks of continuous rain in August, and it was clear the German people would die of famine if there were no bulk imports of food. Such food was not easy to find from abroad. The French consumed more calories than they provided in their zone. The Soviet Union had none. The Americans could provide 940 calories a day out of their own resources, the British only 400—and the British public were opposed to even that. 'HUNS IN CLOVER!' howled a banner headline on the front page of the *Daily Mirror* on 16 May 1945. 'The Germans have everything we in this county have forgotten exists,' moaned one of the popular Sundays a month later, 'their houses being Aladdin's caves of hoarded luxuries.' Meanwhile nineteen out of twenty babies died in the American sector of Berlin in July.

Berlin felt the effects more than other cities. Food could not be brought into the western sectors of the city until the railway link with western Germany had been repaired. In July the daily civilian ration was 800 calories—a ration scale which could not sustain life for long and was indeed worse than that of Nazi concentration camps. The first American-run supply trains did not reach Berlin until the end of the month. Thereafter the daily ration rose gradually to 1,250 calories. This was more than the Germans in the Western zones were getting, but it was still minimal. An

officer on Clay's staff reported in September that the daily diet of the few
fortunate Berliners who had jobs with the US Army consisted of:

> 1 serving spoonful of canned stew, 2 or 3 boiled potatoes the size of golf
> balls, 1 handful of hard-tack crumbs, 1 cup black coffee made from leftover
> grounds from US messes, and 1 spoonful of watery gravy.
>
> A meal two maids were eating in the billet I occupied, which they claimed
> was their only food for the day besides the meal described above, consisted
> of 1½ thin slices of bread, 2 small half-green tomatoes, 2¼ small potatoes, and
> 1 onion half the size of one's thumb.
>
> On several occasions I saw children and old people gathering grass in a
> park, they said for food.
>
> Although many children looked healthy, I saw many covered with sores.
> The sores, I was told, were the result of an inadequate diet—the slightest
> bruise would fester.
>
> I saw no fresh vegetables in the markets and was told there were none in
> the US sector. Only 3 out of 15 meat markets I visited had any meat at all.

In the Western zones of Germany the maximum daily ration for normal
consumers was supposed to be 1,550 calories. In practice it was never as
much as this and varied from 804 calories in Hesse to 1,150 calories in the
Rhineland. In the British zone the basic ration was 1,048 calories for more
than a year after the war. By comparison civilians in Britain got 2,800
calories, German farmers 3,000, and American GIs 4,200—the highest
calorie intake of any human beings in Europe. The ration also varied
according to a person's occupation. There were five or six categories of
ration card. Heavy and very heavy manual workers such as miners drew
one or other of the top two cards, Cards 1 and 2, and with luck might
receive between about 1,750 and 2,500 calories. In the Soviet sector of
Berlin, artists and entertainers were also placed in the top ration category
at 2,500 calories per day. The lowest card entitled the average consumer to
the basic ration, and in Berlin, where it was held by over a million of the
inhabitants, including all housewives, it was known as the 'Death Card'. In
fact, a man who was not working was supposed to be able to survive on
between 1,000 and 1,500 calories a day; but according to the House of
Commons Select Committee on Estimates, 'a diet of 1,200 calories may be
characterised as slow starvation . . . 1,550 calories is probably no better.' If
a man did a day's work his calorie requirement would go up (according to
the UNRRA Food Committee) to 2,650, and in cold or damp conditions it
would go even higher.

Few Germans except the very privileged could count on such bounty in
the first three years after the war. Equally, few could survive on the rations
they did get, except in greatest wretchedness. In the British zone, which
had the least agricultural land but included the second and third biggest

cities in Germany and the largest concentration of industry in Europe (the Ruhr), the task of feeding the Germans was hardest and the weekly ration for a long period after the war was meagre indeed: bread, 2 lb. 3 oz.; cereal, 5 oz.; meat, 3½ oz.; fish, 3 oz.; fats, 2 oz.; sugar, 2½ oz.; jam, 3½ oz.; cheese, ⅓ oz.; milk (skimmed), 1 lb. 1½ oz.; coffee (artificial), ⅔ oz.

To supplement this miserable fare the Germans foraged for extra food wherever they could find it. They poured out into the countryside to barter for potatoes, eggs and meat from the farmers. They swapped family heirlooms and valuables on the black market for tinned food from the British and American army stores. The women slept with the Occupation soldiers in return for candy, chocolate and cigarettes from the PX and NAAFI canteens. The fortunate got jobs as cooks, waiters and cleaners in army messes and billets where the chief reward was the leftovers on the dinner-plates and in the kitchen slop-bucket.

There were few other alternatives. Certainly normal employment was not one. There were not many jobs to be had in any case, but people who did find employment were too exhausted to work for more than a few hours, and men fainted at their jobs in the cities. Even the horses collapsed from hunger in the streets and had to be removed with a crane by the fire-brigade. Many people found it was better not to work, even though the unemployed drew the dreaded 'Death Card', for unemployment gave people greater time and opportunity to go off and barter for better food in the country or on the black market. One German tried to send a letter (in English) to an addressee in Wall Street, New York, which was described by the English officer who intercepted it as 'a wonderful glimpse of the indestructible character of human hope.' The sender requested coffee, tea, chocolate, rice, pepper, cinnamon, nutmegs, cloves and ginger to be freighted to him by air, and 'greater quantities' by steamer to Hamburg. 'I should like to receive six bags of washed milk coffee, either Venezuela, Merida or Guatemala, Costa Rica or Salvador, best quality. Further some sacks of rice, wheat flour, sugar packed in double bags. Two bags of wheat corn, best quality, and two bags of maize-corn, for our hens. Further in chests or boxes tea, chocolate in cakes, and also butter, hog's lard, olive oil, raisins, corned beef, sausages and some boxes of salmon, lobster and sardines; further Stilton or Cheshire cheese and 100 pieces of fancy soap. I beg to ensure against robbery. I thank you very heartily for all your painstaking.'

Ironically, ex-Nazis were among the better-off members of the community. Some still had a lot of cash. Those awaiting investigation in the Allied internment camps were officially entitled to a relatively high daily ration of 2,200 calories. Those who had been convicted, and as a consequence were not allowed to work (except as manual labourers), were free to wheel and deal with the food-hunters. By contrast, for the infirm, the elderly, the very young, the hard-working and those who lived alone—people who found it difficult to go out foraging and scavenging and playing the black market—life became a losing struggle.

The Germans improvised as best they could with what lay to hand. They sowed vegetables over every inch of their gardens and allotments. They learned to eat rhubarb without sugar and developed a taste for unfamiliar delicacies like squirrel, jackdaw and raven.

This was the *Ersatz* epoch of substitute food: rape syrup instead of sugar, beechmast oil instead of lard, rhubarb juice instead of vinegar, and the notorious *Ersatz* coffee, picturesquely nicknamed *Muckefuck*, instead of the real thing, as well as tea brewed from apple peel or strawberry leaves. Unusual properties in common plants and vegetables were discovered. The hungry gathered acorns and ground them into flour to make acorn gingerbread and acorn flan. They ate dandelion as a specific against hunger—typhus and dysentry and sprinkled chickweed from the bomb-sites in their soups and salads. The hard-pressed housewife learned to wash silk and woollen garments in an infusion of ivy leaves, boil up her light-coloured wash with potato peelings, and soak dark-blue and black washing in ox-gall. She learnt to re-cycle old clothes and ex-Wehrmacht uniforms by dying them with the products of the fields and woods: beetroot peel turned them carmine red; birch leaves, yellow–green; sorrel, bright yellow; walnut-shell or alder bark, brown. She discovered the cosmetic properties of lime-blossom tea-slops mixed with rainwater for her complexion. Since next to nothing could be bought in the shops—not even needles or pins or thread—endless ingenuity was employed in make-do-and-mend. Moth-eaten pullovers were unravelled and the wool used again. Glass was taken from picture-frames and used to glaze windows instead. Steel-helmets were turned into cooking pots and gas-mask cases into watering cans. Bricks were salvaged from the rubble by the *Trümmerfrauen* and cleaned by hand—at ten times the cost of new ones. Briquettes of industrial ash and clay, soaked in pitch, gave off heat 'equivalent to not quite dry wood.' So the Germans made do and mended, scrimped and saved, improvised and suffered as the first, and much dreaded, winter of peace drew near.

8

Stille Nacht

As that first winter approached the Allies feared that a further crisis was looming in Germany. It was a prospect that had worried them ever since they had seen the unploughed fields in spring, the coal-mines not working, the transport system and other utility services in ruins. As early as June 1945 the Potter–Hyndley Mission had predicted the possible need 'to preserve order by shooting' in Germany, and Eisenhower sounded a warning note when he told the German populace in August 1945: 'The coming months are going to be a hard test for you. You will have to be tough—there is no alternative. Every sign indicates a severe shortage of food, fuel, housing and transport. So the townspeople will have to go out into the country and help to bring in the harvest. There will be no coal for heating homes this winter. So you will have to go into the woods and cut your own firewood. A third priority is living accommodation. Damaged property must be repaired to offer as much protection from the winter as possible. So you will have to collect scrap material and gather deadwood in the forests. These are all your problems. Their solution depends entirely on your own endeavours.'

There were no materials for building new houses. The British planned to evacuate 600,000 people from the shattered towns of the Ruhr, but in the end found the best that could be done was to patch up the damaged houses so that at least they were waterproof and safe—and wait for the winter to do its damnedest. The American and British press began to write about the coming 'Battle of the Winter'—a struggle to the death against disease, starvation and the deadly central European cold. In Hamburg the Bürgermeister, Rudolf Petersen, one of the big figures in the British zone since the capitulation, appealed forcibly to evacuated Hamburgers to stay in the country and not add to the burden of feeding and housing the people already in the city during the coming winter. In Berlin, where in winter it is colder than the coldest parts of Great Britain, an army of men dug mass graves for the expected victims of the coming winter while the ground was not yet frozen. Rows of black coffins were stacked up in readiness for the surge of dead. In an operation code-named 'Stork', over 50,000 war-shocked children were evacuated to the British zone, where winter conditions were a little better.

'There was an awful hush over the ruined city,' one observer noted early in 1946. 'People were waiting as if for the fulfilment of a curse.' Germany, it seemed, was on the brink of the worst scourge of pestilence and famine since the Middle Ages. In America, thirty-five senators warned President Truman that urgent action was needed to relieve the famine and avoid a terrible human disaster. When the weather turned cold Military Government in the American zone requisitioned all coal supplies, over a quarter of a ton, and ordered all schoolchildren to bring a piece of wood to school each day to heat their classrooms. For the 330,000 inhabitants of Stuttgart it was reported that there were only 71 overcoats and 60,000 pairs of shoes to go round. In Frankfurt there were 900 overcoats for 400,000 people.

The prospects grew bleaker. The harvest, though not a bad one, had not yielded enough food to allow the ration to be increased beyond 1,500 calories, of which 1,200 consisted of bread and potatoes. The Americans authorised the addition of a piece of meat or fish 'one half the size of an egg,' but they knew this would rarely be possible. In November it was announced that there would be 6,650,000 more mouths to feed when ethnic Germans living in Poland, Czechoslovakia, Hungary and Yugoslavia were expelled to occupied Germany at the rate of a quarter of a million a month, beginning in December. 'I don't see how there is going to be room' commented the Third US Army Chief of Staff. 'Even stacking them on top of one another, the facilities are going to be really busting.' Military Government in Württemberg reported that the German populace had begun to sink 'deeper and deeper into despair as they saw a cruel, cold, hungry winter ahead.'

The Germans, having no fires to sit by, took to their beds, and covered themselves with old newspapers and wrapping paper. 'It is an odd experience to wait and watch for people to die,' a 22-year old British lieutenant in the 11th Hussars in Berlin, Richard Brett-Smith, recalled. To fight epidemics British army medics in the capital brought in over 40 tons of DDT, 17 tons of insecticide, 1.5 million units of narcotics and heart stimulants, 5 million units of insulin, 35 litres of diphtheria anti-toxin, 13 million aspirin tablets, 500 tons of general medical supplies, and 4.5 million sulphonamide tablets. The entire population of Berlin was inoculated against typhoid and all children under fifteen immunized against diphtheria. In the British zone a cordon sanitaire was formed to intercept the mass of refugees from the east and dust them with DDT in order to kill the typhus-carrying lice that infested them. Fleets of ambulances were held in reserve for rapid removal of epidemic cases.

And then a miracle happened. Instead of the usual piercing winds and driving snow, the weather turned warm, even spring-like. At Christmas a gentle rain fell. The Christmas spirit revived a little even in the ruins. For 1,000 Reichsmarks—the equivalent of $100 in 1945 and some $600 (or over £500) now—you could buy an old goose for Christmas dinner. For rather less you could indulge in a tin of ex-Wehrmacht sauerkraut re-labelled 'Goulash'. Those who could afford nothing prepared traditional Christmas carp made out of a dough of potatoes and flour and shaped like a fish. On the top of a Stuttgart newspaper office a lighted Christmas tree, the first to be seen in the city since 1938, cast a seasonal twinkle over the ruins. In Frankfurt the local paper reported the scene: 'A few stalls stand on the wet pavement of the main square in the midst of the ruins. Cards are for sale, also a few red and blue pencils, some cardboard toys, a few pitiful things made out of wood, and lots of trashy and expensive ornaments. The old Frankfurter Santa Claus and his arks full of wooden animals is distant as a dream.'

It was not much, but it was better than last Christmas, when the weather had been cold and the sky clear and the Americans had sent nearly three thousand aircraft over Germany on 24 December and bombed thirty-two towns and cities, Frankfurt included, in the biggest air-strike operation of the war.

Not many German children under eleven could remember the famous *Weihnachtsmarkt*, the Christmas Fair, which is the chief attraction of the festival in Germany. For those who survived the horror of the war the first *Weihnachtsmarkt* among the ruins of Hitler's Thousand Year Reich in Berlin was a desperate and moving occasion, as Lt.-Col. Byford-Jones, a British Army officer who had known Germany in better days, discovered:

The coloured lights from the six *Karuselle* (roundabouts) of the first peacetime *Weihnachtsmarkt* lit up the bullet-scarred and shell-blasted façade of the Kaiser's castle. The mechanical music of the fair organ vulgarly blared through halls where Kaisers once lived. There was a vast crowd, mostly mothers, in the Lustgarten, and all the roundabouts were not only packed with people, but beseiged by mothers, who waited hours for their turn to give joy to their children with a morbid compulsion sad to see.

Everywhere in Berlin there were queues—for paper, bread, cinema shows, work, meals—so that it was not out of place that the Germans, their faces blank and pale, formed long queues throughout the day to take their children to see the Lilliput Circus. The small tent where the midgets performed was always full. The cares of the day lay heavy on the shoulders of these women. One could see the strained, pale faces in the glare of the lights, and sense the pathetic efforts they made with their children on the roundabouts to seem to enjoy themselves.

Crowds of children who had no Christmas tree at home gathered round a little one that stood on the base of what had been the statue of Wilhelm IV. They stood in wonder at the 25-metre-high light masts, of which there were four. These children had lived in a world of darkness, in a city of dreadful night, for as long as they could remember. Lights had been something to fear, not rejoice about. Then, the war over, their parents had had to save electricity, and were fined if they used more than a strictly limited wattage. When someone had forgotten and left a light burning all night they had had to sit in the dark to recover the lost current. Now this prodigality . . . indeed, this was a new world!

The weather was not the only miracle to come to the rescue of the Germans in that first post-war Christmas. The American government broke its own rule and authorised private agencies to ship the first relief supplies allowed into Germany in the eight months since the war ended. In some parts of the American zone troops gave Christmas parties and handed out cookies, candy and chocolate to the German children. In Heilbronn the local Military Government detachment were glad to report 'the presence of a traditional Christmas tree in even the humblest cellar home.'

After Christmas, warm damp winds swept across the country. In Frankfurt they reached gale force and tore off the temporary roofing-paper of the patched-up houses and knocked down so many walls that the streets were as choked with rubble as after an air-raid. But the weather stayed warm throughout the mildest winter on record. 'There was hunger but no famine,' Richard Brett-Smith recorded afterwards, 'disease and sickness but no plague.' The Germans began to recover their spirits. What they did not know was that the freak weather had disguised their true position. The food situation had actually grown far worse, and by the spring there were only enough stocks left for another sixty days at 1,550 calories a day.

Germany had reached another point of crisis. Even the Allies grew frightened, although they put a brave face on it. Radio Berlin poured out a stream of cheerful chatter from the Soviet sector. The morning music programme was called 'Let's start the day with a gay heart'. The announcer told his hungry listeners in their hovels and basements: 'For greater pleasure, you should listen on your balcony amid flowers.' But in the coming year even this simple aspiration would remain just a fond dream.

In March 1946 a critical shortage of grain forced the United States to stop all shipments to Germany and the ration in the British zone fell to 1,015 calories and in the American zone to 1,275. It was to continue to fall in the months to come. The Americans foresaw a ration down to 915 calories a day until the harvest in their zone. In the French zone it was even worse and the public health situation was described as 'frightful'. In the British zone by the end of the year it was in some instances down to 400 calories per day—half the figure for Belsen concentration camp under Nazi rule.

Hunger typhus, spread by lice, began to appear among Berliners who were too listless and demoralised to keep themselves clean. The German people were getting closer to starvation every day. By September 1946 their average weight was at its lowest since the beginning of the Occupation. Their faces turned grey or yellow, with dark rings under their eyes. Women cried for bread in the streets. People walked at a painfully slow pace and grew old with dramatic suddenness. Cases of hunger oedema soared—in Hamburg alone there were over 100,000 hospitalised cases in October 1946. Undernourished bodies, living in cold, damp unsanitary conditions, could offer little resistance to disease. The incidence of TB, typhoid and enteric and skin diseases, fostered by malnutrition and over-crowding, rose sharply—in Hamburg there were nearly 17,000 diagnosed cases of TB, fives times the pre-war figure.

'What on earth are you politicians in London up to?' a British medical officer shouted at Victor Gollancz in Hamburg, mistaking his profession. 'Do you know what's going on here? An epidemic of any kind would sweep everything before it. The Army would have a frightful catastrophe: and if you politicians don't do something about it very soon, two problems that seem to have been worrying you will be solved. The size of the German population and manure.'

Women and children were in no way exempt from the state of extreme deprivation that prevailed. The cases of miscarriage jumped sharply. A German gynaecologist attributed this increase to insufficient food, insufficient clothing, lack of fuel, bad housing, homes overcrowded with strangers, queuing for hours for food, inadequate transport and overcrowded trains. 'The wish to have a child is waning,' he reported. 'Instead of wanting a child many women are now succumbing to a deep despondency. The women are weighed down by the anxiety of how to procure the most necessary things for the expected baby. There are no beds, no bedding, no bedclothes and diapers.'

Victor Gollancz, who had taken up the cause of the defeated Germans in the English press, was appalled by the fate of the German children in Hamburg. 'I have just returned from visiting a bunker—a huge air-raid shelter, without daylight or air, where 800 children get their schooling,' he reported. 'In one class of 41 children, 23 had had no breakfast, and nothing whatsoever until half past two, then they had the school meal of half a litre of soup, without bread. Seven of these children had the ugly skin blemishes that are mixed up in some way with malnutrition; all were white and pasty. Their gaping "shoes" mean the end of what little health they have when the wet weather comes.' Many children had no shoes at all and went barefoot—three quarters of a million in Schleswig–Holstein were in this state. Few had winter coats of any kind.

Conditions were so bad in the first eighteen months after the war that Germans in their misery fell prey to rumours of all kinds. A secret agreement had been reached among the Allies at Yalta, they said, to subject the German people to three years of concentration-camp conditions as a punishment. The Russians were starving all the people of Brandenburg to death and no one was allowed to go near the town. All available foodstocks were being kept in Britain, they said, in preparation for another war. The British were planning to invade Russia, that was why British families were brought out to Germany later than American ones. The British were recruiting Germans into the British Army. The Russians were remustering SS battalions. The British were sending the SS to South Africa to build an autobahn to the Mediterranean. The Germans in the American sector of Berlin were going to be made American citizens. The British zone was going to become part of the British Empire and be ruled by King George VI in person.

In fact the Occupation powers probably did the best they could to cope under almost impossible circumstances. A million pairs of boots, a million battle dresses, and half a million greatcoats were sent from British Army stores, and stocks of food that could ill be afforded were imported from Britain and America. In London the Parliamentary Select Committee on Estimates reported glumly on what Germany was costing in grain, raw materials and Occupation expenses: 'It is probably without parallel in history that twelve months after the end of the war Great Britain should be paying £80 million a year [worth nearly £1,000 million now] towards the upkeep of her principal adversary.'

All sorts of measures were taken to increase the amount of food available in Germany. In the British zone, 650,000 acres of grassland were put to the plough. Livestock was slaughtered to provide meat and reduce the demand on arable pasture and animal feed. Luxury crops were prohibited. Vegetable allotments were established in Berlin parks. German farmers, forbidden to possess firearms, hunted the wild pigs which ravaged the crops in herds fifty strong, with bows and arrows. American soldiers hunted the pigs and other pests with Army carbines and burp-guns. British soldiers acted as beaters in a systematic drive to slaughter as many red deer, fallow deer, roe deer and wild boar as possible for meat.

People in America had been prevented by a 'Trading with the Enemy' Act from responding to stories of starvation and misery in Germany. But in January 1946 General Eisenhower gave permission for the Swedish Red Cross to send food to German children and soon private relief was flooding in from American citizens and church and welfare agencies—notably the Council of Relief Agencies and the Council for American Remittances to Europe (CARE)—and from Switzerland, Sweden, Britain, South Africa, Canada and Iceland as well. The CARE packages initially consisted of highly concentrated balanced food packs from American Army surplus, but later other necessities such as lard, baby food, baby layettes, woollens and blankets were included. Week by week private American aid for their erstwhile enemies intensified.

These gifts filled the stomachs and brightened the days of their recipients. From Lübeck a young German woman, Jessica Stolterfoht, wrote to an English pen-friend who had sent her a relief parcel:

> We pounced upon it. You can't imagine what such a parcel means to us. It is much more than the actual value of the food you send, it is the feeling that you are not quite forgotten. We had a long debate as to what to do with the lemon. Pete, my little brother, did not know what it was as he had never seen one. Here people would go crazy if they saw a lemon or some nuts or even a single unrationed apple or plum. Last time I ate a hazel nut was in 1939, last time I had a banana in 1938. My last orange I had in 1942—no, that is not true, a negro threw me one from a truck in 1945!

But the parcels were still a drop in the ocean of German wretchedness and need. Even in April 1947, nearly two years after the end of the war, the calorie level in Western Germany was still only 1,040 calories.

The morale of the German people sank to new depths. The Occupation soldiers noted a curious character trait of the time—the Germans' total disregard for the suffering of their fellow-Germans. With the decline in morale came a degeneration of morality. After the liberated *louche* years of Weimar and twelve years of gangster-rule by the Nazis, morality was not the Germans' strongest point. Under the Occupation many Germans perforce lost touch with it altogether. In the corrupting underworld atmosphere of greed and need, outright crime and prostitution flourished, especially among the young. Tens of thousands of young people, orphaned or separated from their families by the chaos of the war, wandered across the American zone like vagabonds. In the British zone there were 100,000 of them and 80 per cent of the girls suffered from venereal disease, living in gangs in the ruins and surviving on the proceeds of crime. Cases involving juvenile delinquents increased by 400 per cent. In Berlin 2,000 people of all ages were arrested every month, an increase of 800 per cent on pre-war figures. In one month alone in Berlin 199 children aged between eight and fourteen were charged with theft, 23 with breaking and entering, and 58 with black-market offences and causing grievous bodily harm.

By the beginning of 1946 Berlin had become the crime capital of the world with a record number of murders, suicides, thefts, rapes, abortions, frauds and cases of prostitution. Each day there were 240 robberies. Each day five people were killed and six injured by criminals. In March 1946 the civil crime list included 41 cases of murder, 11,000 thefts and 1,551 black-market offences. Scores of gangs of dangerous criminals—ex-Nazis,

Russian deserters, Poles, Frenchmen, Spaniards and Czechs—lived in cellars stocked with stolen uniforms, ammunition, British and American rations, and black jacks. One of the most notorious of the gangs was the Lehrter Bahnhof gang, which was composed of Russian deserters, Russian orphans and Germans. One gang a hundred strong attacked a train at Anhalter Bahnhof in May 1946. Other organised gangs began to operate on a large scale, moving out into the zones and holding up Allied food trains and truck convoys at gunpoint along the autobahn corridor through the Russian zone to Berlin. The Germans submitted a petition to the Control Council in Berlin, begging for assistance in 'breaking up the bands of deserters, criminals and degenerates of every European nation which infested the countryside and bombed cities and towns, stealing and murdering.' The Control Council decided to issue firearms to the German police. Every night after curfew, shots could be heard around the ruins of Berlin.

As another winter approached, the situation was even worse than the year before. West Germany as a whole entered 1947 without stocks of food or coal having been built up or distributed. A large part of the emergency supplies were transported by water. When the waterways froze the rations would run out and gas and electricity plants would run down for lack of coal. The prospect of famine and insurrection overshadowed all else. When the Military Governor of the British zone, General Sir Brian Robertson, was asked if there might be wholesale starvation, he replied: 'Yes, in the urban areas.' In London the government, deciding there was little they could do to help, reacted with apparent complacency.

The winter of 1946–7 was one of the coldest in European history. The cold weather began in mid-December. Driving snow and freezing temperatures continued without remission until March. Germany was seized in the iron grip of a winter for which it was not equipped either materially or psychologically. In Berlin wolves were driven by hunger into the city's outlying woods and signs were put up on the Berlin ring-road: 'BEWARE OF WOLVES!' There was no fuel for heating. Two days after Christmas a German refugee train from Poland was found to contain 16 corpses and 57 cases of severe frostbite when it arrived at the frontier of the British zone. The refugees had travelled in goods wagons which had no form of heating even though the temperature was –20°F.

Schools and workshops closed down. By February industrial production in Germany was down to 29 per cent of its pre-war level. In Hamburg 17,000 people were arrested in the act of pilfering coal transports during February 1947. When the locomotive of a coal train broke down in Mannheim station, 3,000 tons of coal were spirited away piecemeal by a swarm of local citizens. By the end of the winter 352 people had died from hypothermia in Berlin and nearly 55,000 had had to receive treatment for frostbite.

As the winter dragged on food grew scarcer. Rumours began to spread around Berlin of cannibalism and a market in human flesh. There was no hard evidence but no one who knew Berlin at that time seriously doubted the possibility. According to the *New Yorker* correspondent, Joel Sayre, a blind man in an old Wehrmacht tunic was tapping his way along Knesebechstrasse, a well-known street in the Charlottenburg district of West Berlin, when he stopped to ask a passer-by the way. He had a letter to deliver, he explained, to an address in a bombed-out area not far away. The person he stopped happened to be a well-built, good-looking young woman who, when she heard the blind man's story, offered to deliver the letter for him herself. She set off, but when she looked back she was surprised to see that the man was now walking briskly along the pavement and dodging between the traffic with his white stick tucked underneath his arm. Her suspicions aroused, she took the letter to the nearest police station. The police decided to investigate the premises to which the letter was addressed, and found that it appeared to be a shoe-shop run by a married couple. Downstairs in a concealed cellar they discovered a large stock of fresh meat. Evidently the place was a kind of black-market butcher's. Worse, on close inspection the meat turned out to be human flesh. Until now the police had overlooked the letter which the blind man had given the girl. When they opened it they found a piece of paper on which was written a single, chilling sentence: 'This is the last one I shall be sending you today.'

9

Exodus

The displacement of the peoples of Europe was perhaps the most extraordinary phenomenon of the first year after the war. Altogether an unbelievable 60 million Europeans had become displaced persons—or DPs, as they were known—as the consequence of the war and the policies of the Nazi and Soviet governments—ten times the figure for World War One. Much of this displacement had started before the war. Six million Jews had disappeared from their homelands. Three million Russian prisoners of war had been taken west into captivity and death. Whole minorities in the Soviet Union (for example, the Volga Germans) had been forcibly transferred east on Stalin's orders. A huge number of Poles lived in exile in Soviet Central Asia, or languished in British transit camps in Egypt and elsewhere. Ten million forced labourers and several million concentration-camp inmates from almost every occupied country had endured the war years in foreign captivity. Over eleven million German soldiers were held behind barbed wire in prisoner-of-war camps at home and abroad—from the cosseted comfort of their American and Canadian barracks to the hell of their slave camps in Siberia and Central Asia.

Now they were going home. In the first summer after the war the roads of Central Europe streamed with thirteen million displaced persons—forced labourers, concentration-camp survivors—and endless trains of cattle-trucks and freight-cars which had once carried troops, war materials and Jews to the slaughter, now carried whole armies of home-going tramps north, south, east and west along the railway networks of the continent. An immense continent-wide ethnic shake-up was being sorted out and resolved in the aftermath of the war. It posed, in its magnitude and complexity, an unprecedented problem of care and control for the relief agencies.

Germany itself was the central arena. Ten million German city dwellers had migrated to the countryside by the end of the war, and many of these evacuees began to drift home, if they had one, once the fighting had stopped. Often this involved the clandestine crossing of zonal borders, which added to the intense east–west traffic of the uprooted and footloose: by October 1946 nearly two million Germans had crossed from the Russian zone into the west in this way, and over half a million in the other direction. This figure was dwarfed by the ebb and flow of human masses in other categories. Of the ten million foreign workers in Germany at the end of the war, those in the Russian zone were sent home whether they wanted to go or not. So were those in the Western zones—if they were Russian. Half a million Poles were sent home in October following the war. By December there were only 900,000 foreign workers still left, but their numbers were soon augmented by a growing flood of refugees from east European countries seeking refuge from communist life in their own Soviet-dominated countries.

The railway was the main artery for this gigantic circulation of human beings. In the war the Reichsbahn had shunted millions of troops to the front and millions of Jews to the camps. Now it was ferrying the survivors of this continent-wide tragedy to or from their homelands. Captain William Craydon, who ran a feeding station for repatriates at a halt on the main north–south railway line, watched them come and go every day in their thousands in the summer of 1945. A captain who had worked his way up through the ranks of the Middlesex Regiment of the British Army, Craydon had been seconded to the Third US Army to set up a feeding centre for homebound DPs in Bavaria. He had been specially chosen for this task because of his previous experience in running an army soup-kitchen for the poor and hungry when he was in Silesia as a drummer boy after the First World War. The site he chose was the little hamlet of Strullendorf, near Bamberg, on the main line between Frankfurt and Munich. This had two sidings and a branch line which could take three trains at a time, and a river where the passengers could bathe. Heading north came trains carrying Russians, Poles, Hungarians, Lithuanians, Latvians and Estonians. Heading south came French, Belgians, Dutch, Italians, Greeks and Yugoslavs. Captain Craydon recalled:

> I had five or six trains come through each day, 40 trucks to each train, 30 to 40 people to each truck. And I had trains come through at night as well. It worked out I had to feed between 12,000 to 22,000 people a day. I had six big boilers holding 500 litres of soup each, and bread and cheese and American army ration-packs, and little packets of sweets for the children. Some of the people had been on the line two or three days and were very hungry. I felt very sorry for them. Some of them were still in their concentration-camp clothes. Some of the people out of the camps were in a bad way, dying or too ill to move. There was a time when I had to send out an SOS for a medical team to come down because the people on one particular train were so ill and

so covered in sores. Yugoslavs, they were. One fellow died at my station and I buried him next day with full military honours. I buried a lot like that.

I remember another train full of Russian POWs. The Americans phoned me from Nuremberg and said: 'You've got trouble coming. Two thousand Russians on a train. They've got guns from somewhere and they're shooting at people as they pass by.' Probably they were drunk. They'd drink anything—petrol, even. Well, Captain Muller of Military Government in Bamberg heard about it as well and he came tearing along and jumped out of his car and said: 'I hear you're going to have a lot of trouble. I couldn't sleep in my bed and leave you to face all this trouble alone. I've alerted some troops. They'll be here any minute. We'll lay each side of the track. We'll put the lights out and give them a reception.' We waited in the darkness, heard the train coming, heard them shouting and shots being fired down the line. When the train pulled in they were all yelling and jumping about and then suddenly the lights were switched on and they found themselves staring at a hundred automatics pointed straight at them by two companies of American infantry either side of the track. That soon sobered them up and I had no trouble with them after that. So I just carried on ladling out the soup from my six big boilers. By the end I must have given food to nearly a million people and medical aid to many thousands.

By the middle of August the movement of people back to their homes from the former Reich was nine-tenths completed. But as winter approached over a million and a half Poles, Hungarians, Bulgarians, Rumanians, Balts, Central European Jews, Soviet nationals and other Europeans remained in their dismal makeshift DP camps. Those DPs who were waiting their turn to be repatriated or refused to go home put the fear of death into Germans and Allies alike. They were very wild people. In the first two months after the war at least two thousand of them died and many more were seriously ill or partially blinded from drinking poisonous liquor. Many of them were simple, uneducated people and in the boredom and uncertainty of the months of waiting in the dreary overcrowded DP centres many took the opportunity to wreak revenge on the Germans at whose hands they had suffered so much. Not even the Allied authorities were safe from these people. One Military Government officer reported: 'It may help you to visualise the situation if I tell you that on my frequent and long trips about our zone I always had a loaded pistol at hand, and my driver with a loaded rifle! Russians and Poles; Poles and Russians; and both worse than any kind of wild beast.'

These DPs, a hard-core of non-repatriable stateless East Europeans, formed the nucleus of a kind of Army-sponsored underworld and were mainly responsible for the crime wave which swept occupied Germany. They had free rations and free lodging, a privileged status under the Occupation and virtual immunity from the German police. They turned their camps, where they had ready access to Army, UNRRA and Red Cross supplies, into black-market centres and bases for criminal gangs. In

Munich DPs constituted 4 per cent of the population but committed 75 per cent of the crimes. Organised gangs armed with pistols and automatics operated out of the camps in Bremen. In November 1945 one of these groups shot dead thirteen Germans in a single night and when the US Army raided their camp they ran up black flags and hung up a banner in protest: 'AMERICAN CONCENTRATION CAMP FOR POLES'.

Many of the Allied soldiers preferred the Germans, who at least were clean and law-abiding, to the DPs, an increasingly high proportion of whom were found to have been criminals or Nazi collaborators. Even the former concentration-camp victims, who continued to wear their striped camp uniforms and wheedle for special privileges, began to seem a nuisance. Field Marshal Montgomery was forced to issue a warning to the DPs in the British zone: 'I have ordered my troops to take drastic measures against all persons caught in the act of rape or murder or . . . deliberate looting.' British soldiers began to open fire on the DPs they had only recently liberated. Britain's leading hangman, Pierrepoint, arrived from London to hang DPs sentenced to death by British military courts for the murder of Germans. Sometimes they were shot. Stephen Patterson, an ex-Commando with the Coldstream Guards, was a member of a firing-squad detailed to execute two young Poles, aged 17 and 18, who had been sentenced to death by a British military court for the murder of a German farmer and his wife. Patterson remembered it vividly:

We stood at 5 o'clock in the morning in firing position behind Rendsburg Prison and the condemned men were brought in the Black Maria. They were handcuffed and had black hoods over their heads, fastened by a strap around the neck. Their hands were clenched and they were praying. There was a round white piece of paper pinned over their heart. The first one was tied to the stake. He was trembling terribly. The priest, who was Polish, went up to him, prayed, and made the sign of the cross. The signal was then given to aim. With about twenty Military Government officials on stands behind us we took aim. I was against the sentence as I knew how they must have suffered. Their bodies were covered with lice-bites and bruises. I couldn't shoot a person in this manner, so I raised my rifle just above his right shoulder when the order FIRE! was given. The volley of eight shots rang out and the man seemed to be blown backwards, then he hung forwards. Our Captain then had to remove the black hood and shoot him again in the head with his pistol, as this is the regulation. Then the hearse came with a coffin and a man and a woman placed him in the coffin after he had been certified dead by a doctor. He was then buried in the prison grounds. I took the round piece of white paper from his jacket and put it in a home-made leather wallet which a 13-year-old Jewish girl had given to me for a crust of bread just before she was killed by her SS guard.

The same procedure followed for the second man. I again fired over his shoulder and I am very pleased that I did not aim at him as it would have followed me every day of my life. That night most of the firing-squad were drunk, especially the Captain, who had to shoot them both in the head. He was very ill and upset, even though he was a war veteran.

The Occupation authorities tried to do their best for the DPs in Germany. The British tried to teach them cricket, the Americans baseball, neither with any lasting success. For three months after the war a special bomber squadron from England continued to fly over ex-enemy territory, dropping canisters stuffed with foreign-language newspapers, magazines and children's comics. Over 21 million copies of the SHAEF daily newspaper, 2.5 million copies of the SHAEF four-language weekly and over three million other periodicals in French, Dutch, Polish, Russian, Czech and Serbo-Croat were distributed amongst the DPs. Large numbers of priests, rabbis and parsons were air-lifted in, along with 1,000 mouth organs, 1,900 footballs, 10,000 chess sets, 54,000 domino sets, 3,000,000 packets of chewing-gum, 3,500,000 packets of cigarettes, 15,000,000 boxes of matches and 26,000,000 razor blades. Many relief agencies from America, Britain, France, Belgium, Poland, Holland, Switzerland, Italy, the British and Palestine Agencies, the American Jewish and Polish Relief Committees, Catholic Welfare, YMCA and YWCA ministered to the needs of this army of displaced humanity under the supervision of the United Nations relief agency, UNRRA.

By June 1947 over half a million displaced persons remained unrepatriated in the DP assembly centres in the western zones of Germany. These people were to remain implacably opposed to repatriation to homelands which were now under Soviet or communist domination. Even two years later 175,000 were still not resettled and still in care.

Of all the mass population movements that followed the end of the war, none was more tragic than that of the repatriated Russian slave workers and prisoners of war. During the course of the war on the Eastern Front several million Soviet citizens fell into German hands. These included 5,754,000 prisoners of war, only 1,150,000 of whom survived Nazi captivity; 2,800,000 forced labourers, 2,000,000 of whom were liberated by the Western Allies in 1945; about one million refugees of minor nationalities in the USSR who for various reasons (in particular a dislike of Russians and Bolsheviks) had fled the Soviet Union en masse in the wake of the German retreat; and up to a million men, drawn from the ranks of prisoners of war, forced labourers and refugees, who had joined the German side in the fighting against the Soviets. This last category was made of three main groups—the eastern legions (German-officered regiments composed of traditionally anti-Soviet minorities such as Cossacks, Georgians, Ukrainians, Kalmuks, etc.); General Andrei Vlasov's Russian Liberation Army (composed largely of Russian POWs, many of whom had been forced to join by the Germans); and the Russian forced-labour battalions of the Todt Organisation employed on German military construction work.

It might have been thought that the Soviet government, while exacting just retribution from those Soviet citizens who had taken up arms against their own country, might have shown compassion towards the millions of others who had remained loyal to the Soviet Union, in spite of the appalling brutality experienced in German captivity. But this was not the case. In practice, Stalin made little or no distinction between the traitors and the patriots, between the anti-Soviet Vlasov and Cossack armies and the pro-Soviet Red Army POWs and forced labourers—they were all equally guilty of the monstrous crime of having been abroad. All Soviet citizens who so much as caught a glimpse of life outside the USSR, who passed even temporarily outside of Soviet control, no matter under what circumstances, were looked upon as traitors, for it was thought to be inconceivable that anyone who came in contact with the non-Marxist west could retain their Marxist faith intact. Red Army soldiers who were captured in battle, even while unconscious or severely wounded, were doubly despised. To surrender, not to die fighting, was viewed as treachery to the Soviet Union. Soviet POWs were written off as though they were dead, and were deprived of all rights of citizenship and even official recognition of their very existence. The USSR was not a signatory of the Geneva Convention on the treatment of POWs. Red Cross parcels and other relief supplies were denied to Soviet POWs on Stalin's orders, and Soviet POW camps in German-held territory were bombed by the Red Air Force. No exceptions were made to the general rule. Even Stalin's only son, Yakov, was disowned by his father after his capture by the Germans. When Hitler offered to exchange him for his own nephew, Leo Raubal, Stalin refused, and Yakov was allowed to die a squalid death in captivity. Even soldiers who escaped from behind the enemy lines and returned to the Soviet side of the front were punished, sometimes with death.

In spite of this, the Western Allies handed more than two million expatriate Soviet citizens (and a good many Russians who were not Soviet citizens) back to Stalin between 1944 and 1947—many against their will and with the use of force. The fate of almost all of these people once in the Soviet Union was terrible. Many were summarily liquidated. Most of the remainder were sent to slave camps in the Urals, Central Asia, Siberia and the far north where few survived. All in all, the repatriation of Soviet prisoners by the British, American and other western countries was one of the most repugnant episodes to arise out of World War Two. It was, by the terms of the Charter of the International Military Tribunal, a major war crime comparable to that with which the Nazi war criminals were charged at Nuremberg.

The majority of the Soviet citizens involved in this unsavoury business were repatriated during the summer of 1945. They were repatriated not only from the defeated Axis territories of Germany, Austria and Italy, but from the liberated countries of France, Belgium, Holland and Norway, the neutral countries of Switzerland, Liechtenstein and Sweden, from the battlefields of North Africa and the prisoner-of-war camps of Britain and the USA. A number were not even Soviet citizens, and a few were White Russians who had fled Russia after the Revolution, nearly thirty years before. Several nations were thus involved to a greater or lesser extent in forcibly handing Soviet subjects over to the untender mercies of the NKVD (the Russian secret police), and the Gulag.

It was Britain that first formulated the policy of forcible repatriation in compliance with Soviet requirements, and it was Britain that persuaded the reluctant United States government to go along with that policy. In the end though, the Americans forcibly handed back no more than a few hundred Soviet citizens, while the British handed over countless thousands, often amid scenes so harrowing that they have haunted the British soldiers who were ordered to carry them out ever since.

The British made the running mainly because it was they who were first confronted with the unusual problem of captured Soviet defectors en masse. Following the D-Day invasion and the Allied advance through France many thousands of these Soviet troops fell into British hands and were ferried back across the Channel to POW camps in England. As their numbers grew so did the concern of the British government. What was to be done with them? Churchill wanted to postpone the issue until the war was over. It was his Foreign Secretary, Anthony Eden, who forced the pace. 'If these men don't go back to Russia,' he demanded, roughly sweeping aside the humanitarian arguments of his colleagues, 'where do they go? We don't want them here.'

The matter dragged on into 1945. Stalin was not content with Soviet prisoners of war in the German Army—he wanted all Soviet citizens repatriated, including the slave labourers, the concentration-camp inmates, the Red Army prisoners of war, the women and the children. The matter was left to the last great wartime conference of the Big Three at Yalta in February 1945. At Yalta the British proposed to repatriate *all* Soviet subjects, whether they wanted to go or not—a breach of the Geneva Convention on the treatment of prisoners of war. At Yalta in the end it was the British view that prevailed. Eisenhower admitted that one in five prisoners in American hands in France were Russian. The American government reluctantly conceded that 'US policy is to repatriate to the Soviet Union all claimants of Soviet citizenship whose claims are accepted by Soviet authorities. In practice this means ... that Soviet citizens originating within 1939 boundaries of Soviet Union are repatriated irrespective of individual wishes.' So the fate of many thousands of Soviet subjects was sealed to Stalin's satisfaction—and the mass repatriation began.

Advance: Red Army tanks roll past – and over – German dead in East Prussia (*Sovfoto*).

Retreat: (top) German civilians flee west towards Berlin from the advancing Red Army (*Keystone Pressedient*); and (foot) chaos and panic on the great flight to the west (*Carl Henrich*).

A Red Army soldier raises the Hammer and Sickle over the Reichstag (*Novosti*).

(top) For the Red Army it was not all pillage and rapine – this group sings around a piano surmounted by a vase of flowers that have somehow survived in the ruins (*Novosti*); and (foot) a British officer, just visible in the centre of the picture, adds his name to the Russian graffiti on the walls of the Reichstag (*Daily Mirror*).

(top) British Tommies jeer a captured portrait of the Führer (*Associated Press*); and (foot) the arrest of the Dönitz government at Flensburg: left to right – Speer, Dönitz, Jodl (*Imperial War Museum*).

(top left) German civilians are made to walk past dead concentration camp victims at Dachau (*US Army*); and (foot) Russians and Americans drink and dance after meeting on the Elbe River (*National Archives, Washington*).

(top) The heroic *Trümmerfrauen* – the rubble ladies of bombed-out Germany – salvaging bricks from the ruined towns (*Keystone Pressedient*); and (foot) just after the fighting stopped in Berlin, a woman emerges into the corpse-strewn Freidrichstrasse (*Sovfoto*).

Occupation soldiers in action: (top) a GI and a German Fräulein engage in 'frat' (*Hans Schaller*); and (foot) an American lieutenant wears the crown and insignia of the Holy Roman Emperor (*US Army*).

Occupation soldiers in action: (top) the Red Army officer has three watches on his wrist and three medals on his chest (*Keystone Pressedient*); and (foot) the Red Army soldier grabs at the German woman's bike (*Keystone Pressedient*).

Survival: (top left) barefoot German boy rummages for scraps in the British Club rubbish bins at Hamburg (*Victor Gollancz*); (top right) all their worldly goods (*George Gronefeld*); and (foot) rubbish bins at the American barracks in Berlin 1946 (*US Army*).

(top left) deported Germans from Czechoslovakia arrive at a railway station in Bavaria packed into cattle trucks like wartime Jews (*Keystone Pressedient*); (top right) captured German soldiers walk west as American tanks roll east along the autobahn (*US Army*); and (foot) hungry Germans festoon trains on their way to the countryside to barter for food from farmers (*Keystone Pressedient*).

(top) Refugees from the Soviet zone flee through the woods across the border to the west (*Hilmar Pabel*); and (foot) children cheer another Berlin airlift transport into Tempelhof airfield (*Landesbildstelle*).

Among the first Soviet prisoners to suffer this ordained fate, many were not Russians but came from the non-Russian regions of the USSR. Many were terrified of returning to the Soviet Union and expressed great loathing for that country. A British officer responsible for screening the Russian prisoners wrote to the Foreign Office: 'Most of them said they preferred death to returning to the Soviet Union and some even invited the British to shoot them in preference to handing them over.'

The bulk of the mass repatriations took place during the summer following the end of the war in Europe. But sporadic deliveries of groups of Soviet prisoners had been taking place while the war was being fought to its conclusion. Over a thousand were shipped to the Soviet far eastern port of Vladivostok. On arrival they were re-recruited into the Red Army for the final assault on Berlin. Those who survived the fighting were subsequently put on trial and sentenced to twenty-five years' forced labour. Many thousands of Soviet prisoners were also shipped to Murmansk or Odessa. Arrivals not destined for immediate execution were made to put on the rags and footcloths which were the normal apparel of the Gulag slave camps. The remainder were killed as soon as they had disembarked, the sound of execution being drowned by the roar of factory engines, saw-mills and low-circling Red Air Force planes. Many committed suicide on the way.

Repatriations from Great Britain and the USA made up only a tiny fraction of the total repatriations of Soviet subjects, but had to be carried out forcibly amid scenes of violence and anguish. Paradoxically the mass repatriations of Soviet POWs, volunteer workers and slave labourers from Germany, which made up by far the major portion, were accomplished in the main on a voluntary basis and without trouble. This was because they took place immediately after the end of the war, before rumours of their likely fate had filtered back from the Soviet Union. After years of captivity or servitude in Nazi hands, many Russian men and women emerged in the heady days following their liberation imbued with the fond hope of returning home, starting a new life and even helping to build a new Russia. It was bitterly ironic that the fate of these people was exactly the same as that of the traitors who had to be sent back by force. By the end of June 1945, one and a half million had been repatriated from the Western zones; by the end of September 1945, 2,035,000 had been repatriated from the West and 2,946,000 from the Soviet zones.

All repatriated Soviet citizens underwent the same processing once they had been handed over. All their personal possessions were taken and burnt. Known undesirables—anti-Soviet Vlasov men and Cossacks as well as most officers—were executed immediately at their reception point. The remainder were divided into groups—young people under 16, old people over 60, and able-bodied men and able-bodied women between 16 and 60. According to one British Army eyewitness, the old people were taken away and shot. According to another eyewitness, the young people under 16 as well as the old people were shot. The able-bodied men and women were then sent on their way to different forced labour camps deep in the USSR. They were first gathered in immense collection centres (the one at Wiener Neustadt in the Soviet Zone of Austria contained 60,000 people) where SMERSH screening teams roughly divided them again into three groups—those judged to be enemies of the Soviet Union (including anyone found in German uniform), those who could not be proved to be enemies of the Soviet Union, and those few deemed to be loyal. The first group were sent to the forced labour camps, the second to forced labour work outside the camps, and the third to post-war reconstruction sites. In practice the distinctions between these groups became blurred and the vast majority of repatriates ended up as slave labour. According to an NKVD officer who defected to the West, of the five and a half million Soviet citizens repatriated to the USSR, 20 per cent were sentenced to death or twenty-five years' hard labour (which amounted to death), 15 to 20 per cent got five to ten years' forced labour, 10 per cent were exiled to frontier regions of Siberia for six years or more, 15 per cent were sent to reconstruction sites in the Donbas, Kuzbas and other war-devastated regions, and some 15 to 20 per cent were allowed to go home—though most of these were treated as outcasts, could obtain no work and ended up in prison later. The small percentage unaccounted for can probably be put down to those who either escaped or died in transit. All through July and August 1945 the Soviet prison trains—wired and barred cattle-trucks interspersed with machine-gun platforms—could be seen racing through the southern Polish countryside on the first stage of the horrendous journey from Austria and Germany to the Gulag slave camps of Siberia and Central Asia. Numbers did not survive the train journey and few long-sentence prisoners survived the cold, hunger, sickness and brutality of the camps.

The full burden of Stalin's wrath fell mainly on those Soviet subjects who had borne arms against the Soviet Union, notably the Vlasov Army and the Cossacks, though in reality relatively few of these ever fired a shot in anger against their compatriots. The Vlasov Army—the all-Russian military army of the KONR (Committee for the Liberation of the People of Russia) under former Red Army General Andrei Vlasov—only became operational at the very end of the war and did not survive many days after it. In late April 1945, the Vlasov Army marched out of Germany into Czechoslovakia, the only remaining area of Nazi-occupied territory that had not been overrun by the enemy. A day or two before the end of the war, one division of the Vlasov Army turned their arms against their former German allies in the Battle for Prague, thereby hoping to win asylum in Czechoslovakia from a future re-established Czech state. But with the Red Army closing in from the east, the Vlasov Army was forced to retreat westwards towards the advancing Americans. Trapped between the American and Soviet Armies in a space two miles wide, the Vlasovites had few options open to them. More than ten thousand decided to surrender voluntarily to the Soviets. The remainder surrendered to the Americans but were forcibly handed over to the Soviets shortly afterwards. General Vlasov and some of his senior officers were captured by the Red Army on 12 May 1945 and executed in Moscow in August 1946 for treason, espionage and terrorist activities against the Soviet Union.

Not everyone agreed that Vlasov and his followers were traitors. Wilfried Strikfeldt, Vlasov's liaison officer with the German Army, was to write later: 'When an American asked me whether Vlasov was a traitor, I put a counter-question—were Washington and Franklin also traitors? . . . The Russian Liberation Movement was smashed and Vlasov and his friends were executed, just as Stauffenberg and the men of July 20th [the 1944 bomb plot against Hitler] were executed.'

Next in Soviet opprobrium after the Vlasov Army came the Cossacks. A number of Cossack formations ended up in Austria at the end of the war. The two principal groups were the so-called Cossack Division under General Domanov and the rather more formidable 15th Cossack Cavalry Corps under its German commander, General Helmuth von Pannwitz. The fate of almost all of them was uniformly dreadful.

The Cossacks had always opposed the Soviet Russian conquest of their homelands in the Don and Kuban regions north of the Caucasus in 1920. When the Germans arrived in 1942 the Cossacks welcomed them as liberators, and German rule was for the most part benign. But when the Germans were forced to retreat after their defeat at Stalingrad, a large section of the Cossack population was forced to retreat with them for fear of Soviet reprisals. The Cossack 'nation', with its train of wagons, cattle, horses and dromedaries, took part in a great westward migration across Russia, Poland and Germany in its flight before the Red Army. The Cossacks spent the last winter of the war camped in Northern Italy, then in the spring of 1945 withdrew northwards across the Alps into Austria to avoid the advancing British Army. In the valley of the River Drau, near the Tyrolean town of Lienz, the Cossacks finally halted. There were 32,000 in the so-called Cossack Division, but they were only a military formation on paper. They had never fired a shot in anger and in reality constituted a cross-section of the Cossack population from the south of the Don, and included many thousands of women and children. With the war at an end and Germany in collapse, the Cossacks had only two options—they could surrender to the British or to the Americans. In fact, they chose to surrender to the British, on the grounds that they had been the stauncher champions of the White Russian cause between the wars. It was a fatal choice.

On 8 May 1945, the Cossacks began the first stage of the complex business of surrendering to the 78th Infantry Division in the valley of the Drau. To the British troops they presented an extraordinary sight. 'Their basic uniform was German', recalled one eyewitness,

> but with their fur Cossack caps, their mournful dundreary whiskers, their knee-high riding boots, and their roughly-made horse-drawn carts bearing all their worldly goods and chattels, including wife and family, there could be no mistaking them for anything but Russians. They were a tableau from the Russia of 1812. Squadrons of horses galloped hither and thither on the road, impeding our progress as much as the horse-drawn carts. It was useless to give them orders; few spoke German or English and no one who understood seemed inclined to obey. Despite this apparent chaos it was remarkable how swiftly and completely they carried out their orders to concentrate.

Not far away from the Cossacks was the camp of five thousand Caucasians of various tribes, the surviving fragments of national legions formed by the Germans during the war to liberate their homeland. Also in Austria, a few miles to the east, some twenty thousand men of the 15th Cossack Cavalry Corps also surrendered to the British.

Through the spring weather of May 1945 the Cossacks lived a life of almost idyllic peace. There was lush grazing for their horses, a settled life for the families, schools, choirs, church services, newspapers, Red Cross supplies. They were not in a prison camp, there was no barbed wire and no British guards. Very few attempted to escape, for escape seemed unnecessary. None of them had heard of the secret agreement at Yalta to repatriate all Soviet citizens to the Soviet Union; some even hoped they might be invited to join the British and Americans in a new war against Russia. Nobody believed that Field Marshal Alexander, who had fought against the Bolsheviks in the Russian Civil War, would ever be so barbaric as to hand them back to the Soviets. All of them were agreed on one point about their cloudy future: they would never return to the Soviet Union.

On 27 May their dreams were shattered. They were ordered to hand over their weapons and their officers were told to parade the next day before being taken to a nearby town where Field Marshal Alexander himself would communicate to them an important decision about their future. Some Cossack officers believed this was a trick, but more thought the conference was genuine and that they would be back in the camp by evening.

The next morning 1,475 Cossack officers—the cream of the Cossack nation—marched out of camp in their traditional Cossack uniforms, carrying on high the tricolour of old Imperial Russia. Their womenfolk wept as they went. Outside the barrack square they boarded sixty British Army trucks, which were then joined by armoured cars and armed motorcyclists. Together they trundled towards the Austrian township of

Oberdrauburg. Field Marshal Alexander was not there to greet them. Instead Brigadier Geoffrey Musson, the Commander of the British 36th Infantry Brigade, briskly addressed the commander of the Cossack Division, General Timofey Domanov: 'I have to inform you, sir, that I have received strict orders to hand over the whole of the Cossack Division to the Soviet authorities. I regret to have to tell you this, but the order is categorical. Good day.'

It was indeed a trick. The British military authorities in Austria had decided that the easiest way to hand over the Cossacks was first to separate the officers from the men by means of deception. The Cossack officers would spend the night in a specially prepared prisoner-of-war cage at Spittal, lower down the valley of the Drau, and next day would be turned over to the Soviet authorities at the border reception-point at Judenburg. A similar fate would befall the Caucasians.

When General Domanov broke the terrible news to his fellow-officers, they were stunned and panic-stricken. In despair they signed petitions addressed to King George VI, Field Marshal Alexander, the Pope and the International Red Cross. At five on the following fateful morning they were served breakfast and held their last service—'A most impressive affair,' the British officer in charge recorded, 'the singing quite magnificent.' At 6.30 the first truck arrived. General Domanov refused to move as did all the other officers. A platoon of British infantry advanced on them armed with rifles and bayonets or pick-axe helves. The Cossacks and Caucasians resisted passively, sitting on the ground with arms linked. Then the British soldiers launched a violent assault on the resisting prisoners in order to force them into the trucks. A dozen Cossacks committed suicide, three more escaped by crawling out through the wire perimeter. Those remaining were driven at speed towards the Soviet zonal frontier at Judenburg.

A river gorge marked the boundary. British armoured cars and machine-guns lined the approach. One at a time the trucks crossed the bridge over the river to the Soviet side. While the trucks waited for their turn to cross, one Cossack was given permission to use the urinal bucket at the head of the bridge, then suddenly ran forward and jumped over the cliff and fell on the rocks a hundred feet below. With some difficulty the body of the dying officer was recovered and duly handed over to the Soviet forces, along with all the other unfortunates who passed over the bridge at Judenburg that day.

The British soldiers could see nothing of what happened to the Cossacks once they were in Soviet hands—but they could hear. That night and the following day they heard small-arms fire coming from across the river, to the accompaniment of the finest male voice choir they had ever heard. After each burst of gunfire there would come a huge cheer. Clearly, the Cossack officers knew how to die bravely. For several days and nights firing-squads were busy liquidating the Cossack officers in the disused steel-mill at Judenburg.

The melancholy task of informing the Cossack wives that their husbands had been handed over to the Soviets and that they too would follow fell on Major W. R. 'Rusty' Davies, a 26-year old Welshman who had been the British liaison officer to the Cossacks for the best part of the month. On him also fell the task of informing the remaining Cossacks of the arrangements for their own repatriation, due for 1 June.

From that moment onwards the stunned Cossacks began to resist the British. They refused to eat the midday meal provided for them. Many clamoured round Davies, waving passports and documents which showed that they were not Soviet citizens but old émigrés with French, Italian or Yugoslav nationality or registered stateless. Why should they be sent to a country to which they did not belong? Improvised tented churches were set up for confession and communion, and petitions were drawn up. 'WE PREFER DEATH than to be returned to the Soviet Union,' read one such petition. 'We, husbands, mothers, brothers, sisters and children PRAY FOR OUR SALVATION!!!' Black flags hung out from the huts and tents. A hunger strike began, continuous services were held by the priest, weeping mothers clutched their children, knowing that they would soon be separated forever. First to go were the Caucasians. Two hundred had succeeded in escaping through the British cordon during the preceding night. But on 1 June, 3,161 Caucasian men, women and children were sent off to Judenburg in three train loads. The Cossacks followed. On their last day of liberty they bade a bitter and agonising farewell to their families and to their beloved horses and at dawn on 1 June in the damp square at Lienz they prepared to face their ordeal.

The Cossacks resolved to resist the British so that it could never be said that they had been voluntarily repatriated to the USSR. Before a vast congregation of thousands their priests began to intone the liturgy. The arrival of a company of the Argylls did not succeed in stopping the service. When a platoon of soldiers moved in to start moving the Cossacks on to the trucks, the people reacted in a concerted fashion. The younger men formed a ring round the women, children and old people, and knelt on the ground with arms interlocked, an unbreakable human barrier. The battle-hardened British troops, deeply distressed by the repugnant job they had been ordered to do, backed off for a moment.

Major Davies, no less distressed but aware that he had to carry out his orders, ordered his soldiers to prise open the human circle with their weapons. A small group of Cossacks were detached in this way and a gap was opened in the Cossack ranks. Two more platoons were now sent in to keep the gap open while the first platoon attempted to load the detached group of Cossacks on to the trucks. The Cossacks formed into a solid mass. As individuals were pulled away, those who were left were seized with panic and started climbing over each other until they formed a screaming pyramid of human beings. The soldiers were forced to belabour arms and legs with rifle-butts and pick-axe helves to make people loosen their grip and thus try and save those at the bottom of the pyramid from being crushed or suffocated to death. In the end every single one had to be loaded on to the trucks by force.

The soldiers now tried to prise off a second group, using greater violence this time, and the screaming crowd surged away from them— some towards a little bridge over the torrential river Drau which bordered the south side of the Cossack camp. As the crowd poured over the bridge the soldiers lashed out at young and old, men and women alike. The battalion Medical Officer, weeping openly, dressed the wounds of the injured. A mother was seen to hurl her child into the torrent below, thereby ensuring that it would never fall into Soviet hands alive.

The largest part of the crowd was pushed up against a wooden stockade on the eastern perimeter of the camp. When a section of the stockade gave way under the crush of bodies, the people burst out into an open field beyond. Here they began to recover themselves and their priests started up their liturgy again. Lt.-Col. Alec Malcolm, the Argylls' Commanding Officer, who was in charge of the repatriation arrangements, decided to order a halt at this stage for fear of further bloodshed. Both the Cossacks and his own men were in a state of considerable shock and many of the soldiers, including Major Davies, were weeping. With his troops on the verge of mutiny Colonel Malcolm informed his brigade commander, Brigadier Musson, that henceforth he would not use force again and would refuse to issue his men with live ammunition.

By this time 1,252 people had been loaded on to trucks, then re-loaded on to a waiting train bound for Judenburg. The Cossack camp resembled a battlefield. The Argylls' War Diary recorded the casualties in the camp as follows: '5 killed; 3 evacuated with gunshot wounds; 7 head injuries; collapsed 2, women and children 2'—but many more died in the surrounding countryside. A father, for example, had shot his family one by one in the woods, then killed himself. A number of Cossacks had been gunned down as they fled. Twenty to thirty were drowned in the river, including an entire family and a Cossack who plunged into the torrent seated on the back of his horse. How many died on that infamous day will never be known. The British said twelve: more probably it was several hundred.

Similar scenes had taken place at another Cossack camp in the Drau valley where other British units were compelled to use extreme force (including the use of bayonets and machine-gun fire) to load 1,749 frenzied Cossacks on to cattle-trucks for their train ride to Judenburg. During the course of a fortnight 22,502 Cossacks and Caucasians were sent by the 36th Infantry Brigade from the Drau valley to the Soviet-occupied zone of Austria. Subsequent repatriation passed off more peaceably. Over four thousand Cossacks escaped into the forest and over the snow-covered heights beyond. British patrols combed the mountains for them, sometimes assisted by Soviet SMERSH agents. A total of 1,356 Cossacks and Caucasians were thus recaptured, of whom 934 were handed over to the Russians for instant liquidation. A British Army sergeant witnessed the fate of some of these recaptured people when they were handed back to the Soviets at Graz. They were herded, male and female alike, into a huge wired concentration camp. There, drunken Soviet guards in the camp towers fired random bursts of machine-gun fire into the crowd.

The Cossack Cavalry Corps, a regulation formation of the Wehrmacht, with its senior officers, including its commander, General von Pannwitz, drawn from the German Officer Corps, was handed over to the Russians at Judenburg with relative ease. Tricked into believing that they were being sent to Italy and thence possibly to Canada, 17,702 of them were handed over to the Russians by the British 46th Infantry Division. Some ten thousand more were handed over by the British 6th Armoured Division, which had assigned the task to the Welsh Guards—'the most ignoble task,' in the words of the battalion commander, 'which I could ever have given them.' Several thousand Cossacks from this latter group, including all the German officers, made good their escape. The rest of the Cossacks were handed over to the Russians and sent to the death camps in Central Siberia, where few survived.

Some fifty thousand Cossacks were thus forcibly repatriated from Austria. Twice that number of Soviet subjects were repatriated from France and the French zones of Germany and Austria. Other Soviet subjects were repatriated, often forcibly, from Belgium, Holland, Switzerland, Liechtenstein, and Scandinavia.

But by the end of 1945 the whole policy of forcible repatriation had begun to falter. In Germany, General Eisenhower formally queried the whole policy, as did the US Political Adviser in Germany Robert Murphy. In Italy, Field Marshal Alexander refused point-blank to use force and refused to hand over the Ukrainian Division or the thirty thousand Polish citizens in the Polish Corps, and his Chief of Staff, General Sir William Morgan, protested strenuously to the Foreign Office in London that forcible repatriation was 'quite out of keeping with traditions of democracy and justice as we know them.' Eisenhower put a stop to it in the American zone of Germany in September 1945, and in the following month General Montgomery did the same in the British zone. In the following February the Vatican was to join in the mounting protest against forcible repatriation. It was, said a senior spokesman for the Pope, 'a betrayal of the morality and ideals for which the Allies fought.'

The Foreign Office was incensed. On Christmas Day 1945 Thomas Brimelow issued a statement of seasonal goodwill: 'We consider that *all*

Soviet citizens should be repatriated, forcibly if necessary.' The American government decided that proven traitors should still be handed back to the Soviet Union. So the final repatriations took their grim course. In January 1946 in the former Nazi concentration camp at Dachau in the American zone of Germany a shock-force of American and Polish guards attempted to entrain a group of Russian prisoners from Vlasov's Army who refused to be repatriated under the new American ruling. 'All of these men refused to entrain,' Robert Murphy wrote in his report of the incident. 'They begged to be shot. They resisted entrainment by taking off their clothes and refusing to leave their quarters ... Tear-gas forced them out of the building into the snow where those who had cut and stabbed themselves fell exhausted and bleeding into the snow. Nine men hanged themselves and one had stabbed himself to death and one other who had stabbed himself subsequently died; while 20 others are still in hospital from self-inflicted wounds. The entrainment was finally effected of 368 men. Six escaped en route ... eleven men were returned by the Russians as not of Soviet nationality.'

The last operation of this kind in Germany took place at Plattling near Regensburg, where fifteen hundred men of Vlasov's Army had been interned by the Americans. In the early hours of 24 February 1946, they were driven out of their huts wearing only their night-clothes, and handed over to the Russians in the forest near the Bavarian–Czech frontier. Before the train set off on its return journey the American guards were horrified to see the bodies of Vlasov's men who had already committed suicide hanging in rows from the trees, and when they returned to Plattling even the German SS prisoners in a nearby POW camp jeered at them for what they had done. Incidents like this were just too much for the soldiers to stomach, and in Germany and Austria at least they were never repeated.

Officially only thirty-five thousand Soviet citizens were listed as not being repatriated, but it is likely that between a quarter and a half a million evaded repatriation. The eight thousand men of the KONR Air Corps surrendered to Patton's Third Army on condition that they were not handed back to the Soviets. The Americans honoured this agreement and all the Russians found refuge in the West. The British let even more prisoners go free: ten thousand Ukrainians of mixed Soviet and Polish citizenship from the Waffen-SS Panzer Grenadier Division Galicia were not repatriated, on the questionable grounds that they were mainly Polish. The four and a half thousand men of the White Russian Schutzkorps from Serbia—the only surviving formation of the old Russian Imperial Army— who surrendered to the Grenadier Guards in Austria on 12 May 1945, were released by the British after a year and allowed to settle in the West. The 15th Division of the Latvian Legion of the Waffen-SS were allowed by their British captors to escape from POW camps in Germany and find refuge in the relative security of the DP camps. Eight hundred Soviet

Moslems of the Turcomen Division fell under the powerful protection of the International Mohammedan Brotherhood headed by King Farouk and were repatriated no further than Egypt. It is likely that up to eighty thousand Soviet Moslems were stranded in the West in this way by 1946.

Ten years after the end of the war, following the death of Josef Stalin, most of the repatriated Soviet citizens were released from slave labour under a special amnesty. But by then only a relatively small proportion of the 5.5 million who had been handed back were still alive. In March 1982, a memorial to the Russian victims of forcible repatriation was unveiled on Crown land in the centre of London, in a formal atonement for what had been perpetrated with British complicity.

In sum, the Russian prisoners after the war suffered a comparable fate in comparable numbers to the Jews during the war. The Russian and Jewish survivors differed, however, in one important respect. Whereas to the Russians home was anathema, the Jews could dream of nothing else—for home to them was *Eretz Israel*, their Promised Land and the goal of another of the great population movements of the aftermath of the war.

Some five to six million European Jews died in the Nazi Holocaust. But one million survived in Europe as a whole, not counting the many more who survived in the Soviet Union, including two million indigenous Soviet Jews and 730,000 Polish Jews who had sought refuge in the Soviet Union. Some of the survivors were found by the Allies in concentration camps. Thousands of these died soon after the liberation, as a result of disease and starvation incurred before liberation or the effects of over-eating after it. In the concentration camp at Belsen alone, 23,000 people—90 per cent of them Jews—died after the camp had been freed. A number of Jews escaped captivity, however, and emerged at the end of the war from hiding-places in houses and institutions, or remote forests and mountains in Germany, Italy and Poland. Altogether some 20,000 Jews survived in Western Germany, of whom 13,000 were native German Jews. In Poland, where nearly 98 per cent of the pre-war Jewish population had been wiped out, 80,000 Jews were found alive at the end of the war. In every country that had been occupied by the Germans during the war the Jewish losses were extreme, ranging from half to nine-tenths of the pre-war population. The ones who emerged alive from the holocaust called themselves the '*Sharit Hapletoh*'—the Survivors.

The small number of Jews in the Western zones of Germany and Austria were not considered a special problem by the military, UNRRA and the voluntary relief agencies. But from the summer of 1945 onwards their numbers grew rapidly as Jewish survivors from Poland began to migrate westwards across central Europe to the Western zones of Germany and Austria. By October an average of four hundred Polish Jews a week were infiltrating into Jewish DP centres in the American zone of Germany via

Prague, Berlin, Budapest, Bratislava, Salzburg and Vienna. The reasons for this migration were various—their homes and families were destroyed; they saw no future in the prevailing political ferment and economic devastation of Poland; and above all they found themselves to be the targets of a resurgent anti-Semitic hatred as virulent as that which existed in wartime Germany. By the end of 1945 a similar resurgence of anti-Semitism in Rumania, Hungary and Bulgaria caused Jews to migrate from those countries as well.

Then in June 1946 began a mass flight of Jews from Poland. About 200,000 Polish Jews had survived the war as refugees in Russia, where they had been well cared for. At the beginning of 1946 the Russians began to repatriate these Jews, and by June 1946 140,000 had returned there. Few stayed long: though the Polish government was sympathetic to them, the Polish people were not. The migration of Jews from Poland was accelerated by a pogrom in Zielce in July in which forty-one Jews were killed and sixty injured, followed by similar incidents elsewhere in Poland in which thirty-three more Jews lost their lives. By September 1946 over 64,000 Polish Jews had fled to Germany. By November the number that had left Poland for Western Germany, Austria and Italy totalled 120,000—all but 15,000 of them illegal immigrants. By the summer of 1947 247,000 Jews had sought refuge in the Jewish assembly centres (segregated Jewish DP camps) in the Western zones of Germany and Austria, and in Italy—73 per cent of them Polish, the rest Rumanian, Hungarian, Czechoslovakian and German.

Many of these Jews were in an extremely unbalanced emotional state as a result of their ordeals, and their behaviour could be very provocative; it required a considerable effort on the part of even the most friendly non-Jews not to be goaded into retaliatory action. Though the American occupation authorities in Germany and Austria bore the brunt of the burden in terms of numbers (more than 90 per cent of the Jews were cared for by American authorities), the British bore the brunt in terms of provocation because it was the British who were viewed as the obstacle to mass immigration to Palestine.

By now it had long been clear that the migration of Jews from Eastern Europe had been a carefully organised affair, encouraged by agents of voluntary Jewish organisations, most notably the Haganah, the Jewish people's underground militia in Palestine, backed by funds supplied mainly by American Jews. What was in progress was not simply the emigration of Jews from Eastern Europe to Western Europe but a full-scale exodus of European Jewry which used Western Europe and especially the territory of the former Third Reich, as a stepping-stone to Palestine, the Promised (but largely forbidden) Land. It was agents of the Haganah who organised the groups, provided money and documents for them, fixed the border-crossings, arranged the routes, the transport, food and shelter in reception points at the various stages of the journey, and negotiated all the complicated steps that finally led to the clandestine embarkation of groups of emigrant Jews bound for Palestine on board illegal emigrant ships at Mediterranean, Atlantic or Black Sea ports. The Haganah underground route across Europe was the first stage of a Zionist master-plan to force the British to give way over Palestine and step aside in favour of a new Jewish State of Israel.

From the very beginning then, the Jewish DPs regarded their stay in Germany, Austria or Italy as strictly temporary—a necessary stop-over on their way to a new land of their choice. For most of these Jews their first choice was Palestine—or Eretz Israel as they preferred to call it. Their hearts were, as one aspiring Jewish emigrant put it, 'filled with one longing: to go home.' But immigration to Palestine in the first three years after the war presented great difficulties to the Jews. Palestine was governed by Great Britain under a Mandate from the pre-war League of Nations. For fear of provoking a revolt by the Arabs, who still formed the majority of the population of Palestine, the British imposed a severe restriction on the number of Jewish immigrants allowed to enter Palestine. At the end of World War Two, Jewish leaders and the government of the United States, which contained the largest Jewish population in the world, tried to persuade the British government to allow the survivors of the Holocaust to enter Palestine legally en masse—if only for humanitarian reasons. In March 1946 a joint Anglo-American committee on Palestine recommended, among other things, the immediate immigration of a hundred thousand Jews from Europe. Unfortunately the United States government declined to share the military and financial responsibility for the civil conflict which would undoubtedly arise as a consequence of Arab hostility to such large-scale immigration. The British government therefore refused to implement the proposal and continued to limit Jewish immigration to more easily assimilable numbers—specifically 1,500 a month. This meant that the only way most Jews could reach the Promised Land quickly without rotting for years in the DP camps of the former Third Reich was illegally.

Despite the protests of the British authorities, prospective 'illegals' were easily smuggled through to Italy from their assembly centres in Germany and Austria with the active co-operation of the US Army, UNRRA, the International Red Cross and the Vatican; the Italian police did little to intervene. The first Haganah ship attempted to reach Palestine on 23 November 1945, and although it was intercepted by the Royal Navy most of its passengers managed to reach land. Between 15 December 1945 and 15 September 1946, a total of 15,000 immigrants landed in Palestine from the DP camps of Europe—9,296 of them brought in illegally. By the summer of 1946 the trickle of illegal immigration to Palestine was becoming a flood.

The first reporter to travel underground to Palestine on the Jewish exodus was the American I. F. Stone, a columnist on the radical paper, *PM*, himself of Russian–Jewish origin. Stone started his trip in May 1946 with the help of contacts in the Haganah organisation. His first port of call was Germany, where thousands of Jews were arriving from all parts of Eastern Europe to wait for a chance to move on to Palestine. Some had been waiting a year and a half in camps run by UNRRA when Stone met them, in conditions varying from that of a well-run kibbutz to stinking transit camps in bombed-out factories and air-raid bunkers. Even the best camps, like the one at Furth near Nuremberg, reminded the inhabitants that they were still in confinement, just as they had been during the war. 'This camp outside Furth was clean,' Stone reported. 'There were curtains and flower pots in the windows of the houses in the camp, a sure sign of good morale. Many of the people were orthodox Jews from Carpatho–Russia in what was East Czechoslovakia and is now part of the Soviet Union. They had a synagogue and were building themselves a theatre.' They also baked their own bread and grew their own vegetables—but it was still no home. 'When I look out of my window and see the barbed wire' one of the inmates confided to Stone, 'my heart grows cold and when I go with my little pot to get my meals I feel as though I am still in the KZ [concentration camp].'

The Haganah smuggled not only Polish Jews who had found life intolerable in Poland but Jews from Russia—Polish Jews who had fled to the USSR at the outbreak of the war or who had lived in the eastern part of Poland which had been annexed by Russia during the war. These Jews from Russia were legally repatriated with their entire families, unlike the ones from Poland, most of whose relatives had been slaughtered in the Holocaust. Many of them had travelled fantastic distances—from Siberia, the Soviet Far East, even Tibet. From Poland the Haganah underground route crossed into Czechoslovakia, then across the Austrian frontier into the Russian zone and from there to Vienna. From Vienna the Haganah underground would take the Jews to an Italian port where they would embark on a ship to carry them across the Mediterranean and (with luck) through the British naval blockade to Palestine.

'We were not the only travellers of our kind in the wake of World War Two,' Stone commented.

At every station and on the sidings to which we were shunted to let more important trains pass, we saw other trains loaded with refugees. In ancient third class carriages like ours we saw Poles going East, and in battered freight cars Volksdeutsche going West. Sometimes our trains and the trains carrying the other refugees stopped on opposite sides of the same platform, and people from both got out to stretch their legs. But there was no mixing. No one shouted across the platform from one train to the other. Their mutual misery created no common bond between peoples who regarded each other as oppressors and oppressed. The hate and fear that flowed between us was almost tangible.

Night fell. There were no lights in the carriage, and in the darkness the refugees, most of whom had survived the Holocaust but lost all their families in the slaughter, began to sing. 'I have never heard singing that touched me so much,' Stone recalled. 'The songs I heard were songs that had sprung from the Nazi-created ghettos, the concentration camps, and the forest hideouts of the Jewish Partisan bands. Many were spontaneous creations of anonymous longing . . . on their way out of Europe, the songs they sang said farewell to vanished homes and parents.'

Vienna was the great crossroads of the Jewish exodus from central and eastern Europe—an exodus far greater in magnitude and misery than the earlier ones from Egypt and Spain. In Vienna were to be found Jews from Rumania, Hungary, Slovakia, Greece, Yugoslavia, Poland and even Vienna itself. The huge Rothschild Memorial Hospital, run by UNRRA, the DP division of the US Army and a Jewish committee representing the DPs themselves, was the hub of the Jewish traffic. Here the new arrivals were medically examined, then given an identity card with a name and number. This, indicated Stone, was momentous.

> To march across borders illegally, stateless and homeless, without documents, and then to come at last to a place where one meets a friendly reception, where one is given an identity card, is something only a refugee can fully appreciate. One suddenly becomes a person, with a name, a number and a *paper*. One now has a right to move freely in the American zone of Austria. This privilege and this blessing the Jewish refugee owes to the American occupying forces. The United States Army is the best friend the Jewish people have in Europe today.

Jewish refugees arriving in Austria were faced with two alternatives. They could either enter DP camps in Austria or Germany and endure a wait (of perhaps years) for inclusion in the small British immigrant quotas that would enable them to enter Palestine legally. Or they could take a chance and carry on down the underground route in the hope of being able to enter Palestine illegally in a matter of a few weeks or months. Already there were over 34,000 Jews waiting in camps in the American zone of Austria. Some of them were living there in relative comfort—in spa hotels or hostels like camp New Palestine, a former SS-troop residence in Salzburg—but it was still not Eretz Israel.

For those who chose to go on, the next stepping-stone to Palestine was Italy—generally by truck via the Brenner Pass to the port of Genoa, mostly with the connivance of the Italian authorities. Some 70,000 visa-less Jews attempted the illegal underground route to Palestine, roughly half of whom were caught at sea by the British naval blockade off Palestine and turned back or interned. I. F. Stone found the particular remnant of European Jewry which he accompanied on the exodus contained people from sixteen different countries. About two-thirds of them were men, for more men than women survived the Holocaust. All of them were Socialists of one sort or another. Most of them were either travelling alone or as members of fragmented and greatly depleted families: 80 per cent of them were under the age of 30, and 30 per cent of them had served in the Red Army, the Polish Army or the Jewish Partisans during the war.

Illegal immigration became even more difficult when a form of land blockade was imposed in central Europe, comparable to the sea blockade off Palestine. The British had long imposed a restriction on Jewish migration movements across their zones in Germany and Austria. Then on 21 April 1947, a US Army directive ordered the closing of all DP camps to infiltrees who arrived in their zones after that date. Columns of Jewish refugees tramping out of Eastern Europe were confronted by American troops barring the way with bayonets fixed. With the secret underground route to Palestine severely obstructed on both land and sea, the number of Jewish DPs holed up in the DP camps swelled to an all-time maximum of 168,440 by July 1947. These people were looked after variously by UNRRA and the International Refugee Organisation, by the British and US Armies, and by other international Jewish self-help organisations. Many of these Jewish DPs were accommodated in former Nazi concentration camps, and some of them had been in them since the end of the war. Some were even dressed in discarded SS uniforms. Not surprisingly the tension and resentment among the Jewish population of such camps was explosive. When they rioted, machine guns had to be fired over their heads. Banners were hung which read: 'FOUR YEARS UNDER THE NAZIS, TWO YEARS UNDER THE BRITISH.' Captain William Craydon, who took over one of their camps in 1946, recalled:

In September 1946 I was sent as commandant to a Jewish camp at a place called Ziegenhain. The previous four commandants had all left in a hurry. I wasn't very welcome. They swore blind I was in the Military Police. The first thing I did was stop them selling their rations. They got good rations and on Sunday mornings they'd have their tables out on the camp roads selling their stuff—chocolate, cheese, tinned meat—like they do down Petticoat Lane. Right, I said, if you don't eat it, you're not going to sell it. I'll knock it off the ration. Then one day six loads of German food came in. They refused to unload it because it was their Yom Kippur Day. There were crowds of them standing there yelling at me. I said to them: 'All right, if this stuff isn't unloaded in five minutes I'll have to send it all back to the German economy.' There was a minute to go and all of a sudden they broke ranks and unloaded the lorries in about five minutes. Anyway, this hostility went on for about three or four weeks. Then one day the Zionist leader, Dr Chaim Weizmann, who was head of the Jewish Agency for Palestine, came with his wife. He walked round the camps with his rabbis in their long beards and when he'd seen everything he gathered all the people together and he said: 'Do you know you've got the best-fed camp in Germany? You want to think yourself lucky.' And Dr. Weizmann's wife turned to me and said: 'If I dared, I would kiss you.' From that day hate turned to love. The next day they opened the hut they had made into a synagogue and invited me to the party. They got a piano from somewhere and I sat down and played a lot of the old songs and the most surprising thing was they all knew them: *You are My Heart's Delight, Roses of Picardy, My Blue Heaven*. They crowded around and sat on the piano singing their heads off.

In spite of the difficulties, between the end of the war and the proclamation of the new Jewish State of Israel in July 1948, the Haganah chartered fifty-seven ships to bring illegal Jews to Palestine. Forty were intercepted, but the rest, plus others not recorded, managed to bring some thirty thousand illegal immigrants out of the ruins of Europe to find a new refuge in the Promised Land.

Following the British government's abdication from its responsibility for Palestine and the subsequent creation of the State of Israel, several hundred thousand Jews were able to emigrate legally to their new homeland. In the period 1946–51,744,000 Jews migrated to Israel, 387,000 of them from Europe; 165,000 European Jews migrated to countries other than Palestine. By June 1950 a total of 105,000 had gone to the USA, nearly 20,000 to Canada, nearly 5,000 to Australia, 10,000 to South America and some 26,000 to Great Britain, France, Belgium, Sweden and Holland. The numbers of Jews left behind in the DP camps of Europe dwindled. At the end of 1949 there were only 61,000 left in Germany, Austria and Italy, and at the end of 1950 less than 39,000. In the end only the sick, the crippled and the old who could not emigrate—and the 3,000 or so who for one reason or another would not emigrate—chose to stay on in the continent which had witnessed the greatest slaughter of their race in history.

While the Russians and the Jews and the other displaced nationalities crisscrossed Europe in their millions, another vast population transfer was taking place among the Germans themselves.

Figures vary for the total number of Germans who were forcibly displaced from their homelands in eastern and central Europe at the end of the war and afterwards. German statistics give the figure of 17,700,000 (or four times the population of Switzerland in 1945) as the total of Germans living in the areas in which the displacements took place—their seven hundred year-old homelands in the eastern provinces of the Reich (East Prussia, Pomerania, eastern Brandenburg and Silesia), the Hanseatic cities of Danzig and Memel, the Bohemian Sudetenland in Czechoslovakia, and German settlements throughout eastern Europe (especially Poland, Yugoslavia, Hungary and Rumania). It was estimated that 1,100,000 of these people were killed during the war, 2.64 million stayed put and 10–12 million were displaced. Whatever the exact number, nothing alters the fact that this was the greatest ethnic displacement—or involuntary migration—of human beings in modern times, and perhaps even in the history of the human race.

The great majority of these displacements took place at a time when eleven million more Germans were being held as prisoners of war in captivity abroad, including more than four million in the Soviet Union, one million in France and one million in Great Britain. If the total of German displaced people is added to the total of German prisoners of war then it would seem that during the first two years after the end of the war a total of twenty-five million people of the German race—or a little less than half the population of West Germany today—were at one time or another displaced from their homeland.

The mass exodus of the Teutonic race has left little trace in the history books outside of West Germany itself. The fact that over two million Germans lost their lives during the course of this exodus is also largely ignored and even disbelieved. In that melancholy catalogue of modern massacre and genocide, Gil Elliot's *Twentieth-Century Book of the Dead*, there is no mention of it, though its nearest equivalent—the expulsion and massacre of a million Armenians by the Turks in 1914—is included. The expulsion of nearly fourteen million German civilians from their hereditary homelands was carried out amid so much cruelty and suffering that it must be seen as no less a crime against humanity as those for which the Nazi leaders were at that very time being tried in Nuremberg; and the death of two million of those Germans was as much a premeditated act of genocide, if a less systematic one, as the German extermination of the Jews. Almost as many German civilians died as a result of the hardship and brutality they experienced during their flight or expulsion from their homes in eastern and central Europe after the war as the total of Japanese dead for the whole of the Second World War, or twice as many as the total dead on all sides in the Korean war, or four times as many as died in the Spanish Civil War.

These population transfers had their origin in the war. The Czech and Polish leaders came to regard the German minorities in their countries—the *Volksdeutsch*, or ethnic Germans, whose roots stretched back as far as the Middle Ages—as collectively to blame for the German invasions and the brutal oppression of the Nazi occupation that followed. In working out how to settle the score and safeguard the peace once the war was over, the transfer of the *Volksdeutsche* Germans back to Germany seemed the most effective and most final of solutions. The leader of the Czech government-in-exile, Dr Eduard Benes, first put this idea forward as serious policy in 1941 when he proposed that the German minority should be expelled from Czechoslovakia (in particular the Bohemian Sudetenland) after the war.

The British backed the idea and in 1943 the Americans and Russians also gave their approval.

Soon the principle was extended. Not only the disloyal *Volksdeutsche* German minority of Czechoslovakia, but the loyal *Volksdeutsche* German minority of Transylvania (Rumania) were to be expelled. Then the principle of population transfer was applied to an even larger group—the nine million German *Reichsdeutsche* who composed the majority of the eastern provinces of the Reich—the indigenous people of purely German territories such as East Prussia, Pomerania, Brandenburg and Silesia. The ancestors of these people had been living in their homelands centuries before the Pilgrim Fathers landed in America: to resettle them in western Germany made as much sense as resettling Americans in Britain or Britons in Denmark and Lower Saxony.

Nevertheless the Allies agreed to it because it seemed an essential part of their plan to compensate Poland for the loss of her eastern territory to the Russians by giving her an equivalent amount of German territory in the west. This entailed extending Poland's western frontier 150 miles westward to the line of the Oder and Neisse rivers deep inside the Reich and placing many millions of native Germans under Polish rule. Fearing that these Germans would develop subversive tendencies towards the Polish state, the Poles claimed the right to expel some nine million of them to the other side of the Oder–Neisse boundary. The Allies agreed, and at the end of the Potsdam Conference on 2 August 1945 the Big Three issued a Protocol, Article XIII of which declared: 'The three Governments recognise that the transfer to Germany of German populations remaining in Poland, Czechoslovakia and Hungary will have to be undertaken. They agree that any transfers that take place should be effected in an orderly and humane manner.' In this last sentence, the British and Americans naïvely misjudged the bitterness and hatred the Czechs, Poles, Yugoslavs and others felt for all things German.

In the months leading up to the Potsdam Conference many millions of eastern Germans had already left their homelands. In the first wave, six to seven million civilians had fled by land and sea when the Red Army began to advance into the eastern provinces of the Reich during the preceding winter and spring. This mass flight, known to the Germans simply as *die Flucht*, in which more than a million women, children and old men were killed by the Russians or died of cold and exhaustion, has been described many times. More than four million people, who either refused to flee or could not be evacuated in time, remained in the eastern provinces, along with millions of *Volksdeutsche* in the Sudetenland and German enclaves in Poland, Hungary, Rumania and Czechoslovakia. In the three-month period between VE-Day and the Potsdam Conference these people were victims of further waves of forcible transfers, the so-called 'wild expulsions'. It was then that the Czechs and the Poles took their revenge in

138

acts every bit as barbarous as those previously committed by the Nazis. They tortured and slaughtered tens of thousands of Germans, many of them innocent women and children. They violently ejected them from their homes, raping women and girls and forcing the men into slave labour. Others were interned in concentration camps, where the brutality was often indistinguishable from that practised by SS Guards in Belsen or Buchenwald only a few months before. Hundreds of thousands of German civilians died in that first peacetime summer, and the numbers did not abate, even after the Allies had insisted on the terms of the Potsdam Agreement. The expulsions continued through two more winters and two more summers until the only Germans left in their old homelands were fugitives in hiding or technicians dragooned into the service of the new states. Thirteen million of their fellows lived a life of destitution and despair in a starving Germany that was so over-populated that there were nearly three times as many persons per square mile as in teeming China.

Unlike most mass murders, those of the German expulsions are remarkably well documented. In Bonn the Federal Ministry for Expellees, Refugees and War Victims later published the results of a fact-finding commission entitled *Documentation on the Expulsions of the German Population from East Central Europe* which contained hundreds of verified eyewitness accounts running into 5,000 pages in eleven volumes: the English digest of this vast work itself runs into more than a million words. Similar compilations of evidence were produced by the Goettingen Research Institute, the Bishops of Western Germany and others. Obviously it is impossible to cite here more than a handful of specific incidents which typify the range of experiences endured—the long columns of people, battered suitcases in hand, pulling handcarts and pushing prams along the country roads, jeered at, spat on, beaten, eaten up by lice and other vermin; the trains of open cattle-trucks full of mothers, children and old people packed shoulder to shoulder in sun, rain and snow; bewildered, exhausted people at the end of their tether, owning only what they can carry, with nowhere to go and no hope for the future, squatting with their bundles on pavements and station platforms with bowed heads and sightless eyes amongst the ruins of the Reich.

During the first mass transfer of German populations from the eastern provinces of the Reich in the last stages of the war, over a million civilians died as they fled from the advancing Red Army, and more were to die when survivors returned to their homes and were arrested by the Russians and sent for forced labour in the Soviet Union, where some 125,000 perished.

In Czechoslovakia no move was made against the *Volksdeutsche* of the Sudetenland until after the surrender of the German forces there on 9 May 1945. A bloodbath followed, as the Czechs turned to lynch law. Czech citizens who felt the urge to torture or kill could select their victims personally from among the Germans held, like live lobsters in a fish restaurant, in the cellars of the so-called partisans, the main perpetrators of the terror, who went about in German Afrika Korps uniforms armed with guns and rubber clubs.

One of the worst incidents was in the Sudeten town of Aussig on 31 July 1945 when a temporary ex-German Army ammunition dump blew up in the neighbouring village of Schönpriesen, shattering all the windows for three kilometres around. Though the explosion was due to an accident, the local Czech militia claimed it was sabotage by 'werewolves' and attacked all the Germans they could lay hands on. One of the first victims of the massacre that followed was a mother wheeling her child in a pram over a bridge across the Elbe. The woman was surrounded and clubbed to death and both she and her child were then tossed into the river. A German eyewitness later testified: 'Another incident, which stayed in my memory and which will haunt me all my life, was that of a German anti-Fascist who had returned after four years in a concentration camp and was now employed as a mechanic. This German fighter against Fascism—his name was Brainl—had his hair torn from his head and was then shot through the stomach.' Those were three deaths: but within three hours up to 2,700 more Germans had been murdered on the bridge or in the main square at Aussig and their bodies either thrown into the air-raid water reservoirs or loaded on to lorries by other Germans and driven to Theresienstadt for cremation. Those who accompanied the dead never returned.

The 'wild expulsion' of the Sudeten Germans began long before Potsdam. Few British or American observers witnessed it. One of the few was Rhona Churchill of the London *Daily Mail*, who filed an accurate report on the circumstances surrounding the expulsion of the Germans from Brno on 30 May 1945:

Here is what happened when young revolutionaries of the Czech National Guard decided to 'purify' the town.

Shortly before 9 p.m. they marched through the streets calling on all German citizens to be standing outside their front doors at 9 o'clock with one piece of hand luggage each, ready to leave the town forever.

Women had ten minutes in which to wake and dress their children, bundle a few possessions into their suitcases, and come out onto the pavement.

Here they were ordered to hand over all their jewellery, watches, fur and money to the guards, retaining only their wedding rings; then they were marched out of town at gun-point towards the Austrian border.

It was pitch dark when they reached the border. The children were wailing, the women stumbling. The Czech border guards pushed them over the frontier towards the Austrian border guards.

There more trouble started. The Austrians refused to accept them; the Czechs refused to readmit them. They were pushed into a field for the night.

They are still in that field, which has been turned into a concentration camp. They have only the food which the guards give them from time to time. They have received no rations. A typhus epidemic now rages amongst them, and they are said to be dying at the rate of 100 a day.

Twenty-five thousand men, women and children made this forced march from Brno, amongst them one English woman married to a Nazi, an Austrian woman of 70, and an Italian woman of 86.

The Czechs set up a number of internment camps for Germans awaiting expulsion from the Sudetenland or deportation to forced labour in the Czech interior during the summer of 1945. Some of them, like Theresien-stadt, had previously been Nazi concentration camps. Under Czech tutelage they differed only in the nationality of the victims—it was now Germans, not Jews, who were tortured and maltreated in them. A former Jewish inmate, H. G. Adler, reported afterwards of the new inmates: 'The majority were children and juveniles, who had only been locked up because they were Germans. Only because they were Germans ... ? This sentence sounds frighteningly familiar; only the word "Jews" had been changed to "Germans". The rags the Germans had been clothed with were smeared with swastikas. The people were abominably fed and maltreated, and they were no better off than one was used to from German concentration camps.'

The worst excesses were committed by young male Czechs in their late teens and early twenties, most of them members of the so-called National or Revolutionary Guard, who resembled the SS even in appearance and gave themselves over to bouts of the most disgusting sadism. In these places German babies were drowned in the camp latrines while their mothers were forced to look on; German doctors were forced to crawl along the ground eating human excrement; men had their legs and arms systematically broken while they were still alive.

In Poland the situation was if anything worse than in Czechoslovakia. Similar kinds of people seem to have been in charge of the many concentration camps there, the worst of which was Camp Lamsdorf in Upper Silesia, where 6,488 inmates, including 628 children, were killed by starvation, maltreatment and hard labour between the summer of 1945 and the autumn of 1946. The commandant was a twenty-year-old thug by the name of Gimborski, whom eyewitnesses confirmed had personally shot to death at least fifty German civilians. His worst feat of barbarity took place on 4 October 1945, when a barrack hut caught fire. The German inmates were surrounded by a ring of Polish guards and driven into the flames: many were burnt to death, while those who were still alive were shot or beaten to death. The German camp doctor, Dr Esser, made a list of those who died in this inferno: 36 men and 11 women (shot); 25 men and 15 women (burnt to death); 285 men and women (dragged out of the sick-ward and thrown into the mass grave—they were either shot beforehand or bludgeoned unconscious and thrown in alive); 209 men and women (died the next day of injuries or bullet wounds received during the course of the catastrophe).

Twenty years later the West German government attempted, without success, to persuade the Polish government to bring charges against Gimborski. As far as is known the only person to have been charged with crimes against the Germans during the period of mass expulsions was the deputy commandant of the Czech concentration camp at Budweis in Southern Bohemia, Vaclav Hrnecek, who fled to Germany after the communist coup in Czechoslovakia, was recognised by former inmates of the camp and brought to trial before an American Court of the Allied High Commission for Germany. The Court found that though there were no gas chambers and no systematic extermination, the camp was a centre of criminal sadism where human life and human dignity had lost all meaning.

Most of those deportees who were put straight on a transport and thus bypassed the concentration camps counted themselves lucky, as indeed they probably were. But the luck was relative. They still had to abandon without compensation all their property and possessions, their houses, farms, businesses and shops. All their money and capital was seized so that they were left destitute. (In the Sudetenland alone the deported Germans had to leave behind an estimated one hundred thousand million Reichsmarks of assets.) Their families were broken up, for mostly it was the women, the children, the sick and the elderly who were deported: able-bodied males were kept back for forced labour, along with technicians and experts of potential value to the new society.

The expellees were normally deported into the Soviet zone. Some remained there but most moved on, hoping to find distant relatives in the Western zones or build a new life in Berlin. The capital attracted them like a promised land. The Nazis had never revealed that the city had been bombed to the ground, and the refugees still believed it was a city of boulevards, cafés and lights. As they trekked daily in their tens of thousands towards this illusory Shangri-la, the rumour spread that refugees were met at the station by the Oberbürgermeister and taken by bus to their new homes, where they were fed on real coffee and cream cakes. After the horrors of the journey, the reality of Berlin was a disillusionment they could barely endure. One eyewitness, Lt.-Col. Byford-Jones, was at a Berlin station when one of the German refugee trains arrived from the east:

> The train was a mixture of cattle and goods trucks, all of which were so packed that people lay on the tops, clung to the sides or hung on the bumpers. Children were tied by ropes to ventilation cocks, heating pipes, and iron fittings.
> The train stopped and a great long groan rose from the length and breadth of it. For a full minute no one moved a limb. Eyes that were full of anguish examined the people on the platform. Then people began to move, but everyone seemed crippled with cold and cramp. Children seemed dead, purplish-blue in the face; those who had clung to doors and fittings could not

use their hands or arms, but went about, arms raised or outstretched, hands clenched. They hobbled, legs numbed, to fall on the platform.

The people who had arrived days before pressed back to make room, and looked on in silence. Soon the platform was filled with cries of disillusionment as the newcomers learned how they had been deceived. Their hair was matted. They were filthy, covered with soot and grime. Children had running sores, and scratched themselves continually. Old men, unshaven, red-eyed, looked like drug addicts, who neither felt, nor heard, nor saw. Everyone seemed to be a unit of personal misery, complete unto himself.

Some of these people had lived for days on nothing but potatoes they dug up out of fields. Some committed suicide by jumping out of the train at night. New-born babies, the sick and the dying were pushed out on the platforms, where they lay day and night until they were dead. Colonel Byford-Jones met one girl who had been raped on the train by Slavs who had taken off her clothes and forced schnapps into her mouth so that she could not resist. Her handbag had been stolen and with it her passport and ration card and the name and address of the friend of her father's with whom she had been hoping to stay. 'The girl cried as she talked', wrote the English colonel. 'No one could do anything for her. There were scores in the same position. There they sat, night after night on the railway platform, waiting and hoping, looking like a lot of duffle bags.'

It was not until the expellees began to pour into Berlin in an uncontrolled flood—33,000 in one day, 200,000 in one week at the peak in 1945—and thence into the British and American zones that the British and Americans themselves began to realise the extent of the tragedy which was unfolding in their midst. Several foreign correspondents, British and American, filed stories from Berlin in the late summer and early autumn of 1945, when the 'orderly and humane' transfers were in full flood. Norman Clark went to the Stettiner station to watch the arrival of deportation trains from the east and sent the following despatch to the London *News Chronicle* on 24 August:

Under the bomb-wrecked roof of the Stettiner Railway Station—the Euston or King's Cross of Berlin—I looked this afternoon inside a cattle truck shunted beside the buffers of No. 2 platform.

On one side four forms lay dead under blankets on cane and raffia stretchers; in another corner four more, all women, were dying.

One, in a voice we could hardly hear, was crying out for water.

Sitting on a stretcher, so weakened by starvation that he could not move his head or his mouth, his eyes open in a deranged, uncomprehending stare, was the wasted frame of a man. He was dying too.

As I walked about the station a score of others came up to me, all ravenous and starved, for whom also nothing else could be done—until death.

Two women sanitary helpers did what they could in ministering to the small wants of the dying.

The train from Danzig had come in. It had taken seven days on the journey this time; sometimes it takes longer.

Those people in the cattle truck, and hundreds who lay on bundles of belongings on the platform and in the booking hall, were the dead and dying and starving flotsam left by the tide of human misery that daily reaches Berlin, and next day is turned back to take train to another town in a hopeless search of food and succour.

Up to 25,000 more were trekking into Berlin on foot each day, Clark reported, but the city was so overcrowded that they were forbidden to enter. Each day between fifty and a hundred children who had been abandoned or lost both parents were collected from Berlin's stations and taken to orphanages. One small boy from Danzig was found in Berlin with a note pinned to his coat stating that his soldier–father was missing in the war and his mother and sister had died of hunger; a young brother and sister were found on a train roped together; orphan girls as young as 10 were raped by the Poles and the Russians. On one occasion a Polish guard took an infant by its legs and crushed its skull against a post because it cried while the guard was raping its mother. One girl concluded she was pregnant because she had been raped thirty times on the journey to Berlin.

One transport of Sudetenlanders—women, children, old people— arrived in Berlin after having travelled in open cattle trucks for eighteen days. Of the 2,400 who had set out, only 1,350 reached their destination alive. Another train set out from Danzig with 325 orphans and hospital patients on board. They were packed into five cattle-trucks, with no covering on the floors, no medical supplies, no doctors or nurses and no water. For the patients there was no food either, but the orphans had two slices of bread each and a total of twenty potatoes to share between them. Six to ten occupants of each truck died during the journey and were simply thrown out of the train. On arrival in Berlin the orphans looked like the emaciated creatures shown in pictures of Belsen; even after ten days' treatment none of them weighed more than three stone, though they were all between eight and twelve years old.

The news stories had little impact on the British and American publics, who held the Germans as little in regard as the Czechs and Poles did. But the politicians and other influential figures were aghast. Winston Churchill, one of the original proponents of the expulsions, was among the first to express alarm. 'I am particularly concerned,' he told the House of Commons on 16 August, only a fortnight after the end of the Potsdam Conference, 'with the reports reaching us of the conditions under which the expulsion and exodus of Germans from the new Poland are carried out . . . It is not impossible that tragedy on a progidious scale is unfolding itself behind the iron curtain.' Another MP asked the House: 'Is this what our soldiers fought and died for?' In October the British Foreign Secretary, Ernest Bevin, went to Berlin to see the plight of the expellees for himself and reported back to the House: 'It was a pathetic sight . . . the most awful sight one could see.' The British philospher and pacifist, Lord Bertrand Russell, took up the refrain in the British press. 'An apparently deliberate attempt is being made to exterminate many millions of Germans,' he wrote, 'not by gas but by slow and agonizing starvation.' The scenes at the Berlin railway stations were 'Belsen over again,' he said.

The American and British governments were powerless. Even their ambassadors in Warsaw and Prague rejected any serious move to complain or intervene. The American Ambassador in Warsaw telegraphed the Secretary of State suggesting that the Germans were probably exaggerating their ill-treatment 'in keeping with their characteristic of whining after losing war.' The British Ambassador said the best thing he could do was hold his telescope to his blind eye 'like Nelson at bombardment of Copenhagen.' In Czechoslovakia, meanwhile, American troops repeatedly intervened to protect German civilians from the barbarities of the Czech militia and grew increasingly hostile towards the Czech people they had just liberated.

At the end of 1945 the Allied Control Council arranged for the unauthorised 'wild expulsions' to be superseded by properly organised transfers which were to be completed by July 1946. But the nightmare of uncontrolled deportations continued unabated into the first winter following the war. By January 1946 the number of German refugees in Germany west of the Oder–Neisse line had soared to over four million. In February 1946 a special correspondent of the *New York Times*, Anne O'Hara McCormick, became one of the first voices to accuse the nations responsible of the same crime that the Nazi leaders were on trial for at Nuremberg. 'We share responsibilities for horrors only comparable to Nazi cruelties,' she wrote in February. And again, in October: 'The scale of this resettlement and the conditions in which it takes place are without precedent in history. No one seeing its horrors first-hand can doubt that it is a crime against humanity for which history will exact a terrible retribution.'

History did no such thing. History lied and forgave and forgot. The Czechs and the Poles denied, then and later, that anything untoward had taken place other than, as the respected Czech President, Dr Benes, put it, 'some, very few, excesses'. The Soviet-bloc Press denounced any evidence to the contrary as 'provocations' and 'falsifications of history' by revanchists, chauvinists, irredents, even 'Hitlerites'. In fact, according to figures provided by the German Federal Ministry for Expellees in Bonn, a total of 267,000 Germans died at the hands of the Czechs during the expulsions from the Sudetenland; 619,000 died during the expulsion from other countries in Eastern Europe, mostly at the hands of the Poles, but some at the hands of the Yugoslavs, Hungarians, Rumanians and Bulgarians; and 1,225,000 died during the flight and the expulsions from the eastern areas of Germany, first at the hands of the Soviets and then at the hands of the Poles. The suffering endured by the 6,944,000 who survived the flight and expulsions from eastern Germany, the 2,921,000 from Czechoslovakia, the 1,865,000 from Poland and other countries and the 2,645,000 ethnic Germans who remained as outcasts and untouchables in their ancient East European homelands, are incalculable.

These sufferings did not cease when the expulsions petered to an end by the early 1950s. Over 10 million of the expellees had ended up in Western Germany—nearly all of them in the British and American zones. By the end of 1950 Germany, having lost one-quarter of her pre-war territory to Poland and the Soviet Union, had undergone within her reduced, devastated and occupied area a 17 per cent increase in population, made up of people all of whom were destitute and less than half of whom were capable of productive work. In some parts of Western Germany the population increase was over 100 per cent. Within 'Potsdam' Germany as a whole every sixth person was a refugee. In Schleswig–Holstein in the British zone every third person was a refugee. In Mecklenburg in the Soviet zone half the population consisted of refugees.

These people were received with great hostility by the local German population. They were seen as a threat to their own survival and a major cause of an escalation in hardship. Feelings on both sides were bitter. The original inhabitants longed to get rid of the refugees, who were frequently billeted in their dwellings. The refugees resented the reception they were given and yearned to return to their old homes and way of life on the other side of the Oder. The refugees settled mainly in the undamaged country towns and villages where it was hoped they might find food from the farms, but very soon rural crowding had reached fantastic heights. In Schleswig–Holstein one village of 890 native residents was required to put up 2,300 deportees. A local government investigation reported in 1947:

> There is not a barrack, not a summer or garden house, not a public hall, not an air-raid shelter, not a factory room or shop, workshop or skittle-alley that has not been used as an emergency accommodation for the refugees. In one case no less than 6 families were housed in a single skittle-alley. This skittle-alley has 25 windows and all of the panes were out. The skittle-alley has now been vacated and the 6 refugee families have been given other quarters, but only in stables and pig-sties. These stables are dark, yet at least the walls are more solid. The families were very fortunate in being able to move there before the severe frosts of the disastrous winter of 1946–7 set in. In their first quarters they would have frozen to death.

These ten million destitute, downgraded, shattered new arrivals obviously added a huge burden to the ravaged economy of western Germany. As one British Military Government officer put it: 'The problem of the refugees was not that of an industrial proletariat but of rural pauperisation.' How that problem was solved lies outside the scope of this book. Suffice it to say that during the first full fiscal year (1950–1) of the newly formed Federal Republic of Germany, the refugees represented a net budgetary cost of 6.1 million Deutschmarks—or one-quarter of the total expense of the government.

10

Raj

The occupation of Germany by the Western Powers was like a new Raj—colonial, exploitative, but in part paternalistic and well-intentioned. Like most colonial rule it suffered from indecisive, out-of-touch direction from the home government, and its effectiveness—or lack of it—depended in large measure on the quality of the men on the ground, which was sometimes suspect. But there were important differences between Germany and the British Raj in India or the French colonies of Africa and the East. The new Raj in Germany was administered not by one but by four colonial powers. And despite the conditions, Germany was not 'Third World'. Beneath the deathly exterior lay the bones and sinews of a nation that had been—and would be again—the strongest nation in Europe.

Ever since the early years of the war the fate of Germany after her defeat had been an item on the agenda of Allied cabinets and summit conferences. Views varied, depending more on the emotional reactions of individuals to the concept of Germany than on rational collective debate. Roosevelt was a confirmed German-hater, like most of his senior advisers. He disliked their arrogance, their fanaticism, their provinciality. 'If I had my way,' he told the *New York Times* in August 1944, 'I would keep Germany on a breadline for the next 25 years.' At about the same time he wrote to his Secretary of State, Cordell Hull: 'Every person in Germany should realise that this time Germany is a defeated nation ... The German people as a whole must have it driven home to them that the whole nation has been engaged in a lawless conspiracy against the decencies of modern civilisation.' Roosevelt did not want to exterminate or enslave the Germans, nor did he want them to starve—but that was all he would grant them. 'To keep body and soul together,' he wrote, 'they should be fed three times a day with soup from Army soup kitchens.'

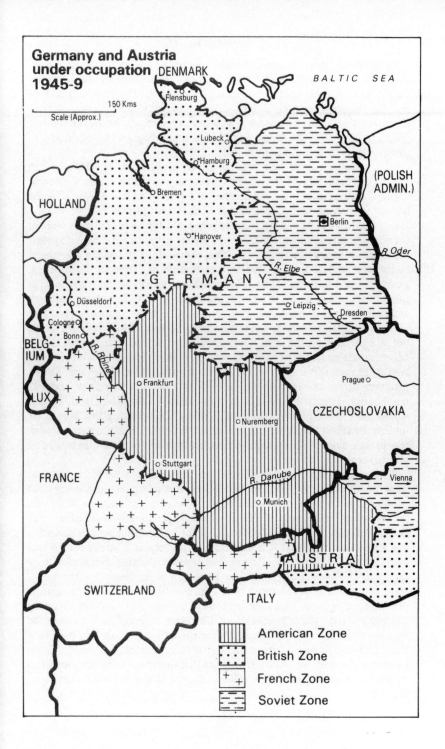

Germany and Austria under occupation 1945-9

150 Kms
Scale (Approx.)

DENMARK

BALTIC SEA

Flensburg

(POLISH ADMIN.)

Lubeck

Hamburg

HOLLAND

Bremen

Berlin

Hanover

R. Oder

G E R M A N Y

R. Elbe

Düsseldorf

Leipzig

Cologne

Dresden

Bonn

BELG IUM

R. Rhine

LUX

Frankfurt

Prague

CZECHOSLOVAKIA

Nuremberg

FRANCE

Stuttgart

R. Danube

Vienna

Munich

AUSTRIA

SWITZERLAND

ITALY

	American Zone
	British Zone
+ +	French Zone
	Soviet Zone

It was Roosevelt who advocated the concept of unconditional surrender and a tough peace. 'The only answer to total war,' he had once said, 'is total defeat and total occupation.' Germany should be dismembered and its leaders punished for their crimes. To what extent the ordinary people of Germany should be punished was a matter of argument. Roosevelt himself seems to have seen the Nazis and the German people as identical and in practice the Western Allies followed this line.

An extreme point of view was embodied in the notorious Morgenthau Plan, the brainchild of Roosevelt's Secretary of State at the Treasury, Henry J. Morgenthau, Jr. Morgenthau was a Jew and was deeply affected by the atrocities being committed against the Jewish people by the Germans. In 1944 he visited London when the flying-bomb raids were at their height and seems to have formed a strong emotional reaction against the German nation as a result. His Plan, therefore, envisaged a Draconian peace and called for the German nation in its present form to be extinguished once and for all. Morgenthau argued that the only way to prevent Germany going to war yet again was to strip her of her industry and turn her into a completely pastoral state for many years to come. The German people, in effect, were to be reduced to a race of peasants eking out an existence off the land. 'Germany's road to peace leads to the farm,' Morgenthau wrote. 'The men and women in the German labour force can best serve themselves and the world by cultivating the German soil. Such a program offers security to us as well as food for Germany and her neighbours.' France would take over the Saar and the Rhineland, Poland would take over East Prussia and Upper Silesia, the Ruhr would be internationalised and the remainder of Germany partitioned. Britain would take over markets that German heavy industry would no longer be able to serve.

The inhumanity of this solution of the German problem brought widespread criticism. No civilised nation, it was argued, could maltreat another in this way. Henry L. Stimson, the Secretary of State for War, who took a softer line, complained to Roosevelt: 'The question is whether over the years a group of 70 million people can be kept within bounds on such a low level of subsistence . . . A subordinate question is whether even if you could do this it is good for the rest of the world either economically or spiritually.' Roosevelt, though he remained a hardliner to his death, retracted a little and in October 1944 declared: 'We bring no charge against the German race, as such, for we cannot believe that God has eternally condemned any race of humanity . . . The German people are not going to be enslaved. But it will be necessary for them to earn their way back into the fellowship of peace-loving and law-abiding nations. And, in the climb up that steep road, we shall certainly see to it that they are not encumbered by having to carry guns. They will be relieved of their burden—we hope, for ever.'

It was the British as much as anybody who softened the American line. Churchill was a redoubtable enemy of the Germans but he was not so much anti-German as anti-Nazi and anti-Prussian. 'Nazi tyranny and Prussian militarism are the two main elements in German life which must be absolutely destroyed,' he declared at Yalta. 'They must be absolutely rooted out if Europe and the world are to be spared a third and still more frightful conflict.' The British, with their tendency for compromise and moderation, were inclined to a policy combining firmness with magnanimity and tempering justice with mercy. It is true that a few British leaders and no doubt a considerable body of the British public believed that there was something endemic to the German character which made them prone to brutality and a lust for domination. But in the main the British argued that the German problem was a matter of finding the right Germans to administer their own country as best they could, and that any attempt to punish the German people as a whole was bound to recoil on the rest of the world. 'We do not war against races as such,' Churchill affirmed—an attitude echoed in Noel Coward's popular song of 1945: 'Don't let's be beastly to the Germans.' The question of 'the good German'—was there such a person or not?—was to occupy the British even more after VE-Day.

Like Roosevelt, Churchill was averse to 'making plans for a country we do not yet occupy.' It would be better he felt, to wait for passions to cool before writing out plans 'on little pieces of paper.' As a result the Western Powers dithered over the formulation of a post-hostilities policy towards Germany. American troops were already on German soil before the Joint Chiefs of Staff in Washington issued their first positive directive for the impending American Occupation of Germany. This was a document known as JCS 1067, which was to form the basis of much future post-war rule in Germany. According to JCS 1067 there was to be no revival of the German economy except where necessary to prevent disease and civil unrest and to prepare the basis of the eventual return to democratic rule. Germany was not to be occupied 'for the purposes of liberation but as a defeated enemy nation,' and 'to prevent her from ever again becoming a threat to the peace of the world.' German living standards were not to be allowed to rise above those of neighbouring nations. The Occupation was to be 'just but firm and aloof' and fraternisation was to be 'strongly discouraged'. The country was to be denazified, decentralised and disarmed. There were to be no German parades, 'military or political, civilian or sports.' No former Nazis were to be employed in Military Government, regardless of administrative necessity. Key industries were to be strictly controlled if not actually eliminated. No merchant ships or aircraft were to be built and no oil or rubber manufactured. No cartels were to be allowed and no research conducted.

JCS 1067 was sent to General Eisenhower as the basis for Allied

Occupation policy in Germany, but it was rejected by other Allied commanders, leaving the Supreme Commander in the odd position of having one set of policy directives for the American forces under his command, another set for his British forces, and none for the French. Indeed it was very soon painfully evident that irrespective of whatever agreement they may have reached in the past, each of the Allies would go their own way in Germany according to their own self-interests and along the lines of their own national character as a ruling power. The French, for example, shared few of the qualms the British felt about the Germans being made to suffer, and they had no hesitation in treating their own Occupation zone, when they got it, as a source of industrial booty which they loosely referred to as reparations.

As for the Russians, they would always go their own way in Germany, pursuing a policy of opportunism dictated by their two abiding obsessions—security and reparations. Right from the very beginning of the war Stalin, unlike Roosevelt, had distinguished between the Nazis and the German people. Immediately after the German invasion his Foreign Commissar, Viacheslav Molotov, stated in a radio broadcast: 'This war was not forced on us by the German people, workers, peasants, intelligentsia, whose sufferings we know so well, but by a clique of bloody fascist rulers.' And less than a year later Stalin declared in an order of the day: 'It would be laughable to equate the Hitler clique with the German people, the German state. The lessons of history teach us that Hitlers come and go but the German people, the German state remains.'

Though privately Stalin might confide to Churchill his desire to have 50,000 German officers shot out of hand when the war was over, he did not share Roosevelt's anti-German sentiments in his public utterances. Unlike the British and the Americans, the Russians knew exactly what they were about when they entered Germany and knew exactly how to organise the industries, farms, unions, newspapers, police and political parties of the defeated Germans to suit themselves. The Russians did not bother themselves with retribution, justice or other lofty moral principles, and did not hinder German freedom of movement by such Western obsessions as non-fraternisation bans or denazification programmes. The Russians were prepared to look favourably on any German who could be useful to them—even, it was thought, the notorious Chief of the Gestapo, General Müller. They had been in Berlin nine weeks when the first Americans got there. By then, a municipal government, a single communist-controlled union, a police force and four political parties were in existence and 80 per cent of the surviving factories had been dismantled and their plant shipped back to the USSR. By comparison, the Americans and the British appeared merely to bumble about, one-eyed men in a country of the blind.

All the wartime Allies continued to argue over the future of Germany even after the war was over and the Occupation had begun. At the Postdam Conference they issued their last joint statement on the matter. By now Roosevelt was dead and Churchill ousted from office, but the Potsdam Declaration embodied more of the decisions they had made previously at Yalta and elsewhere and put forward a view on Germany that was stern without being nihilistic. 'German militarism will be extirpated,' the Declaration stated, 'and the Allies will take . . . other measures necessary to assure that Germany will never again threaten her neighbours or the peace of the world. It is not the intention of the Allies to destroy or enslave the German people. It is the intention of the Allies that the German people be given the opportunity to prepare for the eventual reconstruction of their life on a democratic and peaceful basis. If their own efforts are steadily directed to this, it will be feasible for them in due course to take their place among the free and peaceful peoples of the world.'

Earlier plans to dismember Germany into between two and seven separate states—in effect to destroy the German nation—were rejected in favour of dividing the country into four zones, each zone to be occupied by one of the four Allied Powers—the Russians in the east, the Americans in the south, the British in the north-west, the French in the south-west. The French had been given an Occupation zone, carved out of the British and American zones, at the last minute on the insistence of General de Gaulle. Churchill had supported the French demand, fearful that otherwise the British would have to carry the burden of running the whole of western Germany on their own once the Americans had withdrawn (as he believed they might) from Europe.

The distribution of the Occupation zones did not suit everyone, the Americans least of all. The Russians, it was said, got the corn, the French the wine, the British the ruins and the Americans the scenery. The Americans complained that though the British got the ruins they also got the industry—86 per cent of it, including the Ruhr. This was due to the entirely fortuitous accident of military history which had put the British on the northern flank of the Normandy invasion and the advance into Europe, and the Americans on the southern flank. But in the end it hardly mattered. The superiority of American power and resources ensured that before long they would have the dominant say in the fate of all the Western zones—German industry in British hands included.

On 5 June 1945 the four Allied Commanders-in-Chief issued three proclamations which laid the basis for the organisation of occupied Germany. The first confirmed that unconditional surrender had been effected. The second announced that Germany had been divided into four zones. The third informed the German people that the supreme authority in Germany would be exercised by the Allied Control Council, consisting of the four Commanders-in-Chief sitting in Berlin—initially General Eisenhower (USA), Field Marshal Montgomery (Great Britain), Marshal

Zhukov (USSR), General Koenig (France). Over sixty million Germans and what was left of their country thus formally passed under the control of the Allies. No German autonomy remained, for everything was now in the hands of Military Government, which wielded absolute power. While it was intended that the Commanders-in-Chief of the Allied Control Council should act jointly in matters affecting Germany as a whole, they could also act independently within their own zones, on instructions from their government. In practice the Control Council proved a rather formal and remote body, composed of men who had won their spurs in battle rather than government. The Commanders-in-Chief stayed in their own zones, therefore, and only travelled to Berlin for the monthly Control Council meetings. The real work of governing Germany tended to fall on the shoulders of their Deputies, who stayed in Berlin and bore the brunt of the day-to-day administration. Initially these Deputies were General Lucius D. Clay (USA), General Sir Brian Robertson (Great Britain), General Koeltz (France) and General Vassily Sokolovsky (USSR). At the end of 1945 General Eisenhower was replaced by General McNarney, Marshal Zhukov by General Sokolovsky, and in 1946 Field Marshal Montgomery by Marshal of the RAF Sir Sholto Douglas.

On 15 July 1945 the Allies' wartime Supreme Headquarters, SHAEF, was dissolved and Military Government passed to the zones, whose Military Commanders-in-Chief now became Military Governors. On 2 August 1945 the Big Three signed the Potsdam Agreement. This provided a detailed blueprint for the military governments and listed the main political and economic principles by which Germany should be treated: disarmament, demilitarization, denazification, decentralization, decartelization, re-education, reorganization of the judicial system, restoration of political life at local level, reparations and the dismantling of industry. For this formidable task the four Military Governments equipped themselves with all the paraphernalia of government, including nearly 100,000 civil servants and 175 committees. To the Germans it sometimes seemed they had merely substituted four military dictatorships for their former authoritarian one.

The problems faced by the Allied rulers in Berlin were considerable and in the end insoluble. Their task was to interpret the policies of their respective governments at home in the light of the realities of the current situation in Germany and work together towards the common goal of a new democratic Germany at some unspecified time in the future. Though the Americans and the British saw more or less eye to eye and worked in reasonably close accord, the French and above all the Russians proved a very different proposition. The French had felt snubbed at being excluded from the Potsdam Conference and so blocked the workings of the Control Council. The French were opposed to the unification of Germany and vetoed any proposal of the Control Council which dealt with the country as a whole. So though the Council met every month its authority was almost non-existent, and many of the laws it promulgated were never implemented because the French prevented the formation of any central agencies to carry them out.

As for the Russians, they proved obstreperous from the start, and for every conceivable reason, from ideological and strategical to gastronomical, made themselves almost impossible to deal with. Even their personal habits got in the way of the Control Council's collective functioning. They got up much later in the morning than the Western representatives, ate large breakfasts, and found it difficult to get to the conference table before 11 a.m. As they did not normally lunch till four in the afternoon they usually insisted on working right through the normal Western lunch-time and used the hunger thus experienced by the other representatives as an effective tactical weapon in debate. More serious differences went much deeper than this, and were to lead eventually to an impasse between the Russians and the Western powers that was so total that the peace of Europe seemed once again in jeopardy.

The Four-Power Control of Germany was one of the most extraordinary regimes in modern history. 'The world had never known before a situation in which four peoples lived and tried to co-operate in a country inhabited by a fifth,' a British Military Government officer wrote. 'Although backward peoples have often come under foreign rule, there are few precedents for civilised industrial nations actually taking over the governments of another (instead of giving orders to a puppet regime).'

The planners of SHAEF responsible for organising the Military Government detachments that would follow up behind the front-line fighting troops had always believed that Germany would surrender once the invading armies had reached the German frontier. After the surrender all that Military Government would have to do, it was thought, would be to take over intact an existing system of German government and control it from the top. They had not envisaged that the Germans would fight to the last, that in the process a large part of Germany and the entire system of government would be destroyed, that its records would be burnt and that its Nazi officials would simply melt away, and that they would have to run the whole of the country themselves from the bottom upwards.

Many of the Military Government detachments had already had several months' experience of running day-to-day Germany even before the war ended. As the invading armies swept across the country, spearhead Military Government followed on their heels. Their task initially had been purely in support of the military—to keep the lines of communications open, prevent hordes of German civilians and foreign DPs from jamming the roads, clear rubble, repair bridges, fill potholes, keep law and order to the armies' rear, enforce a curfew, find billets for Headquarters' staffs, mend the telephone system and restore electricity, gas and water, appoint some suitable non-Nazi as Bürgermeister who could pass on their orders to the German inhabitants of the captured towns. These first-wave Military Government detachments performed miracles of improvisation but at this stage any benefit the German populace received from Military Government was purely incidental. But when the front-line Military Government detachments moved off with the advancing armies again, they were replaced by follow-up detachments whose task was much more strictly concerned with civil affairs—and then the Allied Military Government of Germany properly began.

At the beginning Military Government was run strictly as an adjunct of the tactical armies. In the American and British zones the original Military Government teams were generally composed of officers and men who possessed some relevant specialist skill but who were unfit for combat service, normally because they were over-age. The average age of officers in the early American Military government team was 45, but many were older, and some of the most energetic Military Government officers were over 55. Many of these officers were highly qualified, successful and often wealthy men in civilian life, and included lawyers, editors of large newspapers and university presidents. Such men volunteered for Military Government in the expectation that their special qualifications could be put to good use in the task of post-war reconstruction in Europe, and they approached their tasks with an almost missionary fervour. Others, however, were regular Army officers seconded (often against their wishes) from combat units because they were shell-shocked or badly wounded or surplus to their units' requirements after the war. A few crept into Military Government from the ranks of the criminal, and were destined to take advantage of their power in Germany.

Few of these officers spoke German and few had much knowledge of the German people and German institutions they were going to run. The short training course they received in England or America was barely sufficient to equip them for the tough jobs that awaited them. Once in the field they were often looked down upon by their fellow-countrymen in the tactical echelons of the armies and were often impeded in their duties by the incomprehension and prejudice of their commanders-in-chief. General Patton—who was relieved of his command after telling reporters that he used Nazis in his Military Government, adding that there was not much more difference between German parties than between the Democrat and Republican parties back home—was notorious for his contempt of Military Government and his ignorance of what it was about. He preferred to use his own tactical officers from the Third Army in Bavaria for civil tasks rather than trained Military Government officers, whom he regarded as un-military supernumeraries who cluttered up the place. When Colonel Charles Keegan, of Patton's Third Army, took over the Military Government of Bavaria in May 1945, his style of rule owed more to Patton than to

Military Government training programmes back home. 'Rights?' he once
bawled to a group of Germans who had raised the topic. 'You got no rights.
You're conquered, ye' hear? You started the war and you lost. You got no
rights. Tell that thick-headed Kraut that there'll be no changes and that I
will throw that damned bum into the can if he yells again. Tell that lousy
monster I'll put him on ice ... I'll throw you in the can too if you don't
translate the exact words I said and in the same tone.'

This outburst reflected pretty accurately the widespread attitude of the
Allied rulers to their downcast German subjects in the Western zones.
Generals and politicians might make statesmanlike speeches and
declarations, suppressing whatever vengeful sentiments they might feel
privately, but it was the men on the ground, the captains and majors in the
towns and the countryside, who decided the flavour of Occupation rules,
if not its policy.

This policy went through many shifts of direction in the first two or
three years after the end of the war. In the immediate wake of the war anti-
German feeling rode high. All four occupying powers had been involved in
two bloody wars with the Germans in the space of a generation. Evidence
of the brutality and inhumanity of the Nazi regime was still fresh for
everyone to see. Allied wartime propaganda still had its grip on the mind.
For some Allied soldiers in Germany the propaganda catch-phrase, 'The
only good German is a dead German,' was as valid after the war as during
it, and in 1945 the majority of the British, French and Americans would
have regarded the Germans as a race permanently warped by an hereditary
flaw.

It was an attitude that could be found from top to bottom of western
society. In the USA Roosevelt's anti-German feeling was taken over, along
with much else, by his successor, Truman. In Britain, Churchill, who had
preached magnanimity in victory and charity to his country's enemies, was
replaced by a socialist Prime Minister, Clement Attlee, who was a
confirmed anti-German and had a Foreign Secretary, Ernest Bevin, who
was even fiercer. Attlee's was the straight-forward prejudice shared by
millions of his fellow-countrymen at the time. (He had only known one
good German, he confided later, and she was a house maid.) Bevin never
made much of a secret of his anti-German feeling, which dated from the
Great War: it was said he had never forgiven the Social Democrats for
failing to stop the Kaiser making war in 1914, and had disliked and
distrusted Germany ever since.

With people such as these at the helm in Britain the future would seem
not to augur well for the natives of British Germany. When Military
government passed out of the hands of the British Army of Occupation and
into the hands of the civilian Control Commission for Germany, the top job
of head of the Control Office for Germany and Austria was given to a
virtual unknown in government—a former trade union official called John

Hynd, who had been given the sinecure office of Chancellor of the Duchy of Lancaster in Attlee's administration Hynd's appointment characterised the indifference with which the British government—then wrestling with overwhelming problems closer to its home and heart, including the dismantling of the Indian Empire and the socialisation of the now-bankrupt mother-country—viewed the affairs of a defeated rival and enemy. Hynd had little influence in Cabinet. The people under him tended to view the Germans as natives of Empire—albeit exceptionally clever ones. Colonial administrators did indeed join the Control Commission in Germany in large numbers, and when one such gentleman transferred from Nigeria to pick up the white man's burden in darkest Germany, his first act was to ask for a list of staff under two headings: 'Europeans' and 'non-Europeans'.

'Do play your part as a representative of a conquering power,' ran one introductory pamphlet for British sahibs, 'and keep the Germans in their place. Give orders—don't beg the question. Display cold, correct, dignified curtness and aloofness. Don't try to be kind—it will be regarded as weakness. Drop heavily on any attempt to take charge or other forms of insolence. Don't be too ready to listen to stories from attractive women—they may be acting under orders. Don't show any aversion to another war if Germany does not learn her lesson this time.' It could not have been more clearly put in Kikuyuland or the Khyber.

Peter Fabian, a young artillery officer with the 49th West Riding Division at Neheim, recalled one particularly blatant example of callousness towards Germans in the British zone:

One Sunday in June 1945, a farmer's wife—except her husband was dead—came to our camp in a very distraught state. She had run all the eight miles from the farm. She said she had scalded her baby and begged us to help save it. So I went to our Medical Officer, who was a woman, and asked her if she could do anything. She said she thought she could but she didn't have any transport. So I nicked some transport—I took a jeep without proper authority—and drove the MO and the farmer's wife over to the farm. We found the baby almost dead. It was scalded all over. The mother had covered the burns in flour, which was the last thing you should do. So the MO had to spend two or three hours getting the flour off. I think the baby survived but I can't be sure. Anyway, the next day, Monday morning, I was on the carpet sharpish in front of the Colonel, my Commanding Officer, who was a Christian and hated Germans. He said: 'How dare you speak to the Germans! You've absolutely no right. Don't you know there's a law about that sort of thing? Next time you'll be in serious trouble.' This made me very, very angry, so I retorted: 'Well, now I know how you *Christians* feel about these things, but I'm afraid we have other standards.' He didn't answer to that. He just went red in the face and said: 'All right, go.' I never heard any more.

Christopher Leefe was a young subaltern serving with the Green Howards in Berlin in 1946 when a small incident took place which seared his memory:

One evening I was invited to dinner in the Mess of the Royal Hussars ... We were about half way through when there was a terrific commotion in the hall outside and the mess waiter burst in dragging a small boy behind him. The boy had been caught robbing our rooms. He had climbed up a drainpipe and got in through a loo window four storeys up. He had nicked a few cigarette-lighters and a watch and was just about to make his getaway when he got caught. So there he stood, this little German ragamuffin, in front of us grand British officers. He was only about 10, thin as a bean pole, clothes hanging on him like sacks—when kids are starving their clothes always look too big for them. He was stood in front of the senior officer present, a Royals major, and the major asked him, 'Why did you do it?' It reminded me of the interrogation scene in that Civil War painting: 'When did you last see your father?'

The boy just stood there and said nothing. He was blond and Aryan and defiant, and suddenly the major leaned forward and whacked him across the face with his hand. 'YOU FUCKING LITTLE KRAUT!' he yelled. 'Come on, where have you put it all?' Bash, bash! The boy just stood there with the tears streaming down his face and the German mess waiter behind him snarling at him in German. His eyes were so blue and his hair was so blond and he stood there so arrogant and defiant that I've always asked myself right to this day: 'God, I wonder how many of our boys would be as tough as that?'

The point is that none of us could have cared a bit for that little boy. He was probably an orphan, his father dead on the Eastern Front, his mother rotting under the rubble of the bombed-out ruins, and here he was—starving and risking his life climbing up drainpipes in the middle of a British tank regiment. So what? We didn't feel any compassion for him or any of the Germans. They had been public enemy number one. So now we commandeered their horses, commandeered their Mercedes, commandeered their women. I would reckon 60 or 70 per cent of young Englishmen in Germany thought that way. Most of us were for having a bloody good time and believed we could get away with anything.

In the prevailing atmosphere, when every German seemed to wear the mask of a death-camp guard, it did not help much to have been against Hitler and the Nazis, or even an active member of the German Resistance: merely to be German was sufficient condemnation. Peter Bielenberg, a young Hamburg lawyer with an English wife, had been sent to Ravensbrück concentration camp after his arrest following the bomb attempt on Hitler's life on 20 July 1944. He survived the war, however, and in November 1946 was allowed to follow his family to England—the first German after the war to do so. Through his wife Christabel and her family, Bielenberg had a number of powerful allies in Britain, including David Astor (the editor of *The Observer*), Lord Pakenham (the present

Lord Longford, then in charge of the Germany desk at the Foreign Office)
and Sir Stafford Cripps (the Chancellor of the Exchequer), but he was
unprepared for the depth of anti-German feeling among the British. He
recalled what it was like to be a German and a pariah:

> Not long after my arrival in England I had a bad road accident in
> Birmingham. A lorry knocked me off my motor-bike and for a while I was
> quite off my onion. I was suffering from a double fracture at the base of the
> skull and my reactions were unbalanced. Every morning I got the English
> newspapers and primed myself with venom about the anti-German sentiment
> which filled them. By evening I would be so livid that at one time I seriously
> considered swimming the Channel, just to get out of England. I used to see
> Lord Pakenham at least once or twice a week or so—he used to come to our
> house in Regent's Park, more to talk intelligently to my wife, I suspect, than
> unintelligently with me—and I spent my time berating the British
> Government and the British military authorities in Germany for letting my
> mother starve and pretending to give rations of 1,250 calories a day when
> according to the information I had it was only 950 calories or so. And Lord
> Pakenham would say to me: 'You can't be right, you know, you can't be
> right.' Later I discovered neither of us was right—the British were allowing
> 1,050 calories a day. Incidentally, I can't think of any person who tried
> harder than Pakenham to do justice to his job, and do it as humanely as
> possible for the Germans, but his means were quite inadequate at the time.
>
> My wife's family were terribly nice to me. But I was suffering in an
> atmosphere in which there was an unspoken understanding that I belonged
> to a nation of swine and that people only conversed with me because I
> happened to have been in a concentration camp. This didn't appeal to me
> much. There weren't many Germans living in London after the war. There
> were a few German immigrants who had British passports. There were one
> or two Jewish–German friends and non-Jewish German acquaintances. And
> there were others—the kind who changed their names from Heinrich
> Wilhelm to Henry William and got a British passport. I found it despicable to
> dissociate yourself from the background in which you happened to be born. I
> also deeply resented being treated as a beastly German, but I was
> determined to remain a German and hold my head up. That's why I ended up
> in Ireland. My wife didn't want to go back to Germany and I didn't want to
> stay in England. So we bought a derelict farm in Co. Carlow and built it up.
> The gentry in Ireland were worse than the people in England. I mean, they
> were still celebrating the victory in the First World War. But the non-gentry
> population were not anti-German and let me lead a normal life at long last.

Strangely enough the Americans, in spite of their long history of anti-
colonialism, were not far behind the British when it came to playing the
role of colonial governor. Take, for example, the case of Major Everett S.
Cofran, American Military Governor of Augsburg in the first summer
after the war. Major Cofran began his short reign by hanging a sign behind
his desk which read: 'I HATE ALL GERMANS.' When he was asked why

he hated them he replied: 'Were it not for them I would be America's most famous architect.' Before the war he had designed the Bermuda Yacht Club; now as a soldier he was earning 2 per cent of his former income. On his desk he put a large card with the total of American dead on it, explaining to the German mayor: 'If ever I weaken in the fight against National Socialism, a look at the number of the dead always gives me new strength.' For Major Cofran National Socialists and Germans were inter-changeable. He treated them all, including his German mayor, dictatorially, and on a single day attempted to fire 43 of the 48 doctors at the city hospital, 58 of the city's 60 firemen, the whole of the forestry staff and nearly all the policemen on the grounds that they were Nazis. His life-style matched his imperiousness. He took a large apartment for himself and a grand hotel for his officers. He demanded the city hall *Ratskeller* as his restaurant and required flowers to be sent to his office every morning. He demanded two cameras from the mayor as personal gifts and tried to bill the city for 500 bottles of wine. Before long Cofran became too immoderate even for his own superior officers and was transferred. Six months later he was murdered in Passau in his sleep by a fellow Military Government officer who had mistakenly axed to death two other officers before finding the right one.

While the British looked to their Empire for a model, the Americans harked back to the frontier. They went about with pistols slung cowboy-style round their thighs. Like the railroad barons of the Old West, their generals kept lavish private railroad trains fully staffed and under steam twenty-four hours a day, ready to whirl them from one end of their territory to the other at a moment's notice. They drove around in supercharged Mercedes requisitioned from Nazi owners and roared up and down the autobahns in captured pre-war racing motors. Like the British they displayed a predilection for living in castles and baronial villas but unlike the British they developed a dash for adapting them to their own homespun Yankee taste. One Military Government major, whose regal ways earned him the sobriquet of 'King James', had a huge yellow rose of Texas painted on the stone flanks of his pile in Bavaria. One young officer, a certain Captain Carroll Hodges, lived with his wife in a twelve-roomed mansion and estate at Berg near Munich which could be compared with a millionaire's country residence in the States but cost him only $10 a month, the four household servants included. A certain 22-year old staff sergeant Henry Kissinger, an agent of the US Army Counter-Intelligence Corps, and later US Secretary of State in the Nixon Administration, was the absolute ruler of Bensheim, in Hesse, where he lived like a lord in a luxurious villa whose owners he had evicted. 'What a set-up!' an old chum from Washington wrote in his diary on 21 October 1945. 'Like a castle. Had dinner with him. What an intelligent girl friend!' The girl friend was German. So were the cook, the maid, the housekeeper and the secretary—and the white 1938 Mercedes-Benz he had confiscated from a Nazi manufacturer of baby powder. Kissinger, his friend recalled, 'really enjoyed the trappings of authority.'

In this he was not alone, but for pure *lèse-majesté* few Occupation officers could approach the rich young Bostonian whom the German inhabitants of the small Bavarian township of Eichstätt remember to this day as 'the tremendous Hauptmann Toll'. 'Toll' was his Germanised name, a word meaning 'sensational' or 'insane'.

Eichstätt was a small town with a bishopric, a seminary and a pious, mainly Catholic population buried deep in the Bavarian countryside between Augsburg and Nuremberg. In the autumn of 1945 command of the local Military Government detachment of this area passed to an American captain, himself a devout Catholic and an eccentric, flamboyant individualist who was to become the dominant figure in local life for nearly a year and a half and represents the most extreme evolution of the Occupation type: the local potentate and baron. Years later his German interpreter and private secretary described him thus:

> To my knowledge, he was about thirty-two, born in Massachusetts, Bostonian type, Catholic, unmarried, very sophisticated, graduated from a Jesuit college; his parents were owners of a silver mine business and wealthy. 'Toll' was a type of brilliant American playboy. Very casual and extremely independent. His general look, his appearance and habits were, so to say, 'seigneurial'. He impressed the population immensely by all his actions, and his gestures like a sovereign, and the manner in which he presented the victorious USA made him a sort of god of might, brilliancy and power, like Pizarro or Cortes . . . He bacame a mythical personage. He still lives in the memory of the populace as the tremendous Hauptmann Toll, who once introduced himself to the *Beamten* by his unforgettable words, in his also unforgettable German (all substantives always *feminin generis*): 'Ich am eine einfache amerikanische boy, welke khat eine grosse Wagen und so will Gäld zu gehen in every Punkt der Wällt. And this is nikt serr vill in USA.'

'Toll' ruled like a feudal lord—some said an American gangster. He went about with a riding whip, screaming at people to get out of his way. He launched a petty reign of terror. When a local woman made derogatory remarks about the Americans, he ordered her to be stripped and marched naked to the city hall. When the local vet failed to turn up on time, he raged: 'Why you not come at once? My dog sick. When I command, right away, or I arrest you.' He then brought his whip down on the desk so hard that it smashed the glass, whereupon he kicked the desk in a fury and splintered a panel with his boot. He declared war on former Nazis and had them pulled off the streets and thrown into the city gaol, where they were robbed and beaten—but many of his own entourage were ex-Nazis, including the chief of police, the superintendent of schools and his right-hand man, who procured boys for him from the ranks of the Hitler Youth.

Life in Eichstätt was treated as a fabulous and profitable adventure by 'Hauptmann Toll'. Though he seems to have done little else for the community, he did at least generate gainful employment for some of its skilled artisans. Some made the hundreds of boxes in which 'Toll' shipped off vast quantities of requisitioned silver, paintings, works of art, furniture and carpets for sale in the USA. One specialised in making copies of baroque objects for 'Toll' to sell as genuine antiques. Another made copies of antique chairs and a Louis XIV desk for the same purpose.

He lived in style. He requisitioned some twenty-five homes for cronies and seized the furnishings. He ordered his German mayor to requisition china, damask tablecloths, crystal glassware and silver cutlery—enough for twenty-four placings—for the officers' casino. When he went to a service in the Cathedral he sat in solitary splendour in a special chair roped off at the front, wearing riding boots and spurs. Later he metamorphosed himself into the guise of a Vatican Chamberlain, went to Rome where he was received by the Pope and was awarded a papal decoration, the Cameriere Segret di sua Santita, which entitled him to become a member of the papal family. On his return to Eichstätt local craftsmen were commanded to create a papal costume for him, complete with chain and sword—the latter looted for the purpose from the town museum—and a famous painter was summoned from Munich to paint his portrait—first as a papal courier, second as an American officer.

The British too, lived well after their own fashion. The Regional Commissioners, who were a species of colonial governors, dwelt in palatial residences like the Krupp Villa Hügel near Essen. Exclusive clubs were set up in time-honoured style. The smoke of battle had barely died down in Berlin before they had opened their Winston Club for officers on the Kurfürstendamm and a Salvation Army Canteen for other ranks on the once-fashionable Unter den Linden. In Kiel they inaugurated the British Yacht Club for pink-gin and white-ducks types, and in Hamburg, the 'capital' of the British zone, where hundreds of thousands of Germans lived in squalor and degradation in the ruins, they took over the luxury Atlantic Hotel as their principal watering-hole and constructed a lavish Allied Victory Club, complete with ballrooms, shops, gymnasium, dancing clubs, restaurants, bathrooms and lifts, using building materials enough to have housed some 6,000 German civilians. At night the lights of this ostentatious symbol of British might blazed out over the darkened ruins. During the day the windows of the NAAFI gift shops were crammed with luxury goods the Germans could only dream of.

Victor Gollancz found in British messes in Germany in late 1946 much the same atmosphere of privileged caste and dignified well-being he had encountered in colonial Singapore in 1918. In devastated Düsseldorf, where the average living space for Germans was 3.2 square metres per person, he found his private bedroom alone measured over 80 square metres and had a bathroom boasting continuous hot water, central heating and every convenience. In such places people dined well at a third of the cost of comparable meals in Britain. While the vanquished suffered hunger oedema on 1,000 calories a day, the victors regularly ate their way through five-course dinners. A typical menu in an officers' mess in the British zone on Tuesday 8 October 1946 read:

Consommé
———
Fried Sole in butter
Fresh Potatoes
———
Dutch Steak
Mashed Potatoes
Cauliflower
———
Raspberry Cream
———
Cheese
———
Coffee

By comparison the set lunch for German guests at the Mitropa, a so-called 'bunker hotel' in Berlin converted from an air-raid shelter, offered the following: meat broth or vegetables, a 50 gram portion of mince, 400 grams of potatoes, and kohlrabi (turnip-cabbage).

In the devastated cities of the North Rhine and Westphalia the British were the new *Herrenvolk* and lived a life tantamount to apartheid. The officers kept separate from the men, the army from the Control Commission, and everyone from the Germans. '*Eintritt streng verboten*' proclaimed every notice board: 'Entry strictly forbidden'—to Germans. Approval was rarely given for Germans, no matter how worthy or distinguished, to enter these inner sanctuaries as guests. At cinemas and hairdressers they were required to occupy separate cubicles and stand in separate queues. Even a year and a half after the war it was rare for officer-types to meet Germans on terms of equality, and few had any first-hand knowledge of the conditions in which the Germans actually lived. The Germans were the new *Untermensch*, untouchables in a new kind of vassal state.

Nothing made them feel more so than the business of the Dependents—the wives and children of the Occupation soldiers who came out from Britain to join their husbands in Germany once the Occupation got into its stride. To make room for the British families, the best houses were requisitioned for them, the German families evicted and their furniture seized. The same thing happened in the American zone. The *New York Times* reported that on average one American family displaced eight German families and that in the Grünewald district of Berlin one thousand German civilians were made homeless when the Americans requisitioned 125 houses for Dependents. Many of these German families had been bombed out in the war and now they lost all their remaining belongings to strangers in peacetime—to women and children like themselves. The Dependents, meanwhile, settled into the ruins as if they were the White Highlands of Kenya. In Germany they enjoyed a standard of living that was not only very much higher than that of the Germans but of the British living in Britain as well, pampered by German servants, who were happy to serve them, not so much for the pay as the butt-ends in the ashtray and the left-over food in the slop bucket.

All this ostentiously sybaritic behaviour provoked savage criticism from a minority both inside and outside the Occupation hierarchy. George Kennan, a high-ranking official in the US Department of State, wrote in his memoirs of his visits to the American zone:

> Each time I had come away with a sense of sheer horror at the spectacle of this horde of my compatriots and their dependents camping in luxury amid the ruins of a shattered national community, ignorant of the past, oblivious to the abundant evidences of present tragedy all around them, inhabiting the same sequestered villas that the Gestapo and SS had just abandoned, and enjoying the same privileges, flaunting their silly supermarket luxuries in the face of a veritable ocean of deprivation, hunger and wretchedness, setting an example of empty materialism and cultural poverty before a people desperately in need of spiritual and intellectual guidance, taking for granted—as though it was their natural due—a disparity of privilege and comfort between themselves and their German neighbours no smaller than those that had once divided lord and peasant in that feudal Germany which it had once been our declared purpose in two world wars to destroy.'

Arthur D. Kahn, a former chief Editor in the Intelligence Office of Information Control in Frankfurt, roundly denounced the style of life of the American Military Government, which he saw as a betrayal:

> We became an 'India Service'—'poobah sahibs'—masters of a conquered people, rulers of an occupied colonial state. Little people from the States haughtily ordered German mayors and governors to appear before them, delivered speeches on democracy, and received homage and presents. Like India Service personnel, in the midst of ruins and near starvation, we lived well. We wined and dined as we had never done at home. Like conquerors, we affected fancy uniforms and fancy leather boots. The most beautiful women in Germany we had at our price. There were servants to minister to

our every need. For a few packs of cigarettes, we even had music with our meals. And on the streets, before the opera, groups of Germans gathered to fight for our cigarette butts.

The contrast between victor and vanquished was even more extreme in the French zone. The first Commander-in-Chief, General de Lattre de Tassigny, believed that the best way to re-educate the Germans would be to impress them with a show of grandeur on a scale such as they had never seen before. 'Our ceremonies and military displays', he declared, 'ought to show the Germans that we too know how to conceive big ideas, to carry out huge schemes, to achieve the beautiful.' His villa at Lindau was specially landscaped for him, the National Opera Company was brought from Paris to play for him, and the students of the Villa Medici, the French art school in Rome, came to design and decorate the barracks and compose new music for the military bands. When an American general paid a farewell visit, de Lattre arranged for ten thousand Algerian cavalrymen carrying torches to line his route. Baden-Baden, the most renowned of German spa towns, was the seat of French Military Government. At one time there were so many French there that they outnumbered the native Germans and consumed more food than they supplied: each Frenchman, it was calculated, consumed as much meat in a week as fifty-five Germans. French officers and their wives took over the undamaged grand hotels and in the evenings danced in the Casino ballroom to the music of the municipal orchestra playing Viennese waltzes. The French left-wing press dubbed Baden-Baden 'Little Vichy'.

Amongst the ordinary Allied soldiery, fellow-feeling and compassion soon began to stir after the hate and anger of the war and the chilly aloofness of the non-fraternisation period afterwards. 'As the months progressed,' recalled Captain Ian Warner, of the Hampshire Regiment, based at Soltan, near Celle, 'things slowly got better and the anti-German feeling amongst the troops became tempered with a lighter vein of humour and tolerance—the British soldier is, in the main, a friendly, helpful sort of chap, not given to bearing a grudge or hate for long.' Among a minority of more sensitive Allied soldiers it became apparent that most Germans were perfectly normal human beings, and the extent of their catastrophe and depths of their suffering were a cause for inner disquiet. Phil May, an impressionable 19-year old Second Lieutenant in the Green Howards, was quickly disabused of wartime prejudices when he had his first glimpse of the ravaged Fatherland from the train to Osnabrück, and wrote home to his parents in April 1946:

The Ruhr towns are really in the most terrible state. No matter how much one has been told or from what you have read you could not realise how shocking it really is. Mile after mile of absolute ruin and destruction. There's nothing in England to compare. London has had nothing by comparison. Most of the people still look dazed. How some are managing to live I don't know. The children are the worst and all are very hungry. You see them all around the side of the railway line crying out for food and cigarettes. It is sad that this happened to what must have been a wonderful country. I can't help feeling sorry for them, but there are not many that seem to agree with me. You can see that they are a broken race at the moment but there is no doubt that they have got guts. All are working hard on the land trying to grow food, and digging is going on in every garden by the young and old. My gosh, if you hear anyone in England grumbling at what they had to put up with during the war, it is a mere nothing by comparison . . . The Germans don't seem to know quite how to treat us. A few are friendly but most just look blank.

Individual compassion did not amount to universal liking, but an opinion poll among GIs in the American zone in 1946 revealed that nearly 80 per cent of the soldiers interviewed had a favourable impression of the Germans. Half of them liked the English best of all foreigners, 28 per cent liked the Germans best, and only 11 per cent the French. The GIs liked the cleanliness of the Germans, they liked German girls, they admired the way they made the best of their terrible lot. The British, too, respected their 'guts' and the way their girls 'made them feel like a king'. Society had been turned upside down in Germany. Upper-class refugees from the east, career soldiers, and gentlefolk living on savings, found themselves sinking down the social scale, while technicians, opera stars, and *maîtres d'hotel* were becoming a new aristocracy. The daughters of counts worked as barmaids and two Princesses were employed as street-cleaners in Berlin. Flung into this social flux, the Allied soldiers were never certain who they would meet next. Sometimes greater intimacy led to increased respect. In 1948 Christopher Leefe, now a British Army Captain in Hildesheim, started to go out with a local German girl (who eventually was to become his wife) and through her met the rest of her family. They were a revelation to him:

The head of the family—my future father-in-law—was Paul Goerz, a businessman. He had been one of the pioneer inventors of television before the war and had been the head of Goerz Optik in Berlin and a director of Leitz and Zeiss-Ikon. During the war he had been garrison commander in Oslo and was one of the survivors from the battleship *Tirpitz* when it was sunk by the British. At the end of the war he was a prisoner of the British and afterwards he came to Hildesheim where he founded a firm called Blaupunkt which manufactured radios (and still does). His wife, my future mother-in-law, was called Lilli, like her daughter. She was an absolute lady through and through—gracious, elegant, very dignified, very kind, very bigoted, incredibly stubborn, absolutely straight, a stickler for discipline, for correctness. She had spent the last winter of the war with the youngest of her children on the family's estates in East Prussia, where they had four or five farms with shooting and forestry. Then, when the Russians drew near, she loaded the children and all the family possessions on to a couple of tractors and a couple of farm carts and headed west—part of the great trek of German refugees from the east. And eventually they joined up with the father in Hildesheim in the British zone. This was where I met them.

By my standards they were incredibly cultured people. It was they who introduced me to the finer things in life, showed me that there was more to life than wine, women and song, and living in barracks and riding horses and playing a lot of rugger. They took me to the opera in Hanover, taught me about art and antiques. They, defeated Germans, introduced me, a victorious Englishman, to civilized virtues. They had lost everything in the war but by their stoicism they had gained everything. They started with nothing and just fought back. The father worked bloody hard. He was in the factory at 8 in the morning and he was still there at 10 at night, producing wireless set after wireless set. By this time Lilli's husband, Jürgen, had come back from the war. He'd been captured on the Eastern Front and spent a few years in a Soviet forced labour camp. He'd seen a heck of a lot. He was a very nice chap indeed—a very quiet, sympathetic man. I used to hack a horse up there to the house for him to ride and we used to go riding in the woods together. It was still strictly illegal for a serving British Army officer to go around with an ex-officer of Hitler's army, a former enemy. But he was a good bloke. And he was a soldier—he didn't make excuses, he didn't cringe like the rest of the people.

I think that is where my education started, with that family. They were intensely cultivated people—and I? What was I? Just a captain in the army. I used to make a lot of illicit trips in the 15 cwt truck and take them bacon and bottles of gin and packets of washing powder—all these things they couldn't get. And we'd go to cafés and restaurants—but it was they that ordered the food and wine. Looking back, all of us officers in the British Occupation army must have enjoyed a power and a status amongst the Germans far higher than we could have felt entitled to in normal times. We were the conquerors. We ruled the country. Even the lowliest English subaltern carried more clout than the most exalted German. And so for a while we enjoyed a relationship with people whose company we couldn't have aspired to under ordinary circumstances.

For the Germans the relationship with the Americans and British was more often a disappointment. Many had greeted them as liberators rather than conquerors, welcoming the Americans with garlands and wine in Munich and speaking warmly of the 'fair play' of the 'English gentlemen' who had captured Hamburg. Those who had not supported Hitler looked forward to a new era of freedom and democracy, even under Occupation.

But their hopes were not fulfilled, and disillusionment often led to anger. The Germans were angry about hunger and the black market, about the requisitioning of their homes, the dismantling of their industry and destruction of their economy; they were angry about what they considered to be the unjust procedures of denazification, about the Allies' sweeping powers of arrest, which they deemed as bad as the Gestapo's, and about Allied militarism, which they claimed was no better than German militarism before it.

In the American zone the violent behaviour of troops was one of the most frequent causes of complaint. German civilians were beaten up in their homes or on the streets, women molested, pedestrians deliberately run down by American army drivers. Not even women from the Occupation forces were safe in the streets at night unless they carried little flags showing their nationality. Armed robbery, looting and car theft were rife. Violent behaviour by American soldiers was so widespread that Congress in Washington was told: 'The German troops occupying France had a better record in their personal contact with the population than the American troops occupying Germany.' A special study of a typical German town under American Occupation—the old university town of Marburg in Hesse—showed that though many inhabitants had been well disposed to the Americans when they first arrived, most had totally ceased to co-operate with them by the end of 1945. They submitted a long list of complaints to the Military Governor of the town, most of which fell under the headings of violence. They complained that they requisitioned the homes of anti-Nazis, then looted or burned their possessions; did not keep law and order; used Gestapo methods in denazification investigations; starved or beat up German prisoners; caused many accidents on the roads; abused hunting-rights and practices; imposed electricity cuts on the populace while leaving the lights in their own premises 'burning from top to bottom both by night and by day.'

The problem became so bad that the Americans decided to put their house in order once and for all. In May 1946 General Joseph McNarney, who had replaced General Eisenhower as Commander-in-Chief in the American zone the previous November, declared: 'Discipline in various places and under various commands in the theatre has decreased to such an extent that the good reputation of our troops is generally discredited.' A formidable new élite force of troopers called the US Zone Constabulary was formed under the command of Major General Ernest A. Harmon and let loose on the miscreant Army of Occupation. Harmon himself launched a reign of terror among his commanders, roaring up and down the length and breadth of the American zone in his special train. The Army may have been knocked into shape again, but the same could not be said about Military Government.

This was not, in all probability, the fault of the head of American Military Government in Germany, General Lucius D. Clay, a former engineer officer who was once described by Roosevelt as 'the most competent man in the executive departments . . . give him six months and he could run General Motors or US Steel.' Clay was destined to become an independent sovereign in the enclave of Europe under his command and the single most important decision-maker in Western Germany in the first four years after the war. But he was handicapped by the essentially improvised nature of the Military Government organisation he commanded. With a few exceptions, it was short of really first-class men. Policy and plans often failed to reach local commanders in the field, many of whom in any case ignored directives from above and ruled their areas like independent feudal kingdoms. Some were blatant carpetbaggers, others were Americanised German Jews, recruited because of their fluency in the German language, who bore a grudge against the Aryan native and conducted private vendettas against the populace.

It did not help that even the men at the top fell out with each other over major policy directives from Washington. 'The written orders from Washington meant whatever the commanding general at each level said they meant,' wrote the Chief of the Decartelisation Branch, James Martin. If the officials responsible for the programmes did not support the directives they simply did not carry them out. James Martin's own area— the breaking-up of the German industrial cartels which had supplied the Nazis with their war material—was a notorious case in point. Decartelisation had been regarded by American planners as the most necessary of all the economic reforms envisaged in occupied Germany—an essential act of denazification and a vital precaution to prevent Germany from ever waging another aggressive war. But it proved impossible to get Military Government to push it through. Instead a protracted battle ensued between two ideologically opposed groups—the anti-trust group and the big business group who wanted ex-Nazi plants put back into operation 'simply because they belonged to Singer, International Harvester, General Motors, or because an American, Belgian, or British company had a pre-war arrangement.' Though Martin and his group took the case to Congress they lost the battle when General Clay finally turned against decartelisation—even though it had begun as a mandatory order from Washington.

Only the firm of Bosch was proceeded against and fully decartelised. I. G. Farben was broken into three components but ironically nearly fell prey to an illegal undercover 'raid' by a group of three Property Control officers from American Military Government in Bavaria, whose ringleader was Lt.-Col. John McCarthy, Chief of the Investigation and Enforcement Branch. McCarthy's plan was to form a stock-holding syndicate of German financiers, I. G. Farben custodians and American members of Property Control and Farben plants—a plan which would have made them all millionaires. The plan failed and McCarthy and his colleagues were investigated, the resulting report running into twenty-six volumes. Those responsible were then fired and shipped quietly home without publicity. Later the twenty-six volumes were destroyed.

The French were untroubled by the sort of inner rifts which troubled the Americans. In the French view the French zone of Germany existed for only one purpose—to benefit the French. Their avowed aim was the end of Germany as a nation. The Germans had marched into France three times in less than a century and the French consequently did not ever wish to see the re-establishment of the Reich. For their own security they wanted the Rhineland permanently occupied and the Ruhr and Saar taken away from the Germans for ever. They were the only one of the four Occupation powers who charged the Germans money for the privilege of being occupied by them—a huge sum which by the end totalled $737,500,000, most of it in cash. Everything that could be extracted from their zone they extracted. In the early months of the Occupation they made off with machinery, livestock and art treasures as war reparations. Later they extracted reparations from current productions, forcing the Germans to sell them coal, steel, timber, wood pulp, chemicals and leather at a 20 per cent discount, paying in marks which they had either captured or printed themselves, and selling any surplus on the world market for dollars. Though theirs was the smallest and poorest of all the zones, the French managed to extract proportionately more than even the Russians, making a profit out of their Occupation of about 2,000 million dollars. But there was a positive side to French rule too. They never practised non-fraternisation, for instance, and they initiated the most successful of all re-education programmes in Germany—with profound results for the future development of Western Europe.

The British were not as overtly extortionate as the French but they were more hidebound and bureaucratic. The British Element of the Control Commission was the biggest Occupation bureaucracy—26,000 personnel compared with 5,000 Americans at the end—and behaved like it. Its top men were of the highest calibre. Its lower ranks, however, included a mediocre rump of ex-servicemen and civilians who could not get a better job in Britain. Such people brought to German affairs some of the less palatable aspects of the British civil service, and were often officious, obstructive, and inflexible in imposing the letter of the law, but blindly indifferent in exercising the spirit of it. The indifference of this overblown bureaucracy usually baffled and sometimes infuriated the Germans. In November 1947 Jessica Stolterfoht, a young University student, wrote from Lübeck to a pen-friend in England describing a typical case of British bureaucratic inconsiderateness:

> What I tell you now is absolutely true. Denmark and the Netherlands offered vegetables in masses to Germany. They did not want any direct payment. They had a record harvest of tomatoes, for instance, and did not know what to do with it. They asked for permission to bring it to Germany in their own ships. The British Military Government did not allow the import! The tomatoes had to rot and the German population had to be content with a ration of 3 lb. of tomatoes for the whole season.

Of course, it is all right if the Allied nations intend to starve us as a punishment. I could not say a word against it, knowing all our sins. I could understand that we must starve because there is not enough food in the world as a consequence of the war of which we were the origins. All that would be comprehensible to me. But why could we not get the offending vegetable if starvation is *not* meant as an actual punishment?

For a while the Germans were cowed and submissive under the Occupation. Considering the extent of their suffering it was extraordinary that they should remain so disciplined and controlled for so long. But they were not always utterly quiescent. In the spring of 1946 there were riots in Hamburg and the Ruhr: crowds of Germans attacked food stores and coal trains and there were several hundred arrests. There were riots in Hamburg again in the summer: thousands of Germans had eaten up their thirty-day bread ration in twenty days and rather than endure ten days of hunger they had raided shops and bakeries. As winter drew on there were growing signs of fierce resentment or suicidal despair among the populace. In Stuttgart a bomb exploded in an American office and another was thrown into the denazification records centre. American newspapermen reported that Germans were secretly drilling in the woods, and the figures '88'—standing for 'Heil, Hitler', 'H' being the eighth letter of the alphabet—were a common graffiti. The continuing dismantling of German industrial plant, which many regarded as a senseless act preventing the Germans going to work to manufacture goods in exchange for food, provoked bitter protest. In November 1946 the employees at the I. G. Farben Chemical Works at Leverkusen issued a defiant condemnation of British policy: 'We do not intend to suffer further misery without protest. We do not believe that the present economic policy of the occupying powers is dictated only by considerations of safety. We believe that behind many measures stand the egoistic and competitive motives of the great capitalists.'

They may well have been right. Towards the end of the war the British government's Chief Scientific Adviser, Lord Cherwell, had reported to the Cabinet: 'The main advantage which this country could secure from reparations would be the capture of Germany's pre-war export market... I trust we shall do nothing to encourage the rebuilding of German industry.' Though the Cabinet rejected this, at least as an explicit policy, there were times when it seemed this was indeed the Occupation's aim. Eighty-six per cent of German industry lay within the British zone and the British produced a hit list which included much of it. They seemed unaware that democracy could not grow when the means of production had been taken away, or that the German failure to produce was harming the European economy as a whole. The British wiped out the German watch industry and destroyed part of the Hamburg fishing fleet. They blew up the Bloehm and Voss shipyards and Krupps steelworks in Essen, and tried to extort the secrets of the '4711' formula of *eau de cologne* at gunpoint Unilever tried to extinguish the Henkel soap factory. The British motor-car industry declined to take over the Volkswagen car plant, which they saw as a rival, and attempted to have it broken up instead. The British went on tearing down German factories after the Americans had stopped doing so and even the Russians wanted them to remain intact. There were violent demonstrations by German workers at the factory gates and the British prepared to open fire if necessary to keep public order. Konrad Adenauer, the Mayor of Cologne and future Chancellor of the German Federal Republic*, warned the British that morale was at a record low. And what did the British propose to build in place of the factories and workshops they had taken down? A kind of German New Delhi—the so-called 'Hamburg Project'.

The 'Hamburg Project' was the dream-child of Whitehall—a grandiose inner city of towers in the best surviving residential area of Hamburg to concentrate the officers of the British Raj more efficiently and house the members of the British colony in a manner more befitting their station. Seventeen thousand citizens of Hamburg would have to be evicted to make way for this ambitious scheme. A storm of protest greeted its unveiling. In London questions were raised in Parliament. In Hamburg petitions were sent to the German mayor. One read: 'We, the women of Hamburg, entreat you, Bürgermeister Petersen, to beg Military Government not to push misery beyond the limits of endurance. Mr. Churchill and President Roosevelt declared that the Allies would put humanity first in dealing with the vanquished. An English residential quarter of the kind planned, populated by healthy and well-fed human beings amidst the hunger and distress, is a symbol of unbearable contrast and will be a source of jealousy and hatred. We implore the Military Government to put the dictates of humanity in the forefront of their planning.' The British administrators on the spot agreed, and the project was stopped just in time.

It was a matter of popular debate among the Germans as to which zone was the best to live in. 'The Russians promise everything and do nothing', they quipped. 'The Americans promise nothing and do everything. The British promise nothing and do nothing.' On the other hand, the Germans reckoned they were freest in the British zone, best off in the American zone. On reflection, the best zone was judged to be the American zone for the first fortnight, and British zone for ever after.

* In the autumn of 1945 Adenauer, already a leading figure among the German Christian Democrats, was dismissed from his post and banned from politics by the British. At the time the action seemed justifiable —Adenauer had grown obstructive over vital matters like coal production—but in retrospect, as Adenauer grew into a figure of towering importance, it looked increasingly as though the British had made a political gaffe. Adenauer, however, put a good face on it. After he became Chancellor, he thanked the British, without whose efforts, he said, he would still have been mayor of Cologne.

11

Vice

When the fighting stopped the morale of all the Allied fighting men suffered a catastrophic collapse. The reason is not hard to see. All four armies were composed primarily of civilians in uniform. Day after day they had put up with privation and steeled themselves against death for the sake of the greater cause, for victory. And when victory came their *raison d'être*, as they saw it, vanished overnight. They didn't want to be in the army and they didn't want to be in Germany or wherever it was. Clearing up the mess and administering the peace were no concern of theirs. They wanted to go home, but they couldn't.

In the British and American forces demobilisation was based on the principle of first in, first out. Many servicemen found that they had months and (in the British case) even years still to serve. Service life reverted to a barrack routine of meaningless bull and parades. Young men who had achieved high rank on wartime operations were reduce in rank when the services reverted to a more professional peacetime establishment. Not surprisingly such men bitterly resented this and added their own voice of discontent to the growl that was welling up in all the former theatres of war.

The collapse of morale took many forms. On occasion it manifested itself in outright mutiny. In March 1946 there was a major mutiny in the RAF in India because of delays in demobilisation. In Europe and in the Pacific Theatre after VJ-Day certain units of the American Forces came near to mutiny too. In Paris and in the American zone of Berlin thousands of American soldiers marched through the streets carrying placards protesting against not being allowed home for their first peacetime Christmas. In Frankfurt 4,000 American Occupation troops demonstrated outside the headquarters of their commander-in-chief, General McNarny, chanting: '*We wanna go home, we wanna go home.*' Though some two and half million American servicemen were repatriated from

Europe between VE-Day and New Year's Eve 1945, those that remained and those that replaced them grew ever more disaffected. In all the armies such disaffection ran from what King's Regulations would call 'conduct prejudicial to good order and military discipline' to debauchery, banditry and big-time organised crime.

Nowhere was collapse of morale in the Allied forces more widespread and severe than in Germany. This was partly because more Allied servicemen were concentrated in Germany than anywhere else; and partly because the morale of the German people had collapsed as well, so that foreign soldiers and native civilian alike were forced to live in an environment which resembled, to a degree, a landscape and a society in the wake of a nuclear holocaust.

At least two activities in daily service life—the black market and sexual concubinage—were so widespread as to be virtually universal in the American and British zones. The problem was rooted so deep that even the high command was entangled in its tendrils. It was alleged, for example, that very senior RAF officers had been disposing of valuable antiques from the castles of the German nobility and flying them out of the country by the plane-load in RAF aircraft. It was also alleged, that the wife of the Military Governor of the American zone, General Clay was herself involved in large-scale black-market operations. 'It was common gossip that her acquisitions were being sent back to the States by the General's personal plane', one US Army Criminal Investigation Division agent has stated. When the plane flew out of Berlin on a smuggling flight the pilot logged it as a 'training flight', thereby avoiding fuss, and when it landed in Miami the pilot reported the flight as a 'security mission'—thereby avoiding customs inspection. When the case was reported to General Clay by an intelligence agent, it was suppressed as a 'security threat'. Even a former member of the White House Cabinet turned up in Berlin with 50 cartons of cigarettes for trading on the black market.

There had been ominous signs of incipient breakdown even while the war was still being fought. During the Battle of the Bulge in December 1944 the American effort to throw back the German counter-offensive had been bedevilled by some 19,000 US Army deserters involved in large-scale robbery and black market dealings in the rear areas. One group, belonging to the US Army Corps of Transport, even went so far as to siphon off gasoline badly needed for the American tanks at the front and sell it for a huge profit on the French black market. In Italy American soldiers of Italian origin abused their privilege in occupied cities to establish organised crime and gangster rule along mafia lines.

When discipline collapsed at the end of the war, the incidence of serious crime in the Occupation armies rose steeply—not just in the US Army. Berlin was terrorised by armed gangs of deserters and DPs—Russians, Poles, Frenchmen, Spaniards (ex-SS volunteers) and a few Americans. In

175

May 1945, only a week or two after the surrender, one of these gangs, a hundred strong, attacked a train at the Anhalt railway station in true wild west style. Out in the zones British Army convoys were held up at gunpoint, and on one occasion British soldiers fought a running gun battle with American train bandits who had shot their way out of an ambush not long before.

'To the victor the spoils' was an age-old precept of war—never more so than in the first year after VE-Day, when it was put into practice from the top to the bottom of the conquering armies. At the Potsdam Conference in July 1945 even the supreme Allied war lords were not averse to taking material advantage of their brief incursion on to the soil of their former enemies. Thus President Truman's special adviser, Brigadier-General Harry Vaughan, found he could peddle his spare clothes on the Berlin black market for 'a couple of thousand bucks', while the Chief of the Imperial General Staff, Field Marshal Sir Alan Brooke, Marshal of the Air Force Lord Portal, and Admiral of the Fleet Viscount Cunningham took the opportunity to make off with antiquarian tomes from the Royal Library in the Cecilienhof Palace, during time off from deciding the fate of Europe.

Probably every Allied soldier in Germany secreted a few items of loot in his knapsack at one time or another. The Russians set off back in horse-carts piled high with anything down to harmoniums and lavatory-pans. The Americans, having less need for domestic appliances (which to the Russians were treasure on earth), went for collectors' items with investment potential—Napoleon's death-mask, lead soldiers from the War Museum, the Reichspost stamp collection, Goering's Mercedes, the Walther pistol with which Hitler shot himself. A few, however, took advantage of opportunity and the chaos of the time to make a killing in instant riches—jewels, money, gold. It was the dubious distinction of the American zones of Germany and Austria to play host to some of the greatest robberies in history, only one of which was ever brought to court.

The most publicised of these robberies was that of the crown jewels of the former royal family of Hesse. These were stolen from the family seat at Kronberg Castle (then a US Army officers' recreation club) in April 1946—just before the wedding of Princess Sophie of Hesse, youngest sister of the present Duke of Edinburgh. The missing valuables included rubies, pearls and jade torn from their settings, together with two quart jars full of diamonds, a solid gold dinner-service and nine volumes of letters from Queen Victoria. The Army valued this stolen treasure at $1,500,000—worth over $8,000,000 today. But according to the Countess of Hesse, the sister of the late Kaiser Wilhelm II, it was worth twice this amount. Either way the robbery was the biggest known to history at that time and it created a world-wide sensation when the culprits—the welfare officer at Kronberg Castle, Captain Kathleen Durant, her husband Colonel James Durant and his ADC, Captain James Watson—were brought to trial and sentenced. What was not known at the time was that even bigger robberies had been committed in areas under US Army control—likewise on occasion by members of the US Army itself.

Gold and coin were the main targets of these earlier unsolved heists. Six and a half tons of gold from the Ribbentrop Gold Fund of the German Foreign Office, which had been hidden in Ribbentrop's Castle at Fuschl in Austria, was handed over to American troops shortly after the end of the war. According to Dr Robert Kempner, the Chief American Prosecutor at the Nuremberg Trials, German Foreign Office officials had informed him at Nuremberg that the amount allegedly turned over was less than the amount that was shipped to Fuschl, which had been worth nearly $7,500,000. But though the matter was raised in the American Senate the discrepancy was never solved.

At about the same time the bulk of the contents of the so-called *Goldzug*, or Gold Train, disappeared under mysterious circumstances while in American hands. The Gold Train had been found at Bad Ischl in Austria, where it arrived from Budapest near the end of the war laden with some three million dollars in gold, jewellery and other valuables which Hungarian Jews had paid to the SS in attempts to buy their way out of concentration-camp captivity. The contents of the Gold Train were deposited with the Property Control Division of American Military Government in Salzburg but only $30,000 was ever handed over to the Jewish Agency and no trace of the remainder was ever found.

Gold was again the target of a mysterious theft when a cache of gold bullion bars measuring three foot high by three foot wide was dug up in the mountains around Mittenwald in the Bavarian Alps in the summer of 1945 and driven off in two trucks by two American intelligence officers—never to be seen again. At almost exactly the same time and in almost exactly the same place—the forested mountains overlooking the Walschensee near Mittenwald—nearly two million dollars, and possibly a great deal more, in dollars and other foreign currency, was stolen from secret caches by a small group of German Army and SS officers with the connivance of certain US Army officers and German civilians based in Garmisch–Partenkirchen. This huge quantity of paper money, worth over ten million dollars today, was part of the gold and foreign currency reserves of the German State Bank, the Reichsbank, which has been shipped down from Berlin and buried near the Walchensee just before the end of the war. Though the American Department of the Army has always stoutly maintained that no such robbery ever took place, American documentation presented in a recent study of the case,* has shown that in fact an investigation *was*

---

* Published as *Nazi Gold*, by Ian Sayer and the present author.

ordered by the Commander of the US Third Army, General Patton, in whose area the hoard had been hidden, though none of the money was recovered and none of those responsible was ever brought to trial. It was also revealed that gold bullion, diamonds, jewels, foreign currency, and bonds and security, worth nearly two and a half billion dollars by today's values, were forcibly removed from the Reichsbank by personnel from the Russian Army, US Army, German Army and SS immediately before and after the end of the war.

At a lesser but more pervasive level, the black market flourished over much of war-torn Europe but it was never blacker than in Germany—a country where the average German could expect a new pair of shoes every twelve years and a new suit every fifty. It was really the Allies who brought about the black market in Germany. Anxious to prevent the kind of inflation that had ruined Germany after the First World War, they pursued a rigid monetarist policy after the Second, with dire results. An economic survey produced by the United Nations after the war analysed the problem like this:

> The practice of 'suppressing' inflation was carried *ad absurdum*, to the point of strangling economic activity. The military administrations brought with them the respectable dogma that price inflation is wicked and anti-social under all conditions. However, under conditions of starvation, and in the absence of well-established Government machinery, the attempt to run the economies of the different occupation zones by detailed military orders only perpetuated the paralysis of the economy. Money ceased to a great extent to function either as a circulating medium or as a measure of economic calculations. Individual barter, compensation trade, wage payment in kind and other atavistic forms of economic communication took its place. The result was twofold: an extremely slow recovery of industrial production and a wide disparity between easy food conditions in the countryside and starvation in the towns. The social inequalities arising from this policy were probably even worse than those which could have resulted from an inflationary price mechanism.

The average income in Germany after the war was about 200 Reichsmarks a week. In theory this was worth $20 or £5—enough to buy a packet of cigarettes or a bottle of wine. In practice it was worth next to nothing because nobody wanted to deal in Reichsmarks any more. Instead the country reverted to a more primitive form of exchange-barter. Germans no longer bought and sold; they swapped. A Persian carpet could be traded for 100 lb. of potatoes, a Gobelin tapestry for a carton of grapefruit juice, a grand piano for a second-hand suit—anything and anyone, from diamonds to love, for an English or American cigarette.

No article of barter was so highly prized as the cigarette. Indeed, before long the cigarette had almost replaced the mark as the universal currency of the people, and become the basic unit of exchange. The cigarette had some of the advantages of currency in normal times—constant demand, regulated supply, handy size, reasonable durability. The cigarette also had another advantage not shared by currency: in the last resort it could be set on fire and smoked to satisfy the cravings of addiction or quell the pangs of hunger. In reality, cigarettes were rarely smoked by the first person to buy them, but were passed from person to person for profit or barter, changing hands a hundred times or more before reaching the end of the line—the smoker.

Within a short while of the end of the war Germany had become a civilisation based on nicotine. The fate of the nation was enmeshed with the names of Lucky Strike and Camel, Senior Service and Craven A. Tobacco plants soared in vineyards, gardens, allotments and the window-boxes of city flats. In the streets a new race of men appeared—the *Kippensammler*, the collector of butt-ends. Like prostitutes every *Kippensammler* had his beat, usually at places where cigarette ends were thrown away in abundance, such as the entrances to messes, soldiers' clubs and cinemas. Waiters and maids collected butt-ends from ashtrays and sold them to the *Kippensammler* at a fixed price per tumblerful. Waiters in the Café Wein in Berlin averaged 75 to 100 butts a day, for which they received $5. More enterprising people employed hundreds of *Kippensammler* and set up small cigarette factories in bombed buildings where the butt-ends were reassembled into whole cigarettes which were sold for up to four marks each. It was calculated that seven butt-ends made one cigarette and for one cigarette a man could buy his next meal.

In time the German black market developed into a well-organised alternative economy in which supply and demand were regulated between three main groups—the people of the towns, the people of the countryside and the soldiers of the occupation armies. The townspeople traded their valuables (jewellery, furs, cameras, watches, antiques) for the soldiers' PX or NAAFI luxuries (cigarettes, chocolate, coffee, white bread, silk stockings) or pilfered military stores (petrol, coal, bully beef), and the country people traded their surplus produce (potatoes, poultry, bacon, eggs, flour) for the townspeople's valuables or the cigarettes and other luxuries they had obtained from the soldiers. The Germans coined a new word for this barter chain—'*kompensieren*', from the English 'to compensate'. A Berlin newspaper, *Der Telegraf*, described how 'compensating' worked:

A pound of butter was offered to a hungry friend for 350 Reichsmarks. As he did not have enough money on him he bought it on credit. He would pay the next day. Half the pound went to his wife. With the remaining half he went out to 'compensate'. At a tobacconist we got 50 cigarettes for the half pound. Ten cigarettes we kept for ourselves. With the remainder we went into a bar.

For 40 cigarettes we received a bottle of wine and a bottle of Schnapps. We took the wine back to the house, but the Schnapps we took into the country. Before long we found a farmer who would exchange the Schnapps for us for two pounds of butter. Next morning my friend took back the pound of butter he had been offered originally on the grounds that it was too expensive. Our 'compensating' had brought us in one and a half pounds of butter, a bottle of wine, 10 cigarettes and the pleasure of a tax-free bit of business.

High-minded and high-ranking members of the Allied Occupation might look askance at the German black market as something altogether immoral and undesirable. Not so the Germans. 'It was considered most dishonourable to abstain from the black market as long as members of one's family were starving,' recalled an upper-class Bavarian of that time. 'Not to join because of some code of honour or other was not a good thing. One has to be very careful about getting moral issues mixed up with something that was, at this time, a most honourable business.' For most Germans, condemned to starvation rations and lack of fuel, clothing and medicines, it was often the only means of survival and almost the only means of making an intolerable existence tolerable.

In the autumn of 1945, after the first post-war harvest, the whole of Germany went off in search of calories. A Swiss visitor at the time reported: 'Day after day, night after night, the people crowd on to the railway platforms in their hundreds, many with small children, all with suitcases or rucksacks on their backs. They have heard that somewhere—perhaps 100, perhaps 300 kilometres away—there is a village where potatoes or flour or a bit of pork fat can be got on the Black Market. So there they are going. If the trains run at all they run two to ten hours late. They are unlit and, because of the coal shortage, unheated. The people are squashed into the carriages like sardines into a tin ... such is life in Germany today. The German goes hungry. He freezes. He sees his children die. He has become like a helpless, hunted animal.'

More than three-quarters of the train passengers at that time were so-called 'calorie seekers' rather than *bona-fide* travellers, and it was estimated that every passenger carried an average of 50 kilos of hoarded food or black-market goods. Each train was given a nickname according to its routeing. The Calorie Express was the name of the train that ran from the starving cities of Hamburg and Cologne down to the fertile farming country around Munich. The Potato Train ran from the industrial Ruhr to rural Lower Saxony, the Vitamin Train from undernourished Dortmund to the cherry orchards of Freiburg in the Black Forest, the Nicotine Line to the tobacco fields of the Palatinate. The train that ran from Osnabrück on the North Sea coast to Berlin had two names according to the freight it carried: on the run out to Berlin it was called the Fish Express, and on the run back the Silk-Stocking Express.

What most Germans sought on the black market was food and the essentials of existence. But for those who wanted it, the black market offered far more—from caviar and fresh trout to drugs like insulin and penicillin, travel permits and title-deeds to bombed-out houses. In the post-war turmoil many displaced Germans took advantage of black-market documents to change their identity and start a new life higher up the social or professional scale. According to one official report, 392 false doctors, among them the Head Surgeon of Baden–Baden State Hospital, achieved their positions in this way. More prized than a shiny new identity was a respray of the old one—especially if it belonged to a wanted Nazi. The '*Persilschein*', or Persil Certificate, was a genuine Allied-issue document, falsely filled out, which cleared the bearer from having been a member of any Nazi organisation during the Hitler period. Obviously it was eagerly sought after by Nazis on the run, and it gave rise to lucrative rackets among Allied occupation officials. In one case, the US Army Commandant of a Civilian Internment Camp for suspected Nazis near Garmisch–Partenkirchen in Bavaria peddled official discharge papers to the inmates at extortionate prices and when he had run out of bidders he recruited more by the simple expediency of having more Germans arrested in the streets 'on suspicion'.

Evey city, town and village had its special black market rendezvous and safe houses. Some of the most notorious black-market 'pitches' were in the Alexanderplatz and the Tiergarten in Berlin (where 4,000 people would congregate on an average black-market day), the air-raid bunker at Cologne main railway station and the red-light district along the Reeperbahn in Hamburg. For a while Potsdam, in the Soviet zone, was thought to be the black-market capital of Europe, if only because it was beyond the reach of the military police (except Russians, who didn't care) and yet close enough to Berlin to attract a lot of customers. There in the main square on a good day thousands of Russian, American, British and French soldiers, DPs and Germans would be milling about in one huge illegal oriental bazaar in which Meissen china, Rolleiflex and Leica cameras, diamonds and Mickey-Mouse watches changed hands at inflated rates for precious cigarettes, candy, coffee and soap. Probably the biggest of all black markets was at Bulmke, a suburb of Gelsenkirchen. Here black-market business was conducted quite publicly with all the goods on open display as if it were a legitimate street-market: evening gowns and ladies' hats, alcohol, chickens, bicycles, matches. More often the black market was a hole-in-the-corner affair—a whisper in a doorway, huddled bargaining in the ruins, a suitcase with a false bottom, a pig in a pram with a baby's bonnet on, a coffin full of bacon.

A few people made a killing on the black market. These were the *Grossschieber*, or big-time operators, also known as *Süssstoffgangsters* or saccharine-gangsters. They ran large illegal organisations which dealt in the more valuable black-market commodities such as drugs (especially precious penicillin or 'white gold'), industrial chemicals, old masters, and precious stones. Such men were the 'Price Commissars' of the underworld. They fixed the prices and kept order among their followers with the help of professional boxers. In other circumstances they might have become business tycoons, but even now they displayed ambition and imagination. An entire train of thirteen wagons and a loco was stolen in the French zone by one gang, then driven into the American zone where it was loaded with a huge cargo of potatoes before being driven back to the French zone. Another gang, the Duisburg Railway Station Gang, was particularly sophisticated and efficient, with its own embossed and headed writing-paper and typed lists of commodities, with date and prices, like a legitimate trading company.

Professional criminals fed the black market with a wide range of goods pilfered from the US Army. In 1946 $10,000 worth of army stores were being stolen from one Quartermaster's Depot at Ludwigsburg every day. Profits were high. The 'banker' for a black-market ring in Berlin was found to be carrying nearly $300,000 in diamonds when he was arrested, equivalent to $1,500,000 in today's terms.

Even legitimate businesses were forced to embark on large-scale black-market operations in order to pay their employees in kind—wages alone being of little value, owing to the fantastic prices of black-market goods. Thus one of the departments of the German railways, the Reichsbahn, shared out two oxen, five pigs, four sucking pigs, 19 cwt. of grain and six cwt. of flour amongst its workforce over a six months' period.

Many Allied subjects took some sort of part in the black market. Len Carpenter, the British civilian prisoner of war who had sat out the Battle of Berlin in a private apartment in the west end of the city, was more heavily involved than most. Years later he was to recall:

When the British arrived in Berlin in July 1945 I didn't officially report to them and oddly enough none of them ever asked me to. You may find this hard to understand but for some reason I didn't want to appear to be a member of the winning side. Not that I didn't take advantage of it. Near to my house was an army cookhouse, and I'd often troop in and have a good feed, even in civilian clothes—no one ever asked me who I was or what I was doing there. All you needed in Germany was a lot of chits, all well-stamped. Provided you had a lot of stamps you could go anywhere.

Not long after the end of the war I opened the English Academy of Berlin. I knew that the Russians wouldn't have Berlin to themselves for ever and that sooner or later the Allies would arrive, so I thought I'd cash in on this. I had lots of little leaflets printed in German, which read: 'When the British and the Americans come, will you be able to speak English?' I plastered these leaflets all over Berlin and before long I had a flourishing language school going. Then I started giving lectures. My subject was 'The Other

England'. The Germans imagined the English were a race of dashing young men in sports cars with scarves flying out round their necks. They thought their Anglo-Saxon cousins were tall blond Aryans, like they were supposed to be themselves. They were very disappointed when they saw that we were a nation of little dark men who whistled all the time ... So I gave these lectures about the other England—the working class, the people who voted Churchill out of power in the first election after the war, which was something the Germans couldn't understand.

Before very long, though, I found that I could make more money in one black-market deal over lunch than I could in a month of straight work at the Academy. So I went into the black market in a big way. I started by buying NAAFI goods from English soldiers and selling them to Germans, and getting cameras and suchlike from Germans and selling them to English soldiers. Then it developed. A German friend of mine, a German banker's son called Boscherling, had very good connections and established a contact in a town in East Germany where cloth was spun—Leipzig or somewhere. He was able to get hold of an unlimited amount of cloth, and since cloth was hard to come by at home it became one of our main lines on the black market, especially with the girls from the ATS. In fact it became almost like a normal legitimate business. The British soldiers would pay in cash and I would go around with up to 10,000 marks in spare cash in my pocket, which was worth £1,000 then and getting on for £12,000 now. I wouldn't have dared to bank it—I didn't bank anything in Germany.

In time I became very well organised. I started supplying all the officers' messes with spirits. Then I began to fix up the English soldiers with German girls—not at any profit to myself, I assure you. When the British Army first arrived in Berlin there was a non-fraternisation ban in operation. But that didn't deter anybody. The German women were quite willing to give themselves—they just wanted to be where the chocolate was. I remember going up to a group of women outside a railway station and saying. 'You whores! Six weeks ago the British were dropping bombs on you and now look what you are doing!' But very soon the British soldiers were bringing the German girls I had introduced into my flat in Kastanienallee in Charlottenburg, and of course they were doing it all over my furniture and my lovely silk-brocaded chaise-longue—still with their boots on! And then, of course, the girls would come back to me and say: 'I gave these English friends of yours an inch and they took a yard.' And later they'd come back again and tell me they were pregnant. Well, I had a Jewish friend in Berlin whose brother was a doctor and so very soon I was in the market for supplying someone to get rid of these pregnancies. And then, of course, I felt I had to get the market in contraceptives organised.

It was amazing what people were prepared to barter to get things they wanted. One day I did a deal with a German who wanted to escape to the West. I got an Allied army uniform for him—and do you know what he'd given me in exchange? His wife and his home. I went to visit his home. It was in a lovely part of Berlin, a beautiful house with lovely gardens. I had a frank conversation with his wife—well, I had more than enough women in my life. But looking back, I'd have been quite well off if I'd taken up the offer.

By now I was living a lovely life. I'd sleep till about half past eleven in the morning, then Boscherling and I would go down to the Kurfürstendamm where we'd have lunch. We would invariably pick a couple of girls up and taken them back to the flat for the afternoon. We'd push them out of bed at about tea-time, four or five o'clock, and at about seven o'clock at night we'd go out for dinner. Afterwards I would invite more German girls in for a cup of tea or a drink, but some nights really I was so knackered I would just slap their thighs and say 'cheerio' and that was the end of it—I just hadn't the energy.

On top of that I still had my regular wartime German girl friend, a brunette, about 20, 21. She was a presentable girl, but friends told me she had 'traitorous eyes'. When I first knew her towards the end of the war she was working as a laboratory assistant at a place called Buch, just to the north of Berlin, where they did experiments on people. Her father worked for the equivalent of the German BBC as a personnel manager under Heinrich Himmler's brother, Ernst.

I never thought of going home to England. I had always regarded myself as a cosmopolitan. I was glad to be making money and living a good life. I couldn't have lived a life like that back in England. Above all—this is the strange thing, you see—I had found more freedom in Berlin than I had ever known before. I came from a narrow, repressive background. But in the ruins of Germany the permissive society was experienced long before it came to England. Out there in the shattered streets of Berlin I was my own man.

In due course big-timers more ambitious than Len Carpenter progressed from inter-zonal black-market business within Germany to international business outside Germany.

At the time of Germany's collapse the Reich held deposits of precious stones and metals (including gold, silver, platinum, radium and uranium) for trade and industry conservatively valued at $250 million (or at least £2,750 million today). By May 1945 some of these deposits had been variously hidden throughout Germany, while others were in the custody of various banks and firms in Berlin. However, as the organisation responsible for this wealth had disintegrated, the deposits slipped beyond Allied control after the war's end, only to resurface during the next twelve months in a large number of illegal transactions by black-market groups in which officers of the Allied Occupation took part. A Top Secret report by British agents of the Economic Information Section of the Control Commission in Berlin, dated 17 July 1946, outlined the situation.

In the summer of 1946 Allied intelligence organisations launched a special operation, codenamed Sparkler, aimed at the recovery of the German government's precious stone and metal holdings estimated to be worth £75 million (or over £825 million today). Operation Sparkler was placed on a Top Secret basis as it was already suspected that certain personalities in British Military Government could not be trusted and appeared to have been involved in irregularities involving £49.5 million worth of Reichsmarks in connection with the firm of Roges, the Nazi stock-piling firm for industrial metals and alloys. It was also known that two American officers of the Decartelisation Branch of American Military Government, besides being interested in the acquisition of precious stones and metals for their own ends, were involved with Germans in illegal transactions running into many millions of Reichsmarks, and including the acquisition of 20 kilos of platinum today worth the equivalent of £1.4 million for resale to the Russians (who had set up a semi-official agency in Berlin for buying up precious stones and metals and other commodities at very high prices and on a large scale).

During the course of Operation Sparkler a former head of the Precious Metals Department of the Reichsbank, Albert Thoms, who had a complete list of all gold and precious metal holdings lodged in German banks, was arrested. Meanwhile an informant of the Economic Information Section investigation team engineered an illicit sale of a kilo of platinum, the buyers of which later turned out to be the American officers.

Further investigations revealed that the same groups dealing in precious stones and metals were also involved in massive black-market trading in other commodities, including antiques, paintings, furs, carpets, property, opium, cocaine, penicillin, millions of Reichsmarks' worth of radium and nearly £13 millions' worth of optical instruments. These groups were very highly organised. The American connection, for example, had opened a large export–import business in New York, with agencies in Brussels and Paris and confederates in Germany who included former SS personnel and members of the Berlin municipal administration. British officials of the Control Commission were also involved in major illicit deals, or connived in them—as, for instance, the setting up of a whole plastics factory in Belgium by the American group, using machinery transported through the British zone in Russian lorries. Many of these transactions, ranging from industrial chemicals, explosives and railway locomotives to cars and watches, represented criminal offences under German and International law. The British Sector of Berlin had become the centre of these illegal dealings which, according to the report of 17 July 1946, 'have reached unprecedented proportions which threaten to ruin what remains of Germany's financial and economic structure.' Investigations incidentally revealed that even the Swedish Red Cross, the Chinese Military Mission and UNRRA were involved in large-scale black-market dealings in foodstuffs.

Little seems to have been done about this scandalous state of affairs—certainly not by the British. According to a report of the *Berliner Zeitung* on 21 April 1948 a Scotland Yard investigation was quashed by General Sir Brian Robertson, the British Military Governor, on the grounds that 'the revelation of these affairs would start a whole avalanche which could not then be stopped.' The paper alleged that a number of high officials in the

British Control Commission had been involved in the sale of Wehrmacht equipment 'which in an official report was stated to be twenty million pounds, while it was really, as revealed in the House of Commons, fifty-eight million pounds.' Furthermore an English Air Vice-Marshal and a Rear Admiral had shipped huge quantities of valuables stolen in Germany back to England for their own profit. Even the previous Military Governor of the British Zone, Marshal of the Royal Air Force Sir Sholto Douglas, was required to give evidence concerning the wholesale disappearance of art treasures and furniture from Geselfeld Castle, ancestral home of a distant relative of King George VI of England, at Buckeburg in Lower Saxony. When the Head of the Department for Internal Communication in the Control Commission, Julian Simson, tried to investigate these matters he met widespread passive resistance and was forced to resign. However, eight senior officials of the Control Commission, including the chief of the Metallurgical Branch, *were* taken to court to answer thirty-four charges which included conspiracy and illegal export of goods. 'The jobs held by the Britons called for a very high degree of honesty,' the court was told, 'but the abuse of them provided almost unlimited opportunities for private gain.'

Things had got so bad that the Assistant Chaplain-General to the British Occupation forces was compelled to declare, 'Germany will become the cess-pool of Europe.' With some justification he accused the armies of Occupation of exploitation and the corruption of German women. Unless they pulled themselves together, he warned, they would leave behind a shameful heritage in Germany. The British Army responded by reducing liquor supplies and sending its troops off to religious retreats for spiritual regeneration. But so long as the German population was obliged to starve and survive by barter, the black market would continue to be the warp and woof of life in Germany.

Aachen was the centre for black-market smuggling on a huge scale. Across the Dutch and Belgian borders whole columns of Germans, many of them small children, smuggled goods in bulk for the home black market, especially coffee. Fantastic profits could be made in black-market diamonds. In Berlin, where prices were always highest, speculators would pay as much as 50,000 marks for one carat—a black-market motor-car by comparison cost only 25,000 marks. Unusually, these speculators paid in crisp, new, apparently completely genuine Reichsmark notes. In fact these were not Reichsmarks at all but German Occupation marks, introduced into Poland by the Germans following the Polish defeat in 1939. After the German collapse in Poland some 30,000 million of these marks were bought for a song by Polish and Polish–Jewish entrepreneurs who swarmed into Berlin after the war with cases stuffed with them and proceeded to buy up all the gold and diamonds they could lay their hands on. A few were caught by the military police with fantastic sums in their flats, but most made their getaway with their fortunes intact.

Perhaps the most successful of all black marketeers in Germany was a Jewish DP, a survivor of the death camps, who got hold of a million sewing-machine needles after they had vanished from the Singer factory in Darmstadt while under American Military Government control. The DP was able to smuggle the needles to Italy and sell them to the Necchi Company in return for the American sales rights in the Necchi sewing machine. He then emigrated to America, set up a commission order office in New York, and within two years had made more than a million dollars.

But in general, it was the Allied soldiery that profited most easily from the German black market. At the black-market prices then prevailing, a packet of 20 cigarettes fetched $10, sometimes as much as $20; a candy bar $5; a bar of soap $3; a small bottle of perfume $150; a bottle of cognac, whisky or gin $75–$100; a camera $1,000. Every week an American soldier could buy 10 packets of cigarettes for 50c and sell them for $100—or $5,200 a year. He could sell his weekly issue of seven candy bars for another $1,820 a year, his minimum ration of four bottles of spirit per month for $4,800 a year. So far he would have made $11,726 profit on top of his take-home pay. But this was only a beginning. From the black-market sale of parcels from home he would reckon to net a further $20,000 a year, bringing his total trading profits to over $31,000—which in today's terms would be worth around $175,000. A British private who was sent 500 Gold Flake cigarettes for his birthday sold them to a German hairdresser in the Kaiser Allee for the equivalent in marks of £125—worth more than a year's wages in his pre-war job in Britain. More ambitious soldiers could improve on this figure by importing French lingerie and perfume or Swiss watches, and then investing some of the profits into profitable deals in antiques, Persian carpets, porcelain and so on. Even a really valuable diamond could be bought for a couple of pounds of coffee.

The Russians themselves were a further source of wealth to the Americans. It had always been the Allies' intention to replace Nazi currency with an Occupation currency common to all the zones. The original plan had been for all the notes to be printed in the USA, but early in 1945 the American government handed the Russians a set of printing plates so that they could print the new money themselves and reimburse the American Treasury afterwards. But instead of presenting a proper account of their new currency issue, the Russians printed an unlimited quantity of Occupation marks and used them to pay off their troops, most of whom had not been paid for months or even years. When pay day finally came the Russian soldiers' haversacks were stuffed to overflowing with American-origin Occupation marks. These marks had to be spent in Germany, since the Soviet government had issued orders that they could not be exchanged in Russia.

The result was a fantastic explosion of private dealing in goods and marks between Russian and American soldiers, especially in Berlin, where contact was closest. The Russians would pay $300 to $400 for an American fountain-pen, and as much as $1,000 for a simple Mickey Mouse watch from the PX. The Russian soldiers' demand for watches was inexhaustible and the American soldiers made fortunes out of it. In July 1945 they were paid nearly $1 million in Allied Occupation marks but sent home almost $3 million in hard currency dollars. The balance of $2 million came from Occupation marks acquired from the German black market and from the Red Army, converted perfectly legally into dollars in the Army Post Offices. In the first four months of the Occupation American military personnel sent home $11,078,925 more than they were paid. In October, $5,470,777 excess pay was sent back to the USA. When a maximum $100 was put on money orders, some men would fill in five hundred at a time. Before the breach was plugged, the total US Army liability to the US Treasury for Allied military marks without dollar backing totalled a staggering $300 million. In effect the American government had virtually paid off the Red Army's debts in Germany.

In November 1945 the Army and Treasury put an end to the loophole by decreeing that no American soldier could send home more than he had been paid (plus 10 per cent for gambling winnings). The American soldier countered this by converting his black-market earnings in marks into goods which could then be shipped home and sold at a good profit. No customs declarations were required for packages sent to the USA and soon a stream of valuables was pouring out of Germany and across the Atlantic. One man even sent home a dismantled German motor-cycle in three separate shipments. By the summer of 1946 Americans were buying an average of one million marks worth of antiques in Berlin each month, and one general was known to have sent home in a single shipment a total of 166 crates and boxes full of silver, tapestries, paintings and ceramics acquired from various German castles and estates and worth tens of thousands of dollars. Not everyone sent his ill-gotten gains home. In Berlin a few bought up apartments, and one became the owner of a cinema.

When two American economists arrived in Berlin from the USA in late 1945 to advise Military Government on war reparations problems in the American zone, they were dumbfounded. 'Those conditions,' they wrote,

> created an atmosphere so unreal, so nightmarish, so demoralizing that official work was almost impossible . . . The whole situation—the aftermath of the war—was such that it gnawed at all men's character like maggots. The ever-prevalent destruction all about, the demoralized state of the German people, and the demoralizing influence of the black market—the entire environment made life profoundly depressing. No one could escape the completely disillusioning conditions which prevailed. On first arrival one would refuse to believe what he heard. Then, as he began to see for himself, it was necessary to struggle with his own conscience, his own integrity, to

determine to what extent he would permit himself to be dragged into the cauldron.

But the black market was not the only cauldron.

When the soldiers of the Western Allies first entered Germany a very strict order was enforced forbidding them to fraternise with the enemy. American soldiers were required to carry this order—embodied in a pamphlet issued by the Morale Services Division of the War Department, entitled *A Pocket Guide to Germany*—inside the liner of their steel helmets. The order directed that outside the strict requirements of military duty they should have nothing to do with any German, be it man, woman or child. There was to be no shaking hands with Germans, no talking with them, no visiting German homes, no playing with German children, and, it went without saying, no going with German women. Germans were to be ignored, shunned. It had to be driven home to them as directly and harshly as possible that they had lost the war that they had started and that they must suffer the consequences. 'Don't get chummy with Jerry,' the Army newspaper *Stars and Stripes* exhorted its GI readers. 'In heart, body and spirit every German is Hitler,' the troops were warned. 'Don't make friends with Hitler. Don't fraternize. If in a German town you bow to a pretty girl or pet a blonde child, you bow to Hitler and his reign of blood.'

While the war still raged the non-fraternisation rule was generally observed and for a time the horror aroused by the discovery of concentration camps like Belsen and Buchenwald turned many soldiers against the German people as a whole. But such a ruling could not last, and once the war was over the rule was widely disobeyed. In the American zone it was estimated that some 90 per cent of the soldiers ignored it, especially black GIs, who were among the most enthusiastic fraternisers, and the first to coin the colloquial American English term of abuse 'motherfucker'.

Very soon the question of fraternisation boiled down to one thing—sexual relations between Allied soldiers and German Fräuleins. In US Army language 'non-fraternisation' became known as 'non-fertilisation' and Fräuleins as Furlines or Frowlines or Fraternazis. To go out with one was 'goin' frattin' ' and to go to bed with one was to 'frat'. In the British Army an army-issue cheese or corned beef sandwich—a proven way to a hungry Fräulein's heart—was known as a 'frat sandwich'. There was even a 'frat' song, set to the tune of 'Lilli Marlene', which went—

> Underneath the bushes,
> You take your piece of frat,
> You first take off your gas-cape
> And then remove your hat . . .

and continuing through half a dozen verses to conclude

> . . . And to your chums relate
> The total cost of all of it
> Just one chocolate date.

As far as Fräuleins were concerned the non-fraternisation law was unenforcible. Not since the days of Prohibition in America had a law been so flagrantly violated.

It is not hard to see why the German Fräulein was in such universal demand. She was often unemployed and homeless, usually hungry, cold in winter, and lonely. Many of the women were war widows or wives or girl friends of soldiers who were missing or prisoners of war. Some had children to look after. Many were prepared to become mistresses for a night, a month or eternity in return for cigarettes or a night in a warm room. As for the Allied soldiers, they were young, spirited, far from home and family ties—and well provided with the good things of life. The two, it seemed, were made for each other. No soldier need be without female company if he carried a few packs of cigarettes, or a can or two of bully beef, or a pair of silk stockings in his knapsack.

A young married English private soldier later recalled his poignant affair with an 18-year-old German girl in the ruins of Berlin in the autumn of 1945—an experience common to tens of thousands of Allied soldiers in those weird havoc days: 'She looked every bit like an English girl of twenty-two or three,' the soldier recalled:

Fair, with blue eyes, but very pale. I'd seen her several time in the same café drinking coloured water, and she'd always been alone. She couldn't speak a word of English and I couldn't speak any German. I met her several times and we always did the same thing, went to a cinema and had a drink or danced. All the time I could see she was hungry. Somehow I began to feel sorry for her; then I felt responsible for her. It was forbidden to go into German houses, but one night, because it was raining, she took my arm and led me to the block of flats where she lived. The block had been hit by artillery, the top rows were burnt out. She lived on the third floor. There were two rooms and a small kitchen. There were no panes in the windows. One room was a bedroom, but there were no beds, only two settees, which she pushed together. She had lived with her mother, whose photograph was there. Her mother had poisoned herself on 25 April, when the Russians were attacking Berlin. There was a photograph of her father. He had been killed. The Russians had taken much of the furniture for their barracks. The place was cold—no wood or coal. I made a sign to ask if there was any food in the house, and she thought I wanted to eat. She went to a cupboard. In the cupboard were a few potatoes, a cupful of flour and some salt. Half a loaf was wrapped in newspaper. I felt a bit sick at times about the power I had over that girl. If I gave her a three-penny bar of chocolate she nearly went crazy. She was just like my slave. She darned my socks and mended things for me. There was no question of marriage. She knew that was not possible.

The first two years after the war witnessed in Germany a social phenomenon without precedent in the history of modern Europe—that of universal concubinage, and 'frat' became synonymous with another more explicit four-letter word. This practice was widely observed from the lowest to the highest ranks of the Allied Armies. Among the top brass the spate of high-class German mistresses, many of them of dubious political background, threatened to spill over into public scandal. One general in US Army Intelligence, part of whose job was to root out such politically unwise liaisons, was himself deeply involved with the former mistress of Dr Joseph Goebbels, Hitler's Propaganda Minister, and once brought her over to New York for a 'furlough' in the Waldorf and Ritz hotels.

Bowing to reality the Allied commanders rapidly relaxed the non-fraternisation laws. First General Eisenhower conceded that it was permissible to talk to German children. In July troops were allowed to stand, walk or talk with German adults, but not hold their hands or sit on park benches with them. In August 1945 Eisenhower declared: 'Members of my command are now permitted normal human contacts.' On 1 October, 1945, non-fraternisation ceased to be an official Occupation policy. Shortly afterwards German girls were allowed to stay overnight in the men's quarters at the US Army HQ in Frankfurt, in spite of the strict security surrounding this nerve-centre of the American zone—much to the astonishment of the rest of the German populace, who began to believe that democracy was synonymous with corruptibility.

In December 1945 a German police official had stated: 'It is impossible to distinguish between good girls and bad girls in Germany. Even nice girls of good families, good education and fine background have discovered their bodies afford the only real living. Moral standards have crashed to a new low level. At the present rate, in two months I wonder if there will be a decent moral woman left.' By December 1946 the number of girls selling love for goods in Berlin was getting on for half a million—one-sixth of the total population of the city—compared with less than 50,000 during the war.

There were many cogent reasons why even good girls should become good-time girls in Germany at the end of the war. It was not simply because they were lonely and hungry, without money or a job. It was also because they had no future and had lost their self-respect. Berlin after the war was called a 'sentimental desert'. Everywhere women went about alone. When the winter came, one in three women in Berlin went out dressed in the trousers of her absent husband, brother or son. The catastrophic losses suffered by the German forces had produced a critical shortage of men in Germany, particularly in Berlin, where the number of men had been halved. In Tempelhof, for example, there were 717 girls but only 71 men between the ages of 18 and 21. Out of a population of 15,000 in Lichtenfelde, only 81 were males between 16 and 21. Overall, as a result of war casualties, there were nearly three women to every man (or seven million more women than men). Many of the men were in any case too old or too young to be supportive, many were wounded and maimed and nearly all were abject, penniless and unemployed, as bereft of money or work as the women, and often despised by the women on that account. Marriage bureaux sprang up in the ruins, but they met with scant success, and many couples were unable to produce evidence that their previous spouse— missing in the air raids, say, or at the front—was actually dead. Lesbian bars began to spring up in Berlin, as they had done after the defeat of 1918.

So in cellar dives and basement bars the tribe of Fräuleins mingled with the Allied soldiery and plied their trade in half-destroyed rooms among the ruins. 'At such places as Bobby's, The Tabasco, Rio Rita, Casino and Femina,' reported a British Intelligence colonel in Berlin early in 1946, 'young widows' who had yet to shed the mourning they wore for their dead soldier husbands, were partnering Allied officers, who gave them articles of food, either to eat or sell on the black market. The scenes in these halls were reminiscent of Bacchanalia, and depressed the democrat.'

Such were the insalubrious arenas where conquering male and conquered female collided in the pursuit of love and bread, and where five cultures—American, British, French, Russian and German—wrestled for rapport amid the cigarette smoke, the beer and body smells, the dance-band music and clink of glasses. In those low-lit low-life oases in the deserts of wretchedness outside, 'Viennese' bands and 'international' dance orchestras of emaciated German musicians in Hawaiian shirts gamely banged out mock be-bop, Kraut jazz and that evergreen GI favourite—'*In München steht ein Hofbraühaus, eins, zwei, g'suffa!*'—while ex-Volkssturm waiters scuttled about with trays of beer and highballs to American cries of '*Mak snell, mak snell!*' Here out-of-work sopranos from the State Opera House struggled with their G-strings in the strip-tease show, taciturn Red Army officers guzzled their way through gargantuan steaks they had foraged themselves, and English majors tossed down whiskies and sodas at a price that equalled the wage of a German supreme court judge. Here a vast army of foul-mouthed and extraordinarily resourceful and courageous German girls from every walk of life and class of society sat, drank, necked and jitterbugged with their foreign *Schatzis*, and from time to time babbled out in their bizarre parrot American– English such amorous innuendoes as: '*Kommon, Schatzi, you dutti Yanki bastid, less go ficken!*'

Perhaps never before in modern times had the womanhood of a nation fallen so low—or fought back so defiantly. James McGovern, who had served in American Intelligence in Germany, later recreated a scene outside one of these night spots which vividly encapsulated the fate of German women and of the German nation itself:

> There, lying on a slab of concrete six feet square, once part of the façade of a beauty salon, lay the constabulary private and his Frowline, half-hidden behind a pile of ruins. The young American was naked except for his combat boots and the bright yellow scarf round his neck. The Frowline, whose chubby, cheese-white body, and short, powerful piston-legs, completely enveloped him, was completely naked. A pitiless moon had suddenly emerged from behind black clouds to light up their bodies like a police spotlight.
>
> They lay coupling, groaning, moaning, on a concrete slab in bright moonlight in the dead centre of Berlin at the dead centre of a dead Germany . . . until the air was split by the Frowline's sudden wail of pleasure and pain. The grunts and moans stopped. The Frowline rose from the concrete altar of German–American relations. She stood like an avenging Valkyrie, an indestructible Earth-Mother, rising out of the Prussian soil, the bright moonlight shining on the red nipples of her sagging breasts, standing triumphantly over the jagged ruins, living proof that Germany, in whatever form, and by whatever terrible means, was going to survive.

'Frat' had some unfortunate by-products. Some twenty to thirty thousand illegitimate children were fathered in the American zone alone, and in Germany as a whole the number of illegitimate births rose by nearly 10 per cent. Venereal disease spread like a medieval plague till it had reached epidemic proportions, infecting an average of more than one in four of the troops in the American zone, and rising in a few units to 100 per cent. The women in Germany were as badly infected: nearly one-third of girls examined in a spot-check in Berlin in the first winter after the war were found to have the disease.

An Occupation officer in the British zone recalled that

> the Russians had brought over a particularly virulent type of Asiatic syphilis which was rather unpleasant because you tended to swell up. It was like elephantiasis, all your joints and limbs and face and everything swelled up—water, you see—and you just got bigger and bigger until you were just like a sort of Michelin man. Very different from the normal American blob-on-your-knob kind of stuff.
>
> Penicillin was around but not yet in general use at this time. At the end of the war the cure for VD was still very severe. If our soldiers got it there was not much quarter given. They got detention, they got sent to hospital, and they got given mercury treatment and the 'umbrella' and things like that—all quite horrific, really. So they had to be terribly careful. As a matter of course they were all given ET packets—ET stood for 'Early Treatment', I seem to remember—which were full of tubes and swabs for squirting and dabbing and so on, and a list of instructions as to what to do before, during, after and on the way home. French letters were on free issue, too. There was a great

black-market trade in French letters. Many Medical Officers augmented their income by trading army-issue French letters by the gross.

The size of the VD problem was brought home to me when I met my first Platoon Sergeant in Berlin. His wife was due to come out and join him in two days time and he told me that he'd got a full house—the clap. 'What the hell am I going to do?' he asked me. Well, we got it sorted out. His wife was put off and he was put in hospital to be cured by mercury treatment. But a lot of soldiers in the battalion were hardened cases who were known to have had VD eight or nine times and weren't deterred by it.

You see, once a German girl had got it she had no way of getting rid of it, really. It was no good going to a German doctor because very few German doctors could get hold of the penicillin, sulphur drugs and other medicaments in those days, except for black-market stuff smuggled out of Allied military hospitals. All the chemists sold was face cream and talcum powder—if you were lucky.

When the German men came home at last from the prison camps they were aghast at the behaviour of their womenfolk. Some were beaten, some were threatened, a few had their heads shaved as a punishment for collaborating with the Occupation troops. Angry posters appeared on walls and doors. One read (in English): 'What German women do makes a man weep. One bar of chocolate or one piece of gum gives her the name German whore. How many soldiers gave their lives for these women!' One letter written (in English) to a German girl in 1946, read: 'You are a very filthy creature, an American whore. Don't flatter yourself by thinking you are pretty. When one looks at your rouged-up puss one thinks they are seeing a worn-out cow. Just like you the following girls are hated.' The names of seven more German girls followed. In the first case of head-shaving ever heard before an American Military Government court (in Heidelberg) a 20-year old German ex-POW was accused of cutting off a girl's hair in the street with a pair of nail-clippers and was sentenced to nine months' imprisonment—the length of time it would take for the hair to regrow.

Back in the USA there was a vehement public reaction against the Fräuleins and the hold they were supposed to have on the GIs 'over there'. But it did little to change the attitude of the average GI. 'No one could help it,' stated one. 'The girls were pretty and they didn't wear much, and we'd been through hell, living hard, in the open.' Said another: 'When we came up against our first 19-year old Rhineland blonde with blue eyes, pink cheeks, plaits, and very desirable, we were just clean bowled over. There's no doubt about it we just had our frat.'

12

Purge

When the Occupation powers took over the running of Germany in the wake of the Third Reich's collapse they brought to their task two broadly opposite but complementary aims: to wipe out the past and build for the future. 'We shall obliterate Nazism and German Militarism,' Eisenhower had declared in his Proclamation to the German People. And at Potsdam the Allied leaders had promised: 'It is the intention of the Allies that the German people be given the opportunity to prepare for the eventual reconstruction of their life on a democratic and peaceful basis.' Like Hindu gods the new rulers of occupied Germany were avowedly both destroyers and creators. Though 'four-power control' was a failure and each power went its own way within each zone, it was agreed that there could be no future for the German people and no restoration of Germany to the community of nations without the eradication of Nazism and the restoration of democracy through re-education and the inauguration of new institutions. The trouble was that each power had a different view of the meaning of democracy and varying degrees of conviction as to the actual possibility of eradicating Nazism.

It was to prove easier, in the event, to eradicate the material products of Nazism than the Nazis themselves. What was left of Germany's military might was relatively easy to locate but harder to dispose of. Sometimes it was difficult and dangerous work. Hundreds of thousands of tons of ammunition had been stored in salt-mines in the north of Germany, in depots which could be nearly 3,000 feet deep. Sometimes they were booby-trapped, or the explosive material was in an unstable condition. Many of the mines were in the British zone where teams of Royal Engineers and Enemy Ammunition Depot Control Units worked for months and even years to clear them, using local German and Polish DP labour. Inevitably there were mishaps. Several mines blew up, sometimes with loss of life. In the summer of 1946, 9,000 tons of explosives blew up while being removed from a deep mine near Hanover, killing over eighty German and Polish workers, all of them resident in the area. An even bigger explosion took place on 18 April 1947 when the fortifications and U-boat pens on the German island of Heligoland were demolished with a gigantic explosive charge of 3,797 tons of TNT set off by a Royal Navy demolition team on a ship lying nine miles out to sea. This was the largest conventional (i.e. non-nuclear) explosion ever recorded and changed the physical character of the island. (Along with other major man-made tremors in occupied Germany, such as those caused by the blowing-up of the underground war factory at Haslach in the Black Forest, the Heligoland blast was used by British scientists for the study of seismic waves.)

Not only U-boat pens were destroyed. Some 156 U-boats of the undefeated U-boat navy were towed thirty miles north of Malin Head, Northern Ireland, and sunk by their British captors, while 221 other U-boats were scuttled at sea by their own crews. Munitions factories, minefields, rocket sites, and all the rest of the installations and paraphernalia of the German military machine were removed, along with the outward symbols of Hitler and his National Socialists. Nazi flags, portraits and emblems, Nazi street-names, text-books and uniforms were smashed, burned or pulped. Hitler's Chancellery in Berlin was rased and his bunker blown up with high explosive by the Russians. The ruins of his house on the Obersalzberg were blown up by the Bavarian government. As for his body, which had been retrieved by SMERSH intelligence officers of the Red Army shortly after the surrender of Berlin, this was eventually removed to an unknown hiding-place in the USSR, so that the Germans might be permanently deprived of a martyr's relics. 'Like Alaric, buried secretly under the river-bed of Busento,' wrote Hugh Trevor-Roper, the British Intelligence officer who was detailed to investigate the details of the Führer's fate, 'the modern destroyer of mankind is now immune from discovery.'

What the Allies did not destroy, they kept—from Hitler's scorched cadaver to the secrets of the V-2 and the super cannon. Often in desperate competition with each other, teams of American, British and Soviet scientists and investigators in uniform raced through Germany in a scramble for German military and technological secrets and hardware. During the drive into Germany and the early weeks of the occupation the T (Target) Sub-Division of SHAEF sent out special T-Forces of American and British investigators who examined some three thousand planned targets and discovered two thousand more. High on their list of targets were jet- and rocket-propelled aircraft, naval equipment (including the revolutionary new Walter U-boats), synthetic rubber and oil catalysts, supersonic wind tunnels, patent records, documents and scientific and industrial personalities who were experts in biological and

chemical warfare, ballistics, bomb sights, poison gases, radar, communications systems, and much else besides. The most prized target of all
was the huge underground V-2 rocket plant at Nordhausen in the Harz
Mountains, from which four hundred tons of equipment were removed for
shipment to the USA. As well as the V-2s, T-Forces located over four
hundred scientists who had helped develop the rockets under Werner von
Braun. The first fruits of this rich haul, which was to lead directly to the
space flights and ballistic missiles of today, came in October 1946, when a
wartime V-2 rocket with a solar spectograph in its tail-fin climbed to a
then-record height of 55 kilometres over New Mexico and took detailed
photographs of the sun. The Russians had their own form of T-Forces and
dispatched groups of German scientists to the Soviet Union with their
families, there to work in comfortable seclusion at twice the salaries of
their Russian colleagues. In general it could be said that the Allies made a
good job of demilitarising the former Reich by plundering and exploiting
what was of use to them and destroying what was not. The same dual
approach could be seen in their handling of the denazification programme,
which must rank as the greatest of all the Allies' failures during the
Occupation.

The idea of excluding former Nazis from positions of influence in post-war
Germany was theoretically feasible and desirable, but in practice it was an
unsatisfactory business. The sheer magnitude of the task was daunting.
The Nazi Party had had a total of twelve million members; in addition an
estimated three-quarters of the German population had at one time or
another been Nazi sympathisers and probably a proportion of the German
middle class were still Nazis at heart. Virtually the whole adult population
thus had to be screened.

In the American zone every German over the age of 18 had to answer a
questionnaire—a *Fragebogen* (or *Meldebogen*)—containing over 130
questions. These questions dealt with the person's past career and
affiliations, not only in relation to Nazi organisations but to income,
ownership of land, titles of nobility, education, military rank, civilian
employment, nature and size of business and much else besides. The
purpose of the *Fragebogen* was to determine whether the person
concerned had been associated with the Nazi Party or its supporters and
adherents (including the Junkers, the nobles, the industrialists and the
German General Staff) and, if so, to what degree. In the early days of
denazification most Germans attempted to tell the truth. The penalties for
not doing so were severe and in any case the Allies were able to check the
answers against a complete card index of Nazi Party members which had
been found waiting to be pulped in a paper-mill in Munich in the summer
of 1945. After the *Fragebogen* had been filled, it was assessed by a
denazification court and a classification was made within five categories:

major offender, offender, lesser offender, follower, and exonerated person. A variety of penalties, from imprisonment to fines, forfeiture of all property, forced labour and exclusion from every job except manual labourer, were provided for the first four categories.

In the American zone alone thirteen million questionnaires had to be distributed, filled in, processed and judged. The justice that was dispensed by the denazification courts on the basis of these questionnaires was by any standards a very rough and ready one. Not many of the Allied officials involved spoke German or understood the nuances of the Nazi background to each case. They were easily misled by informers who denounced individuals in order to settle old scores or gain advantage. They did not appreciate that some of the most culpable and Nazi-minded servants of the Third Reich may not have been members of the Party at all, or that membership alone did not make a person a real Nazi. Many of the Nazis penalised by the denazification courts were small fry, so called *Muss-Nazis*, like postmen, whose continuing employment was conditional on their joining the Party—as was that of judges and university professors. When the Germans began to see how many big Nazis escaped retribution, denazification became a joke. 'Did you play with toy soldiers as a child,' they quipped in a parody of the *Fragebogen* questionnaire. 'If so, what regiment?'

The Americans were by far the most zealous denazifiers among the four Occupation powers. By the time they had finished 930,000 sentences had been handed out to German nationals. Of those arrested for more serious Nazi or military crimes the Americans tried 169,282, the British only 22,296, the French 17,353 and the Russians 18,000. In the American zone denazification sentences had serious consequences for the future running of the zone. By Christmas 1945, 141,000 Germans had been dismissed from their jobs and thousands more languished in internment camps. This entailed the loss of 80 per cent of all the school-teachers in the zone, 50 per cent of all the doctors, and in some of the towns nearly 100 per cent of the public health staff—people whose services could not be spared given the conditions prevailing at the time.

The Germans had been told that the Allies would restore justice to Germany after the tyranny of the Nazi era. What they saw of denazification under the Occupation gave them no confidence that this would happen. To have the aristocratic prefixes '*von*' or '*zu*' before one's name, to have owned more than 250 acres of land, or been director of a firm employing more than 3,000 people or a member of the General German Staff, condemned a man in American eyes—even though many of the people who risked (and lost) their lives in the attempts to overthrow Hitler in 1938 and 1944 would have fallen into these categories. In the spring of 1946 a *cause célèbre* occurred when the Americans forbade Wilhelm Fürtwangler, the conductor of the Berlin Philharmonic Orchestra, to return to Berlin, on the grounds that he had performed during the Hitler regime and was therefore a tool of the Nazis. Though the decision was rescinded after a few weeks, the matter was long remembered with derision.

If the denazification process itself was unjust enough, the internment camps, certainly those in the American zone, were often an affront to civilised values. Some 150,000 suspected top Nazis, members of the SS and Gestapo, and high-ranking officers of the armed forces were incarcerated in these camps to await investigation and trial. A few of these places, like the one at Dachau, were former Nazi concentration camps. Some of them were run on distinctly Nazi lines by their American guards. Inmates were not allowed visits from their family or lawyers. They had nothing but the clothes they stood up in and they were forbidden to buy or forage for food. Some of the guards mistakenly believed that it was part of their job to give the Nazis a dose of their own medicine. Ernst von Salomon, a right-wing nationalist writer and old freedom-fighter of the 1920s, was arrested and thrown into such a camp near Nattenberg, north of Munich, with the Jewish woman with whom he had lived in the war. He later described his experiences in his book, *Die Fragebogen*. According to von Salomon, when they arrived at the camp, men and women were taken into a room where the men were beaten and the women raped by the military police before an excited audience of GIs staring through the window. Von Salomon himself had his teeth knocked out. When he picked himself off the floor, his face pouring with blood, he gasped to a gum-chewing officer who was looking impassively on: 'You are no gentleman.' Guffaws of laughter greeted this remark. 'No no, no! We are Mississippi boys!' the officer chortled proudly as they booted him out of the door. For eighteen months von Salomon was imprisoned in the camp without any charge being made against him or any interrogation being conducted. When he was finally released he emerged so emaciated that he looked like a skeleton. Other inmates have confirmed von Salomon's description of American internment. Carl Blessing, later President of the Bundesbank (Federal Bank of West Germany) admitted before his death in 1971 that he had been treated in just the same way.

The Nattenberg camp was not exceptional. Robert Murphy, political adviser to General Clay, the Military Governor of the American zone, reported:

> One day a senior American medical officer dropped into my Berlin office and said he wanted to show me something if I could spare an hour. We drove to an internment camp in the suburbs, where the occupants were 'little Nazis' awaiting classification. These were former Party members who held insignificant jobs in the Party organisation, including even charwomen in the Nazi offices. The commandant of the camp was a serious young American officer who showed us round conscientiously. I was startled to see that our

prisoners were almost as weak and emaciated as those I had observed in Nazi concentration camps. The youthful commandant calmly told us that he had deliberately kept the inmates on starvation diet, explaining 'These Nazis are getting a dose of their own medicine.' He so obviously believed he was behaving correctly that we did not discuss the matter with him. After we left, the medical director asked me: 'Does that camp represent American policy in Germany?' I replied that of course it was contrary to our policy. When I described the camp's conditions to Clay he quietly transferred the grim young officer to a post for which he was better suited.

On another occasion we were informed that the Nazi torture camp, equipped with devices to extort confessions, was still operating under American auspices. A zealous American intelligence officer had found out how effectively Nazi devices persuaded Nazis to confess their own misdeeds. He was chagrined when ordered to close this establishment.

In June 1946, under the 'Law for the Liberation from National Socialism and Militarism', the Americans turned over denazification proceedings in their zone to German tribunals whose members had themselves been denazified and were subject to Allied supervision. The Americans simply did not have the manpower to carry denazification through on their own, and in any case it was reckoned that Germans were better at assessing suspected Nazis than the Americans. But the task soon proved beyond the Germans' capacities. In the American zone Military Government Law No. 8 made it mandatory that anyone who had ever been a member of the Nazi Party had to be dismissed from his or her job and could only be re-employed as a manual labourer—a ruling which provoked widespread resentment. Though people born after 1 January 1919, were later exempted from denazification—the so-called 'youth amnesty'—this still left 3,000,000 chargeable and 72,000 in prison awaiting trial. By January 1947 there were 450 German denazification tribunals in action in the American zone. Over 200,000 cases had been tried and 370,000 Nazis had been removed from their jobs; but 1,300,000 cases still remained to be heard and the internment camps were still full of desperate SS men—many of whom had been drafted into the Waffen-SS whether they liked it or not—who at the present rate of processing would have five more years behind barbed wire before their cases could be heard.

So the tribunals dragged on. At its peak there had been 545 tribunals at work in the American zone with a staff of 22,000, yet by the time the Occupation era was over denazification was an admitted failure. It was too broad a programme and it had gone on too long. By 1950, a year after the Western zones of Germany had evolved into the Federal German Republic, and the denazification programme had ground to a halt, the American High Commissioner, John J. McCloy, reported that thirteen million had been involved in denazification in the former American zone—the most extensive legal procedure ever undertaken. Over a quarter of the population, 3,700,000 people, had been found chargeable, and the great majority of them had been tried by special courts known as *Spruchkammern* and 930,000 sentenced. In retrospect, it would have been better to have punished the real activists more swiftly and left the great mass of lesser Nazis alone. As it was, the reverse was true. Lesser offenders were brought to trial and often punished severely. Major offenders, with complex cases and hefty dossiers, were able to postpone their trials and get off lightly when the initial hatred and hostility died down. By 1950, indeed, it seemed that the ex-Nazis had won out. Of Party officials removed in Bavaria 85 per cent had been reinstated; 60 per cent of the civil servants of Baden-Württemberg were ex-Nazis. In contrast the officials of the denazification tribunals became the new outcasts of society and found it hard to obtain jobs. As soon as the western Allies relinquished all control over the young democracy of West Germany, the old brigade of the Third Reich era began to seep back into positions of prominence and power. Old Nazis gave jobs to other old Nazis, and before long a large proportion of the West German civil service, foreign office and legal system consisted of people who had served in the Hitler regime. Thus the Hitler state, which it had taken a world war to remove, remained *in situ* in post-war Germany: Not an evil memory, but flesh and blood. Even the outright criminals, the sadists and psychopaths remained at large in comfortable bourgeois anonymity.

In spite of denazification and Allied propaganda about the horrors of the concentration camps, the majority of the German populace remained surprisingly unconvinced about the evils of Nazism and the moral responsibility of the German nation for what had been done in its name. According to intelligence surveys in July 1945, the Germans looked back on the Hitler era as being a beneficial one and blamed their hardships under the Occupation on the fact that the Allies could not run things as well as the Nazis had. Six months after the end of the war the US Army Information Control Division ran an opinion poll which revealed that 50 per cent of all the Germans polled still thought that 'National Socialism was a good idea badly carried out' and only 40 per cent thought it a 'bad idea'. At the same time 70 per cent rejected the idea that Germany had in any way been responsible for the war, while only 20 per cent accepted responsibility. By 1948 a similar poll revealed the alarming fact that the percentages had hardly changed—even after three years of denazification.

In the Soviet zone, the future German Democratic Republic of East Germany, the purging of Nazism was undertaken differently, though the final effect was much the same as in the western half of the country. Instead of an elaborate legal process of denazification, the Soviets went in for extermination or elevation. SS men who had been denounced were summarily executed and their bodies dumped in the streets with an X stitched across their backs by machine-gun bullets. Members of the German armed forces, whether they were Party members or not, were deported to the Soviet Union as forced labour, or dragooned into work-gangs in the ruined cities of Germany. But Nazis who could be of use to their new masters and were prepared to serve under them were able to make an easy passage from one totalitarian system to another. When Molotov jeered at the ineffective denazification programme of the Western Allies at the Foreign Ministers' Conference in Moscow in 1947, the British Foreign Secretary, Ernest Bevin, riposted with a list of top-ranking Nazis now serving the Russian cause in the Eastern zone—men like Markgraf, former SS commander on the Eastern Front, now Chief of Police in Berlin, and Lundwehr, former Nazi Trade Commissioner in the Balkans, now head of the Economics Department of the Berlin city government. Even the head of the Gestapo, General Heinrich Müller, last seen in the Berlin bunker shortly before Hitler's suicide, was reportedly working as an adviser on state security in the USSR. 'As we are unlikely to be affected politically,' a Soviet officer was recorded as saying, 'we use the brains of the Nazis as much as possible.'

The denazification of former Nazi Party members and associates was one thing; the investigation and prosecution of war criminals was another. It was estimated that no less than a quarter of a million Germans had been directly involved in the murder of millions of men, women and children in Europe. The great majority of them were not punished. Many of them escaped investigation altogether and are now flourishing in industry, banking and government in West Germany, while in the early 1960s more than sixty former Party members who had helped in the Hitler regime were Ambassadors of the West German government. Thanks to the cynicism and pragmatism of the Allied authorities justice was not done. There were two main reasons. One was that many Nazi war criminals had expertise which was desperately needed by the Occupation authorities for rebuilding Germany after the war. The second was that the Allies were sick to death of the war and wished to rid themselves of further entanglements in the aftermath of it. This was particularly true of the British.

At a summit meeting with Roosevelt in June 1942 Winston Churchill had proposed setting up an international agency—later known as the United Nations Committee on War Crimes—which would assemble evidence and witnesses in preparation for post-war trials of those responsible for war crimes against Allied nationals. 'Retribution for these crimes must henceforward take its place among the major purposes of the war,' he declared four months later. In Britain the Foreign Office was made responsible for the organisation of the Commission and planning the work. The trouble was that ever since the beginning of the war the Foreign Office had been opposed to a war-crimes policy of any description. This view was shared by the Foreign Secretary, Sir Anthony Eden, who protested: 'I am most anxious not to get into the position of breathing fire and slaughter against war criminals and in a year or two find pretext for doing nothing.' Basically the Foreign Office did not want a repetition of the 'Hang the Kaiser' campaign after the First World War which ended so humiliatingly in the failed and derided war-crimes trials at Leipzig in 1921.

Nevertheless, the Foreign Office's reservations were brushed aside by Churchill and the Allied commitment to prosecute the Germans responsible for the murder of over ten million Europeans was broadcast throughout the continent. The Foreign Office, however, knew that the commitment was going to prove a hollow one. For one thing, the Russians who had borne the brunt of the mass killings and other atrocities, refused to join the Commission because they believed the British were more interested in talking than in doing, and this was undoubtedly true—the Foreign Office prevaricated mightily. They refused to hand over the list of war criminals which had been compiled up to that date and they refused to allow mass atrocities to be considered as war crimes. Crimes could only be listed if the evidence was highly detailed (under most circumstances a virtual impossibility) and if the victim's nationality was known (since crimes against Axis nationals were not to be investigated). Even organisations like the Gestapo could not be presumed to be collectively guilty. More seriously, the Foreign Office rejected a proposal to have the Commission's investigative agents attached to SHAEF. In all, the obstructive attitude of the Foreign Office threatened to cripple the Commission altogether. In August 1944, following the commotion aroused by the news that the Nazis were planning to arrest half a million Hungarian Jews and deport them to concentration camps in Poland, the Commission gave its first Press conference. It was a disaster. The head of the Commission admitted that the list of war criminals was very short—in fact it only had 184 names on it—and that Adolf Hitler was not on it. The Western world now knew that next to nothing had been done to further Churchill's promise of retribution.

By now the whole issue was become an operational matter of some urgency. Reports of elaborate Gestapo and SS escape organisations were reaching Allied intelligence. Neutral countries had not declared publicly that they would refuse asylum to Nazi war criminals who sought refuge across their borders. Since the Foreign Office rejected the idea of an investigatory agency to accompany the Allied Expeditionary Force to track down the wanted men, the military would have to do it themselves, and this they were disinclined to do. The Minister for War had been advised against the War Office being saddled with such a massive responsibility at the last minute, and only accepted responsibility for war crimes against British subjects, which formed a tiny minority of cases. The Foreign Office continued to be indifferent to the subject.

It was believed that there were only between one and two hundred criminals involved and all that had to be done was identify them amongst the mass of German prisoners. Not until March 1945, when the Allies had crossed the Rhine and were already racing across Germant to the Elbe, did the British decide to set up a special organisation in the Adjutant-General's Department to deal with the war-crimes problem. Its brief was to ensure that the British commitment to war crimes was 'not to be bigger than absolutely necessary'. More war criminals were expected to be in the American zone so the Americans could undertake the lion's share of the action. The Judge Advocate-General, Sir Henry McGeogh, was himself reluctant to become involved in war crimes work and deliberately constructed a tortuous procedure for the preparation of each trial.

The British and Americans were ill prepared when work started. A Central Registry of War Criminals and Security Suspects, or CROWCASS for short, which was to become the largest register of criminals in the world, was set up in Paris but from the beginning proved incapable of coping with the task and produced a list of suspects that for the time being was valueless. The US Army's programme in Germany lacked a clear policy for prosecution. Investigators in the field, many of them soldiers who overnight had become detectives, were not properly trained and produced cases which could not be brought to trial because of insufficient evidence. By August 1945 not a single German had yet been tried in the American zone for war crimes and atrocities. This was attributed to lack of organisation, equipment and trained staff—deficiencies which likewise handicapped the British war crimes headquarters at Bad Oeynehausen, whose head complained to the War Office at Christmas 1945: 'We have nothing, not even a typewriter.'

The first test was Belsen. The initial reaction of the War Office to news of this place was to deny that any war crimes had been committed at Belsen at all. In any case, they said, the victims were not British nationals (in fact several were). But the reality of a concentration camp in British Army hands, and a total death toll of over 70,000, could not easily be brushed aside. Whatever the War Office in London felt or said, the people on the spot, the Judge Advocate-General's department in Germany, could not ignore the horrors of the case and felt compelled to hunt down those responsible. But they were not equipped for the task. 'The evidence flowed in like a deluge and we were submerged by it,' recalled a JAG lawyer, Colonel Gerald Draper. 'We were failing because the wave of criminality was so great and our resources were so inadequate.' In the face of deliberate prevarication by the JAG department in London, which took up to two months to vet the sworn statements of evidence by inmates of the Belsen camp, the witnesses were allowed to leave rather than wait almost indefinitely at the place of their captivity and torture. In desperation the JAG in Germany sent a cable to London: 'There is a need for rapid action before there is any weakening of the present determination on the part of the public that war criminals be brought to justice.' The response of the Adjutant-General was to go off on two weeks' holiday in a huff.

The Belsen trial, the first major war-crimes trial in occupied Germany, opened on 17 September 1945 at Lüneburg in the British zone. On trial were Josef Kramer and forty-four of his staff. The purpose of their arraignment was threefold: to punish the guilty; to demonstrate to the German people what had been perpetrated in their name; and to provide them with an example of impartial justice under the aegis of a democratic court. Tragically, the trial achieved none of these goals and was to prove a disaster for the image of British justice. Kramer and his guards were not charged with murder but with having ill-treated the camp's inmates and having failed to provide for their well-being. The British Army officers who acted as defence lawyers used techniques which, though routine enough in an ordinary trial in Britain, seemed outrageous, even sick, in the context of the Holocaust. They set out to establish that the camp inmates who gave evidence against their SS torturers were liars. They justified the beatings by claiming that the prisoners had to be restrained because of the shortage of food. They exonerated Kramer's brutality because he had to deal with 'the dregs of Eastern Europe'. At the end of the trial eleven of the accused were sentenced to death, nineteen to prison terms ranging from one year to life, and fifteen were acquitted.

There was an international outcry at both the verdict and the conduct of the trial. There was also concern at home. The Prime Minister, Clement Attlee, expressed his concern at the delays that had occurred in prosecuting the Belsen criminals and urged that war-crimes investigations be given a high priority. Sir Hartley Shawcross, the Attorney General, and Ernest Bevin, the Foreign Secretary, agreed—unlike their predecessors. But the failure of the War Crimes Commission and the War Office to set up any organisation for the investigation of war crimes left the British Army in Germany in a poor position to follow up this more positive attitude. Only after the discovery of Belsen did the British Army organise three war crimes investigation teams, each of four men, to undertake what amounted to the biggest manhunt in history. (The Americans had twelve teams). There had been 81 camps like Belsen in the British zone. Only three had been investigated and only 50 of the 20,000 SS staff had been arrested. The War Office, moreover, continued to sabotage the efforts of Hartley Shawcross and the British Cabinet in their efforts to increase the rate of prosecutions for war crimes in Germany. 'There are tens of thousands of Germans responsible for millions of murders,' Shawcross had declared at an inter-departmental meeting in London following the Belsen trial. 'We must set ourselves an absolute minimum of prosecuting at least 10 per cent of those criminals in the British zone. I am setting as an irreducible minimum that we try 500 cases by 30 April 1946.'

But by the beginning of 1946 only twenty cases involving ninety-one war criminals had been tried, and investigations into thirty of the concentration camps in the British zone had been terminated because of lack of evidence.

Many of the most wanted Nazis succeeded in getting clean away—some by living under assumed names in Germany, some by escaping abroad, generally to the Middle East (Egypt and Syria), or to South America (where Argentina and later Paraguay granted them political asylum). Escapes for top Nazis had been arranged some weeks before the German collapse and the people involved provided with large sums of money, false papers and useful addresses abroad. Several Nazi escape organisations have been named from time to time, including Die Spinne, Die Schleuse, Kreis Rudel, Stille Hilfe, Bruderschaft, Verband Deutscher Soldaten or Kamaradschaftswerk—and, more popularly Odessa.

There were three main routes abroad. The first led from Germany to Austria, then to Italy, then to Spain; the second led via Austria and Italy to the Middle East; the third led via Austria and Italy to South America. The routes out of Germany seemed generally to take the same courses southwards. They all initially focused on Memmingen in the Allgäu, a secluded wooded region in southern Bavaria near the Austrian and Swiss borders. From there the route led to Lake Constance, where it divided into two, one route leading to Switzerland, the other to Innsbruck in Austria and thence to Italy via the Brenner Pass. In Italy the main goal was nearly always Rome, for no organisation gave greater help to escaping Nazi criminals than the Vatican in that city. During the war Pope Pius XII, who was both pro-German and anti-Semitic, had condoned the extermination of the Jews and the gypsies and the Nazi murder of millions of Russians and Poles (both Christians and Jews) on the grounds that the Nazis were the main bulwark against the godless Bolsheviks and that any protest to Hitler might threaten the future of Catholics in Germany. After the war a number of the Pope's officials in the Vatican (almost all of them Germans and Austrians) quite deliberately set out to aid individuals implicated in Nazi crimes. A number of national committees were set up in Rome to help their own fugitive nationals down the Vatican escape route—not just Germans but refugees from Stalin and Tito as well. A Papal Assistance Agency was established for such fugitives, with warehouses full of clothes, food, toilet articles and 2½ million cigarettes left behind by the Brazilian Army (which had fought with the Allies in the Italian Campaign). Escaping Nazis were welcomed by the Catholic clergy, who accompanied them to Rome dressed in monks' habits, gave them money and sheltered them in convents and monasteries. The principal escape organiser in the Vatican was the pro-Nazi Rector of the Santa Maria del Anima, Bishop Alois Hudal, who was also priest–confessor to the German Catholic community in Rome. This was the man who arranged accommodation for the fugitives, gave them meal tickets for lunch at a mess run by nuns, provided them with money (generally $100), a false International Red Cross passport, an entry visa to a foreign country, a boat ticket, and generally a job in the country to which they were going.

Among the Germans who benefited from this *Römischen Weg* (Via

Romana, or Roman Way) escape-route were two of the most wanted Nazi criminals of all—Franz Stangl, the Commandant of the Sobibor and Treblinka extermination camps, and Adolf Eichmann, who was responsible for the running of the Jewish extermination programme. Stangl, who was responsible for the murder of about one million human beings, was captured by the Americans shortly after the end of the war and put in an SS camp at Bad Ischl, in Austria, under his real name. In July 1945 he was transferred to another camp at Glasenbach and kept there until May 1946. Although some American officers knew that he was the commandant of Treblinka death camp, he was arraigned not for this but for his work on Hitler's euthanasia programme. At the end of May 1948 he escaped from an open prison in Linz, Austria, crossed the Tyrol and entered Italy. From Florence he took a train to Rome, where he contacted Bishop Hudal. This obliging cleric duly provided the mass murderer with a Red Cross passport, an entry visa to Syria, $100, a boat ticket and a job in a textile mill in Damascus. In May 1949 Stangl was joined by his family in Syria and in 1951 was granted a visa, made out in his real name, to emigrate to Brazil. In Brazil, still using his real name, he was able to get a good job as an engineer at the Volkswagen plant in São Paulo and lived in reasonable contentment with his family until he was arrested in 1967 by the DOPS (the Brazilian Alien Police) and extradited to Germany to stand trial. Sentenced to life imprisonment in 1970, Stangl died in prison in Düsseldorf in 1971.

At the end of the war Adolf Eichmann, head of Section B-4 of Bureau IV of the RHSA (Head Office for Reich Security) and the man responsible for the practical implementation of the Final Solution of the Jewish Problem, was at Alt-Aussee in the Austrian Alps, where his RHSA boss, Ernst Kaltenbrunner, had taken refuge. Shortly after the end of the war he was captured by American troops and thrown into a prison camp for SS men. The Americans did not know who he was, but several of the inmates did, and it was they who early in 1946 helped him escape after his name had begun to crop up with uncomfortable frequency during the trial of the major war criminals at Nuremberg. For the next four years he lived on Lüneberg Heath, fifty miles south of Hamburg, where he worked as a lumberjack under the name of Otto Heninger. Early in 1950 he got in touch with the Römischen Weg organisation and in May was passed through Austria to Italy. In Rome a Palatinate priest, Father Anton Weber, of the St Raphael Society, who knew his true identity and the nature of his crimes, gave him a refugee passport in the name of Richard Klement and shipped him to Buenos Aires in July.

In Buenos Aires Eichmann obtained identity papers and a work permit in the name of Ricardo Klement. He worked in a laundry and on a rabbit farm and after his wife and children joined him there in 1952 he got his first steady job in the Mercedes-Benz factory as a mechanic. He lived a dreary life in one of the poorer suburbs of Buenos Aires, and never took great pains to hide his identity—certainly the city's Nazi colony knew precisely who he really was. So did the Time–Life correspondent in Buenos Aires, who was offered his life story in 1956. It was surprising, therefore, that it took the Israeli Secret Services so long to track him down. Not until May 1960 was he kidnapped and flown out of the country to stand trial in Jerusalem for his complicity in the murder of over five million Jews. In May 1962 he was hanged for his crimes.

Many top Nazis fared better and got clean away. The most notable of these, probably, was the Chief of the Gestapo, Heinrich Müller, who succeeded in escaping without trace and was thought to have been given employment by the Russians in the Soviet zone of Germany and later in Albania. No Nazi criminal, however, has raised greater public interest than the infamous SS Head Doctor at Auschwitz, Dr Joseph Mengele, the so-called Angel of Death, a Nazi who had performed many horrendous medical experiments on inmates at the Auschwitz death camp. Between 1945 and 1948 Mengele lived in Czechoslovakia, Austria and Switzerland. In 1948 he returned to Germany with an International Refugee Organisation pass made out in his real name and in the summer of 1950 acquired a West German passport also made out, unbelievably, in his real name. With this he travelled to Italy in the course of 1950, and the following year travelled to Marseilles where he caught a ship bound for Tangier, and thence to Argentina. In Buenos Aires Mengele joined the family agricultural machinery firm of Karl Mengele & Sons, again in his real name. After his arrest and extradition was demanded by the West German government in 1959 he went to ground, allegedly under the protection of the Römischen Weg. In fact this organisation no longer existed in its original form. Instead, fugitive Nazi VIPs and fascist Croats, Italians, Belgians, Norwegians, Dutch and French belonged to an organisation called SDI (Sicherheitsdienst International) designed to protect them from secret agents, especially Israeli ones. Mengele then fled to Paraguay, where he is still believed to be living. All attempts so far to kidnap him and bring him out of the country to stand trial have failed.

Strangely, though the topmost Nazis of the Third Reich had been provided with the means of making good their escape at the end of the war, none of them succeeded—indeed hardly any of them tried. The top four—Hitler, Himmler, Goebbels and Bormann—killed themselves. The rest were easily found. Some of them, like Dönitz, Keitel and Jodl, had been in direct contact with the Allies and were simply put under arrest, others just waited resignedly at home for whatever fate had in store for them. At the end of the war few expected they would be put on trial for their lives. But that is precisely what happened.

The trials of the major Nazi war criminals at Nuremberg, which opened on 20 November 1945 before the International Military Tribunal, were seen by the victorious allies as a symbolic act of collaboration which was intended to promulgate a new law for the society of nations.

The indictments with which the Nazi leaders were charged fell into two parts. One part charged the defendants with having committed war crimes and crimes against humanity. In fact, the aberrations of the Nazi regime were so monstrous that it could be argued that only by bringing such charges could the conscience of the human race ever be cleansed at all. The other part of the indictment, however, was more controversial, for it charged the defendants with something quite different—with waging aggressive war (i.e. crimes against peace) or conspiring to wage it. Many observers of the trials felt uneasy about this, for it could be argued that such charges could be laid at the feet of the military leaders on the Allied side as well.

The trial of the leaders of a vanquished nation was without precedent in the modern history of the West. Although both Napoleon and Kaiser Wilhelm II had been branded as war criminals by their enemies, neither had ever formally been charged under law. But the concept of war crimes' trials was not altogether new and was not invented simply for the sake of bringing top Nazis to book. After World War One, for example, the Allies had drawn up a list of nine hundred Germans to stand trial as war criminals, including the military leaders, Hindenburg and Ludendorff (though eventually only sixteen, including U-boat officers who had violated the rules of war, were brought to court). In the 1920s and 1930s the Americans had been foremost in campaigning against military aggression and affirming the criminality of going to war. In 1932, for example, White House cabinet minister Henry Stimson had declared war 'illegal throughout practically the entire world ... It is an illegal thing.' In 1945 at Nuremberg the American prosecutor Robert Jackson described the trials as 'mankind's desperate effort to apply the discipline of the law to statesmen who have used their powers to attack the world's peace.' The British prosecutor, Sir Hartley Shawcross, put forward the same view: 'It is a fundamental part of these proceedings,' he said, 'to establish for all time that international law has the power to declare that a war is criminal.'

The Nuremberg trials conducted jointly before four judges (with four deputies) represented the four victorious allied powers, the USA, Great Britain, France and the Soviet Union. The President of the Tribunal was Lord Justice Lawrence, one of Britain's leading jurists. It was made clear from the outset that it was not the German people who were on trial, but their leaders. The defendants were to be tried not only as individuals but as symbols. Hans Fritzsche, the relatively inoffensive head of the German Broadcasting Service, was brought to court as proxy-defendant for the dead propaganda minister, Joseph Goebbels. Similarly, when it was ruled that Alfried von Krupp, the arms tycoon, was too old and senile to stand trial, the prosecutors wanted his son, Gustav, to stand trial in his place as a symbolic head of the German armaments and munitions industry. (In the end, Alfried von Krupp was tried by a later American court and sentenced to twelve years' imprisonment and confiscation of his property.)

Twenty-three men were listed to be tried at the Palace of Justice in Nuremberg, but in the end only twenty-one actually ended up in the dock, since the alcoholic Robert Ley, the Nazi Labour Leader, hung himself before the trial began, and Martin Bormann could not be found and was tried in absentia.* The defendants, who had until recently enjoyed immense power and privilege as leading members of the Third Reich, were now kept in solitary confinement in primitive stone-floored cells in Nuremberg Prison (adjacent to the Court Room) where they lived lives which were both austere and humiliating. The military men were deprived of their rank and status. No talking was allowed between prisoners at any time, except in the dock. At nights they were kept under permanent surveillance and had to sleep with their faces and hands always visible to their guards. They were marched into the court in fours, into the showers in twos, and into the small counsel room, where they could discuss their cases with their lawyers, in twelves. Their food was plain—watery soup, vegetables, potatoes, powdered eggs and coffee. On this regimen, and deprived of the narcotic drugs to which he had been long accustomed, Goering lost weight rapidly; the more his body shrank the sharper his wits became, till he emerged (in Sir Hartley Shawcross's view) as the most dominating personality in the courtroom.

The Nuremberg trials were a prodigious exercise in logistics and cost the formidable total of $4,435,719. Each of the four prosecutors had a staff

---

* The defendants were—Herman Goering (former Luftwaffe Chief, Reichsmarschall, and President of the Reichstag); Rudolf Hess (formerly Hitler's Deputy); Joachim von Ribbentrop (former Foreign Minister); Constatin von Neurath (former Foreign Minister and Ambassador to England and Italy); Franz von Papen (Reich Chancellor before Hitler and Ambassador to Austria and Turkey during the Nazi regime); Alfred Rosenberg (Reichsminister for the Eastern Occupied Countries and chief Nazi ideologist); Hjalmar Schacht (before the war President of the Reichsbank and Economics Minister); Walter Funk (Schacht's wartime successor); Wilhelm Frick (former Minister of the Interior and Reich Protector of Bohemia and Moravia); Baldur von Schirach (Hitler Youth Leader and Gauleiter of Vienna); Ernst Kaltenbrunner (Head of the RHSA, including the Secret Police, Gestapo, Security Services, extermination camps, etc); Julius Streicher (Gauleiter of Franconia and Nazi's chief Jew-baiter); Wilhelm Keitel (Field Marshal, Chief of Staff of the High Command of the German Armed Forces); Alfred Jodl (Chief of the Operations Staff of the High Command of the Armed Forces); Erich Raeder (former C-in-C of the German Navy); Karl Dönitz (Raeder's successor and Hitler's successor, former Commander of the U-Boat Navy); Hans Frank (Hitler's lawyer as Minister of Justice and Governor-General of Occupied Poland); Artur Seyss-Inquart (Austrian Chancellor, and deputy Governor of Poland, Reichskommissar of Holland); Albert Speer (Minister of Arms and Munitions); Fritz Sauckel (Plenipotentiary for the Allocation of Labour—i.e. slave labour); and Hans Fritsche (Head of German Radio Propaganda).

of some six hundred. A corps of interpreters provided simultaneous translations in any language spoken in court. Many tons of documents were processed during the preparations of the prosecutors' briefs, and by the time the trial had ended the court transcripts totalled ten million words. The accused underwent continuous psychological investigation, which included intelligence tests—the professional Jew-baiter, Streicher, achieved the lowest score with 106, the banker Schacht the highest with 143, narrowly beating Goering and Dönitz, who both scored 138. The security arrangements were formidable. Sherman tanks guarded the Palace of Justice and American soldiers armed with machine-guns crouched at the ready behind sandbag emplacements in the courtyard and corridor. Every spectator coming into the courtroom was screened and searched by military policemen.

Day by day for month after month, an endless stream of witnesses, documents, photos and newsreels revealed the disgusting and unimaginable nightmare of the Holocaust and the terror war launched by the Nazi tyranny. The evidence constituted an almost limitless inventory of infamy. 'A thousand years will pass,' even the notorious Nazi Governor-General of Poland, Hans Frank, was to comment, 'and still this guilt of Germany will not have been erased.'

Considering the circumstances, the trial was conducted with reasonable, though not meticulous, fairness. The Allies were determined to have Nazi blood even before the trial began and in the event they got it. Judgement was passed on 1 October 1946. Eleven of the twenty-one accused were sentenced to death (Goering, Keitel, Kaltenbrunner, Rosenberg, Frank, Frick, Streicher, Seyss-Inquart, Jodl, von Ribbentrop and Sauckel), seven to prison sentences ranging from ten years (for Dönitz) to life (for Hess, Raeder and Funk). Three—von Papen, Schacht and Fritsche—were acquitted, to the outrage of the Russian and American prosecutors.

President Truman thought the trials blazed a new trail to international justice and Walter Lippmann, the American political commentator, compared them to the Magna Carta, Habeas Corpus and the Bill of Rights. But not everybody was happy about the outcome of the Nuremberg trial. The Russians, who had wanted all the defendants executed, were upset at the verdicts. The German people, who found themselves implicated in the accuseds' crimes by the notion of collective guilt, came to see the trials as a ritual act of revenge. British and American politicans and service chiefs— uneasily aware that they too had conducted submarine war like Dönitz and aerial war like Goering and, even worse, dropped two atom bombs on civilian populations—were dubious about the ambivalence of some of the charges, particularly the charges connected with waging war and preparing to wage war.

The men sentenced to imprisonment were incarcerated in the old prison of Spandau, in Berlin. Nearly forty years later the last of them,

Hitler's ancient and possibly half-mad deputy, Hess, who had already been a captive of the British between 1940 and 1945, was still serving out his time alone. The men condemned to death were hung in the prison gynmasium at Nuremberg in the early hours of 16 October 1946. The American hangman in charge of the executions, Master Sergeant John C. Woods, was either very bad at his job or a sadist, for the hangings were very messily carried out. The condemned men hit the framework of the scaffold as they fell and the faces of some of them were lacerated and bloodied in this way. Not all of them were killed outright. Former Foreign Minister von Ribbentrop, the first to be hanged, dangled for ten minutes on the rope before he expired. Jodl was still alive when he was cut down, Keitel took twenty-four minutes to die, and Streicher groaned for a long time after his execution. After the hangings the dead men, including Goering, who had poisoned himself with a concealed cyanide capsule on the preceding night*, were cremated and their ashes were taken by two US Army lorries into the German countryside and poured down a conduit in a quiet country lane.

After these and subsequent lesser trials at Nuremberg there was a growing feeling against any intensification of war-crimes prosecutions. The distaste was shared by the Commander-in-Chief of BAOR, Field Marshal Montgomery—and for that matter his successors as Military Governors in Germany, Air Marshal Sir Sholto Douglas and General Sir Brian Robertson, who were anxious to bring the whole business to an end at the earliest possible opportunity. By the end of 1946 only 447 more cases were ready for trial—though none of the 1,341 suspects had been arrested. By the end of 1947 General Robertson was trying to persuade the new Secretary of State for War, Emanuel Shinwell, to put a complete stop to the war-crimes trials. In fact they dribbled on till the end of the Occupation, culminating in the trial of one of Hitler's most brilliant Field Marshals, Erich von Manstein, on charges of having committed war crimes against civilians and soldiers in Russia and Poland during the German campaign on the Eastern Front. By now there was widespread opposition to the continuation of the trials in Germany, but Ernest Bevin and Sir Hartley Shawcross remained adamant that they should go ahead. According to Shawcross the issue was a trial of strength between the government and British Army officers who did not wish to see highly placed fellow-officers from the profession of arms submitted to the indignities of a

---

* The mystery of how Goering got hold of the capsule has baffled the world for the best part of forty years. According to the meticulous researches of Ben E. Swearingen the capsule was taken from Goering's luggage in the baggage-room in Nuremberg Prison with the connivance of an American officer of the guard, Lieutenant Jack G. 'Tex' Wheelis, whom Goering rewarded with his gold watch, gold pen and gold cigarette-case. The truth of the matter was known to the US Army board of inquiry that investigated the suicide in 1946, but was suppressed because it was too shameful to reveal.

judicial process—'owing to the fact that for the most part the victims were, after all, only Russians or Poles.'

Originally two other of Hitler's outstanding military leaders, Field Marshal von Rundstedt and Field Marshal von Brauchitsch, were to have been tried with von Manstein, along with a lesser figure, General Adolf Strauss. But even the War Crimes Group of the British Army were opposed to these proceedings and during von Rundstedt's journey to Hamburg to stand trial they went to the extraordinary length of throwing a full-dress dinner in the Field Marshal's honour at Bad Oeynhausen as a mark of respect for a fellow-officer of his calibre. Afterwards most of the war-crimes investigators resigned rather than help the prosecution prepare a case against him, for in their view he was no war criminal. In the end both von Rundstedt and Strauss were found unfit to stand trial and von Brauchitsch died before the trial could begin. But the trial of Field Marshal von Manstein continued in spite of vociferous protests in Britain both inside and outside of Parliament. A public subscription was opened to raise funds for von Manstein's defence by British lawyers in what was described as 'the belated trial of an aged German general'. Churchill himself contributed £25 to the £2,000 that was raised and the poet T. S. Eliot was counted among von Manstein's earnest supporters. But there were many who saw the support for the exponent of *Blitzkrieg* and the conqueror of France as clear evidence that the British were looking to the Germans, above all the German officer class, for further help against the Russians.

Von Manstein's trial opened in Hamburg in August 1949. He was found guilty on nine of seventeen charges, including failure to protect civilian life, and sentenced to eighteen years' imprisonment. He served only three years and was released in 1952.

The statistics of the promised retribution were unimpressive. In the American courts in Nuremberg itself 199 such persons were tried between July 1945 and July 1949, 36 of whom were sentenced to death (and 18 actually executed), 23 to life imprisonment, 102 to shorter terms and 38 acquitted. In the American courts at Dachau, which worked in parallel with the ones at Nuremberg, 420 Germans were sentenced to death. Similar trials were conducted in the other three Occupation zones and in other countries throughout Europe. Between the autumn of 1945 and the spring of 1948 over 1,000 trials involving 3,500 people were conducted before Allied courts. Up to 1963 nearly 10,500 Nazi criminals had been sentenced by Allied and German courts, several hundred of whom had been executed. In addition it was estimated that more than 10,000 Germans had been sentenced to imprisonment or death by the Soviet Union.

The general failure of denazification could have cut off at the roots the

Western Allies' attempts to re-plant democracy in post-war Germany. At the heart of re-democratisation was re-education. Yet even here old Nazis continued to flourish. Field agents reported that without exception universities and technical colleges in the American zone were employing professors who were ex-Party members and under the denazification laws should have been dismissed from all jobs except that of common labourer. In July 1946 it was found that professors at Erlangen University in Bavaria were denigrating democracy, criticising the Jews, and discussing the virtues of Nazism. In one lecture Auschwitz extermination camp was described as paradise compared to future plans. Much the same was true at Würzburg University, which a year after Hitler's death was largely staffed by active Nazis, one of whom taught the same course of 'Germanics' (the basis of the 'master race' theory) that he had taught during the Third Reich.

Similarly in the police and legal professions ex-Nazis continued to find employment. When the leader of the West German Social Democrats, Kurt Schumacher, who had been crippled as a result of the twelve years he had spent in concentration camps, arrived in Hanover for a political meeting, he was aghast to discover that most of the police guard the British had given him were former SS men—even though the Hanover police were officially reported clear of Nazis. From Schleswig–Holstein, Hamburg, Kiel, Oldenburg and Westphalia came similar reports of British officers of the Public Safety Branch recruiting former Nazis and SS officers who had served in Russia and Poland in the war and were even listed on the CROWCASS files as security suspects. Former Nazi judges were allowed to return to the bench and sit in judgement in trials involving Nazi crimes. In Bremen, for example, not one of the fifty-nine judges and prosecutors was ever denazified and nowhere did the British or French ever fire a German judge because he was a former Nazi and gave judgements which favoured former Nazis on trial. Within a year or two of the fall of the Third Reich it could be said that the judiciary in the Western zones had been well and truly *re*nazified. Likewise, many leading financiers, industrialists and administrators with indirect complicity in the Nazi terror as 'armchair murderers' were allowed to resume their place in the hierarchy of power because the Occupation authorities—the British in particular—believed they were indispensable in helping to get Germany on its feet again.

Not that the occupying powers seemed to view German recovery with desperate urgency. The restoration of democracy may have advanced ponderously, but the economy was fossilized. While exhorting Germans to step up production to help pay their way, the Allies continued to take away their means of livelihood by dismantling the nation's industrial base.

One of the chief bridges to the future was the re-education of Germans in schools, universities and prisoner-of-war camps. For the British this was one of the real achievements of the Occupation in which they took special pride and for which future generations of young Germans had reason to be grateful. The problems were considerable. Quite apart from failures in denazification which permitted Nazi professors to give Nazi lectures, there was an acute problem of text-books, since even in relatively unideological subjects like mathematics existing text-books from the Hitler era were heavily impregnated with Nazi propaganda, as in this arithmetic question: 'If it takes 50,000 members of the Wehrmacht three days to conquer Holland [area of the country stated], how many days will it take 80,000 men to conquer England [area stated]?' A remarkable American and British crash programme in the writing and bulk printing of new 'democratic' text-books for German schools did not completely solve the problem. German history, for example, was not taught in the schools for a while because the four Occupation powers could not agree on the facts of German history, let alone their interpretation. The harsh conditions of life in Occupation Germany also hindered the re-education programme. In the American zone, for example, there were often as many as eighty children to one teacher. There were so few classrooms that children in some areas had to go to school in two-hour shifts, and the children of some families were so short of shoes and proper clothing that they had to take turns going to school, sharing what little there was to wear.

The Germans were allowed to take the first step towards governing themselves when elections took place in January 1946 to choose local councils to take over the day-to-day running of the administration, under Occupation government supervision. A large proportion of the population turned out to vote but there was some scepticism about their motivation on the part of Military Government. One American detachment dismissed the elections as 'a bum's rush into what passes for democracy'. The Germans themselves were suffering from what they called a 'burnt fingers complex'—a reaction against the disaster of their last venture into politics and an awareness that whatever the result of the present venture none of the German parties could exercise any influence over the things that mattered, such as denazification or the political and economic future of the country. Some observers thought the main reason the Germans had flocked to the polls was 'to convince themselves and their neighbours that the stigma of Nazism had been eradicated, not because it was their patriotic duty to elect men who could lead them to democracy.' According to American Military Government, one thing had become clear—'the German people had not suddenly shaken off the past and embraced democracy. They had voted but the political principles were obscure and the faith of the people frail and uncertain. The fact remains that the average German does not yet recognise the personal responsibilities which go with political freedom.' Throughout the Western zones, however, the first German elections for thirteen years demonstrated a firm anti-authoritarian view which resulted in an overwhelming victory for the non-communist parties.

But Germany continued to drift under Occupation rule. The Western Allies continued to tinker with the schools, universities, trade unions, financial reform, a free German press, the revival of the churches and civil services at local level, but fundamentally there was little change in Germany's state of frozen prostration and apathy, a state which was to last for the best part of two years after the end of the war. The ruins of the Reich were tidier than they had been, but they were still ruins, not foundations for a new Germany. The British and Americans were no nearer to a clear policy for Germany or a common view of the kind of Germany they would like to see.

The rift between the Western zones and the Soviet zone grew steadily wider. By the spring of 1946 it was evident that the Americans and the British were actually paying for the Soviet Occupation, since the Soviets had still not delivered any foodstuffs from their zone, though the Western zones had continued to send them reparations in the form of coal and dismantled industrial plant to the value of $14,000,000,000 (according to the US State Department's calculations). The American and British zones were costing the American and British taxpayers $600,000,000 a year. The USA and Great Britain together had sent $64,000,000 worth of aid to Germany in 1945 and $468,000,000 in 1946 simply to keep the German people alive. According to the *New York Times*, in no other country, not even the USSR, was the ruin so general and the level of life so low as in Germany two years after the war. It fell on General Clay, the Military Governor of the American zone and the most powerful Allied officer in occupied Western Germany, to make a decisive move.

In May 1946 Clay halted the shipment of reparations to the Soviet zone and sent a memo to the American Secretary of State, James Byrnes, suggesting that if the Russians continued to refuse an exchange of commodities between the Western and Eastern zones then Western Germany should be federalized and the American, British and French zones merged. In essence Clay was proposing the formation of what more than three years later was to become the Federal Republic of Germany. In July the Soviet Foreign Minister, Viacheslav Molotov, sprang to the attack over American policy in Germany. Germany, he claimed, was being used as a pawn in international power politics. What the Soviet Union wanted to see was not a federation of German states, which meant a divided Germany, but a strong centralized government—preferably, it went without saying, under Soviet control in much the same way that government of the Eastern zone was under Soviet control.

Unlike the Russians, who had a very positive idea of what they were about in their zone, and were already busily engaged on the preliminary steps for the Sovietisation of East Germany—the break-up of the great estates of the Junkers, the redistribution of land and the take-over of big businesses—the Western Allies had no clear plans for Western Germany. The Americans, for example, appeared to be facing two ways at once. On the one hand they benevolently fed the German populace and made arrangements for free elections. On the other hand they continued their harsh policy of dismantling, requisitions and arrests.

General Clay now proposed that the State Department should, as a matter of urgency, define a more positive American policy in Germany. 'We face a deteriorating German economy', Clay wrote in his memorandum, 'which will create a political unrest favourable to the development of communism in Germany and a deterrent to its democratization. The sufferings of the German people will be a serious charge against democracy and will develop a sympathy which may well defeat our other objectives in Germany.' In September, Secretary of State James Byrnes accepted Clay's invitation to come to Stuttgart from Paris, where he had been attending a meeting of the Council of Foreign Ministers, to address an audience of Military Government administrators on the subject of US policy towards Germany. This speech is generally regarded as the first admission of a an American volte-face on Germany, and the start of a new way forward for the people of Western Germany.

Byrnes and his party arrived in Stuttgart in September, travelling via Berlin in Hitler's own armour-plated train. In essence Byrnes held out the hope of a revived, free and independent Germany run by Germans. But he wanted no misunderstandings: Germany would remain disarmed and the USA was prepared to keep American troops on German soil for many years to come to assure the peace in Europe. He made it clear that the present suffering of the German people, largely as a consequence of the failure of the Allied Control Council to agree, could not go on much longer. 'Germany is a part of Europe,' he declaimed, 'and recovery in Europe will be slow indeed if Germany with her resources of iron and coal is turned into a poor house.' If Germany could not be reunited, the USA would do all it could to unite it as much as possible. The United States was willing to unify her zone with any or all of the other zones. This offer, he said, had to date only been accepted by the British. And he concluded: 'The American people want to return the government of Germany to the German people. The American people want to help the German people to win their way back to an honourable place among the free and peace loving nations of the world.'

Byrnes' speech was a great occasion—'the major development of the Occupation so far', according to Clay—and it was heard not only by the 1,500 people present in the auditorium of Stuttgart opera house but by millions of Germans listening to a simultaneous translation on the radio. Most were deeply moved, for here at last was the outstretched hand they had been waiting for.

217

At the end of the speech the band struck up *The Star-Spangled Banner*, and everybody, including the invited German officials in the audience, stood. As Byrnes left the podium many of the Germans were openly weeping. 'I walked backstage', Clay recalled later, 'to congratulate him on a speech which I believed would live through the years. Senator Vandenberg, whose eyes were moist, as were mine, remarked: "They played The Star-Spangled Banner with the same authority as if they were on the steps of the Capitol." '

The speech marked the end of the negative phase of Occupation government and the beginning of a more positive one. In response a newly elected deputy in the Hesse parliament in the American zone declared later in the year:

> Today's misery comes from the shutting out of democracy. The spirit of militarism and of National Socialism must die if Germany is to live. The Germans must feed themselves and pay for their own goods or every word about democracy is meaningless and a nation goes under. Not every German is guilty but the majority made great mistakes. Collective guilt is to be rejected. The German people have contributed much to the world, and Germany freed from the ideology of the past should have a place in it, and a change in its unbearable fate. The Byrnes speech was a ray of hope for the possibility of a state, a community for Germany. It breached the iron ring of helplessness. Without the food the United States has given Germany it would have starved. This is the first time in history that a conqueror has given such help to the conquered. We stand before the winter solstice.

Ahead lay the reconstruction of Germany, the Marshall Plan, German self-government and the economic miracle. But it would be another two years before the essential ingredients of change—large imports of food and raw materials, and currency reform—would come about. Until then there could be only hope.

13

Reds

The Hotel Lux in Gorky Street, Moscow, was not a place where a casual visitor could book a room or go to the bar for a drink. It was, rather, a special kind of hostelry for special guests of the Soviet Union. For twenty-five years it had been the home of the Comintern, or Communist International, but towards the end of the war, after the dissolution of the Comintern, it became the home of a group of expatriates known as the National Committee for Free Germany. This National Committee was composed of dedicated members of the German Communist Party, men like Wilhelm Pieck and Walter Ulbricht, the future President and Chairman of the German Democratic Republic, who had spent the years of the Hitler regime in exile in the Soviet Union, where they had devoted their time to planning for the golden day when they could return to their Fatherland and inaugurate a new communist state.

At 6 a.m. on 30 April 1945, the day of Hitler's death, the ten men of the Ulbricht group, each carrying a small bag and 3,000 Reichsmarks for expenses, boarded an American Douglas aircraft with a Red Air Force crew at Moscow Airport. They landed on an emergency airstrip near Kustrin on the Oder and carried on towards Berlin in a little convoy of Red Army staff cars. On the morning of 2 May, the day the Germans surrendered the capital, Ulbricht and his party made their way through the shattered streets of Berlin to a boarding-house in Lichtenberg that was to be their temporary headquarters. That afternoon Ulbricht established contact with old Party members who had survived the war in Berlin. Wolfgang Leonhardt went with him to meet them in the Neukölln district of Berlin:

> We were in a simple room of a worker's house. An oil lamp stood on the
> table—there was of course no electric light at that time. On chairs or on the

219

floor sat twelve Neukölln Party members. The whole atmosphere was entirely different from that of meetings of the Soviet *Komsomol* or Party. It was like pictures I had formed to myself of meetings at the time of the October Revolution and during the Civil War in Russia.

One could feel the genuineness of the enthusiasm. Brief, clear-cut proposals came from all sides. Someone was noting down the details: names of Party members to be looked out; rough plans for working parties to unload and distribute food, for contacting engineers and mechanics to get the light, water and gas put in order, for organising more working parties to clear the wreckage, for writing out identity documents—all done without any agenda or excitement or unnecessary talk. The only thing I disapproved of was Ulbricht's manner. Ulbricht behaved like a dictator. The way he put his questions was very different from the tone I would have expected of an émigré returning after twelve years to meet the survivors of the party who had spent years living under the Nazi terror.

So the Party began to spread its tentacles. At the beginning not only communists but social democrats and independent anti-fascists were invited to join the local administration. As part of the step-by-step approach the members of the Ulbricht group were sent out into the streets to find anti-Nazi bourgeois Germans who might be suitable as mayors of the twenty Berlin districts. But key positions in the local administration—including that of Deputy Mayor and the officials in charge of education and the police—were always given to communists. When the time came to form the administration for the city as a whole and someone objected that the nominee for Mayor was 'not quite right in the head', Ulbricht replied: 'That doesn't matter. The Deputy will be one of our men.' It was, in fact, one of the group of ten who had recently arrived from Moscow. When the administration of the city of Berlin was finally complete, only six of the seventeen officials were Communist Party members, but there was never any doubt that the administration was in Communist Party hands. Nor was there ever any doubt that it was the Ulbricht communists and not the old Berlin communists who were running the show. A demonstration of this occurred at one of the regular weekly conferences of Party functionaries.

'A question has been put to us by some doctors,' one official told Ulbricht from the back of the meeting-hall, 'about what course they ought to take with women who have been raped and come to them for abortions. I've promised the doctors a reply.'

Another official spoke up: 'The question's very urgent. It's being talked about everywhere. We must give officials responsible for public health a clear directive. In my view, abortion ought to be permitted officially in such cases.'

Ulbricht sharply interrupted the discussion. 'There can be no question of it! I regard the discussion as closed.'

Then something happened that would have been impossible in Moscow—open cries of protest against a senior Party official.

'We can't do that! We must discuss it!' shouted one.

'We must give working-class women the right to abortion,' cried another.

Before long the clamour had gone beyond a simple question about abortion. What was being demanded was a clear and public statement about the German communists' attitude towards the excesses of the Soviet Army. Ulbricht faced the meeting with an angry frown.

'I repeat,' he said sharply, 'I regard the discussion on this subject as closed. Any concession to these emotions is, for us, quite simply out of the question. I will not allow the debate to be continued. The conference is adjourned.'

What this meeting revealed was not simply Ulbricht's attitude towards his own Party members and his contempt for initiative from below, but Moscow's attitude towards him and their intention of imposing a Soviet system from above, for the Ulbricht group and the German Communist Party were acting under the direction of the Kremlin and with the backing of the Red Army in Soviet-occupied Germany. For a while the German communist leadership dallied with the theory of a separate German road to socialism; not even they then understood the exact nature of Soviet communism under Stalin. They should perhaps have picked up a clue when the so-called anti-fascist committees, anti-Nazi groups and socialist offices, which had sprung up spontaneously in eastern Germany after the defeat, were ordered to be dissolved. Essential to Stalinist policy was the repression from below of emerging independent communist or socialist organisations because of the danger that such organisations would escape the Kremlin's direct control. Probably Ulbricht himself understood this well enough—in Spain during the Civil War his job had been to liquidate anti-Stalinist revolutionaries in the Spanish Republican Army.

After the arrival of Wilhelm Pieck from Moscow the stepping-stone progress towards communist rule proceeded apace. First came the formation of new political parties, including the bourgeois parties of the right and centre as well as the KPD (German Communist Party), which in April 1946 merged with the more popular SPD (German Socialist Party) to form a new Socialist and Unity Party, the SED. The plan was to achieve communist domination by parliamentary means. The communists had genuinely believed they would win the elections for the provincial parliaments held in the autumn of 1946. Their groundwork was more thorough, they argued, and they had enlarged their catchment area by extending the vote to the great mass of former minor Nazis, one of whom had even come up with an election slogan: 'LONG LIVE THE *SED*—THE LITTLE NAZI'S BEST FRIEND!' The elections were a shattering defeat. In the elections for the regional parliaments in the Soviet zone the SED received on average less than half the votes. In the Berlin elections held in October 1946 the SED received less than 20 per cent of the votes. The explanation was not hard to see. Wolfgang Leonhardt commented: 'To the man in the street we were known as the "Russian" party. In practice, we had supported all measures taken by the Soviet Occupation authorities. They had supplied us with paper, vehicles, buildings and special food rations. Our leading officials lived in large country houses hermetically sealed from the rest of the population and guarded by soldiers of the Red Army. They travelled in cars which carried Russian marks of identification. The result of the elections was the logical consequence of our dependence on the Soviet Occupation authorities.'

Logically the next step would have been for the SED to publicly distance itself from the Soviet Occupation. But in fact the reverse happened. The links with the SED, which was clearly regarded as the old KPD under another guise, grew steadily stronger. In November 1946 it celebrated Soviet National Day, in December Soviet Constitution Day and Stalin's 67th birthday. 'The far-sighted genius of the Soviet Union's great leader,' declaimed Wilhelm Pieck, 'shows the German people, too, their way.' By the end of 1947 it was clear that since parliamentary means had failed Soviet communism would have to be imposed on the Eastern zone by other means—and from above.

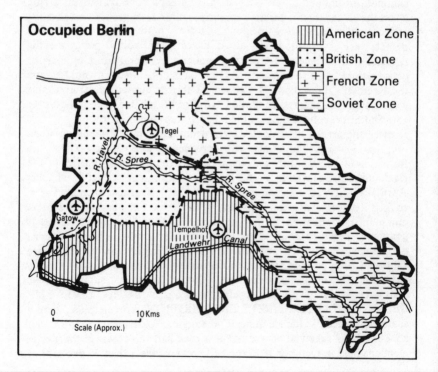

By now it was clear that Allied plans for a common policy in Germany and for the treatment of the country as a single economic unit had failed. One reason for the failure was the growing divergence between the policies pursued by the Occupation powers in their various zones. Another, more important reason was the breakdown of the old wartime alliance between the USA and Great Britain on the one hand and the Soviet Union on the other. As far as Germany was concerned the major issues in dispute were reparations, the future of the Ruhr (which the Soviets wished to see internationalized), the economic unity of Germany and the functions and power of a future German government. Almost the only significant agreement reached by the Allied Control Council in Berlin was a law promulgated in January 1947 which declared that 'the Prussian state, which from its early days has been the promoter of militarism and reaction in Germany, has *de facto* ceased to exist.' Otherwise the Allies were locked in stalemate and mounting recrimination which mirrored the mounting tensions of what had already become known as the Cold War.

In Germany the comradely regard with which the majority of British and American soldiers had held their comrades-in-arms in the Red Army was soon dissipated. Before long the mutual suspicion spilled into actual hostility. In no field was this more apparent than in intelligence. Western intelligence units like the US Army Counter-Intelligence Corps (CIC) began to turn the main weight of their endeavours away from the pursuit of Nazi fugitives to covert operations against Soviet intelligence manoeuvres in the occupied zones. A striking example of the escalation of fear and the exploitation of intelligence opportunities among the drifting population of uprooted souls occurred at Aschaffenberg in the American zone, where Captain William Craydon of the Middlesex Regiment, on loan to the US Third Army, worked as a liaison officer between the DP camps and American Military Government, and from time to time passed on useful information he gleaned from refugees from the Soviet zone to the local CIC detachment. One morning in the spring of 1946, Craydon found a man waiting for him at his office with another batch of papers. The man informed Craydon that he had worked for the Russians in the Military Mission in East Berlin, but had stolen some secret papers and defected. He was nearly caught at the border and as he knew Russian he decided to read the papers, memorize and destroy them in case he was captured. However, he succeeded in crossing the border illicitly at Hoff. Craydon continued:

> I sent my secretary back to her camp for the morning, hung a 'Do Not Disturb' notice outside my door and turned the key. He then began his detailed report. I took it all down on paper. Later the man left, saying he must get back to his family. I gave him food and money, telling him we were grateful for his co-operation. He said he felt it was his duty to the West.
>
> I sent this off the next day in a large envelope addressed to Mr E. Bevin,

the British Foreign Secretary. I also sent a copy to Sir Winston Churchill. So that I was sure the letters would arrive safely I put them in another envelope addressed to my sister, asking her to post them in London.

Craydon's report was as follows:

> Papers together with verbal information came into my possession of Stalin's plans to make a five-prong attack on the West, the Middle East and Alaska by 1952. First to build up a front-line army consisting of 250 divisions, and huge reserves. These numbers do not include the Baltic States, Poland and other countries taken over. To build a huge submarine force numbering 750, to work in packs of 4 or 5 to prevent troops returning to Europe, to divert all food ships to Russia under escort. The land attacks, to move three prongs down the West and through Eastern Europe to the Middle East, the fifth prong to Alaska. All communist civilians to be driven in front to block roads and cause confusion and hamper movements of troops of the Allies still left in Europe. The names to be filed of all prominent persons in the West, who would be arrested and sent to Siberia.

Captain Craydon was not a trained intelligence officer and the peddling of information, both genuine and spurious, was a well-recognised method for some DPs to gain favours of one kind or another from the Occupation authorities in Germany. It would be tempting to think that Captain Craydon had been duped, as many CIC agents were also duped, by 'intelligence' confidence-tricksters looking for a quick meal and a helping hand westward. But by a curious coincidence reports reached the West many years later that the Soviet Union had indeed contemplated a pre-emptive military action of the kind described in Captain Craydon's letter and on approximately the same time-scale. According to a high-placed Czech government official, Karel Kaplan, who had access to documents of the highest secrecy in the archives of the Czechoslovak Politburo and Central Committee, Stalin had announced in the Kremlin in January 1951 that the Americans had to be swept out of Europe by armed force before their increasing political and military strength made it impossible to do so. According to Kaplan, who defected to Munich in 1977, Stalin had never lost sight of his ambition to advance Soviet hegemony from the Elbe to the Rhine and thence to the Atlantic. Europe in his view was a great power-vacuum and Russian military power was over-whelming. What defeated his plan was the inability of the communist economic system to support his demands on it—and his sudden death in 1953.

Meanwhile on 1 January 1947 the British and Americans merged their zones for economic purposes into a single unified zone called Bizonia and handed over much of the administrative responsibility for running it to the Germans—in particular to an elected economic council of fifty-two Germans who, under Allied supervision, shouldered the task of economic reconstruction. These developments were bitterly opposed by the Soviets, who rightly saw in them the embryo of an independent German state. The British and Americans were nevertheless determined to push through their plans for western Germany irrespective of Soviet opinion. On 7 January the composition and the powers of the German Economic Council for Bizonia were changed in order to create the nucleus of a future German government, and plans were made for the economic merger of the French zone with Bizonia to produce a federated West Germany.

Six months later the USA, Great Britain, France and other West European countries agreed on a plan to create a West German state which would enjoy a limited degree of sovereignty by 1949. A prerequisite for an independent nation was a revival of its economy. In West Germany the only active economy was then the black market. This now had to be destroyed, and this could only be done by currency reform—the substitution of the almost worthless Reichsmark for a brand new currency, the Deutsche Mark, with a stable and universally accepted value.

The currency reform operation was carried out in the utmost secrecy, for any leak would have led to grave international repercussions. One of the few people in the European Command entrusted with prior knowledge of the operation was the civilian head of the US Currency Bank in Frankfurt, Frank C. Gabell, whom we last met as an American Military Government officer wrapped in an SS flag in the front-line town of Homberg in 1945. On Gabell fell the responsibility for directing the shipment and distribution of the new currency in the western Occupation zones. Twenty-thousand cases of the new notes arrived in Frankfurt from the USA, where they had been printed, each case weighing 90 lb. and marked 'Bird Dog'—the operation's code-name. Only Frank Gabell and five others knew what they were. 'Some of the soldiers who helped load them thought they were dog food,' Gabell recalled. 'Others figured they were atom bombs. But it was only money. We thought about it in truck-loads. For eleven days and nights the distribution went on . . . Then on 18 June the new currency was announced to the world.'

The result was electrifying. West Germany's economic miracle began on that day. The black market was wiped out almost overnight, and the black-market barons were beggared. The cigarette, which for three years had been Germany's only valued unit of exchange, became once again merely something to smoke as confidence in money was restored. Traders abandoned the barter system and returned to selling goods for cash. But for the ordinary German the greatest wonder of currency reform was the magical, virtually immediate stocking of shop-windows with a variety of foodstuffs and consumer goods which had not been seen legally for years.

The Soviets were caught off-guard and reacted angrily. The first step towards the independence and economic revival of the western zones aimed at the heart of their German policy. Hot on the heels of the Marshall Plan (the American aid programme for European recovery) and the Treaty of Brussels (the European mutual defence pact which preceded NATO), currency reform goaded the Soviets into massive retaliation. Their target was the isolated outpost of Berlin. The first sign of trouble had been at a meeting of the four-power Allied Control Council in Berlin on 20 January 1948, when the Soviet Military Governor, Marshal Sokolovsky, formally condemned the British and American plans for an economic merging of their two zones. Bizonia, Sokolovsky complained, amounted to the establishment of a separatist German government in western Germany, and was a violation of agreements reached by the Allies at Yalta and in the Control Council. At subsequent meetings of the Control Council in Berlin efforts were made to reach a joint agreement with the Russians over currency reform, but without success. Finally, on 20 March, Sokolovsky brought matters to a head. Britain and America, he said, had in effect broken away from the system of Control Council rule in Germany by making a bipartite agreement between themselves which was in contravention of existing Allied agreements. That being so they would have to face the consequences of their actions. From now on, said Sokolovsky, the Control Council had ceased to exist as an organ of government. He then adjourned the meeting and the Council never met again.

Shortly after the 20 March meeting General Clay's political advisor, Robert Murphy, sent a report to Washington containing a very shrewd interpretation of the situation. The Soviets, he claimed, were now embarked on a programme to force the Western Powers out of Berlin in order to liquidate this remaining 'centre of reaction' east of the Iron Curtain. Sokolovsky's charge that Britain and America had destroyed the Control Council was the first step. The second step would be to make a formal demand for the withdrawal of the Western Powers from Berlin. If the Western Powers refused, the third step would be to apply pressure tactics to make it difficult for them to stay—for example, by interfering with the fragile lines of communication between Berlin and the Western zones. 'Our Berlin position,' Murphy wrote, 'is delicate and difficult. Our withdrawal, either voluntary or involuntary, would have severe psychological repercussions which would, at this critical stage in the European situation, extend far beyond the boundaries of Berlin and even Germany.'

The day after Murphy wrote his report the predicted Russian interference began. The Russians demanded the right to board and enter Allied trains coming to Berlin from the West. At the same time they interrupted vital telephone links. These actions were trivial in themselves but were clearly sighting-shots in a more ambitious campaign. Murphy advised against hasty concessions; Clay advised against the evacuation of

American dependants. Any compromise, he said in a phone-call to Washington on the evening of 2 April, would have a serious adverse effect for the Western Powers throughout Europe. But the British and American governments were against any retaliatory action—certainly nothing as drastic or potentially catastrophic as the course put forward by Winston Churchill, who proposed that the Soviets should be forced out of Berlin and eastern Germany while America had the atomic bomb and the Soviet Union did not, and that their cities should be rased to the ground if they failed to comply.

Though four-power government had come to an end for Germany as a whole, the four-power Kommandatura which controlled Berlin struggled on for a little while longer, though the meetings grew chillier and more ill-tempered from week to week. Finally, after a futile and petulant meeting lasting thirteen hours on 16 June, the Russian Commandant walked out and never returned. This marked the beginning of the division of the city. Two days later the British and Americans launched the new currency in the Western zones.

The Russians' reaction was instantaneous. On the evening currency reform was announced they stopped all passenger traffic between the Western zones and Berlin by road and rail. On the autobahn at the Helmstedt checkpoint, Soviet guards turned back all eastbound traffic. At the border station of Marienborn trains carrying German passengers were also turned back. Patrols of Russian and East German frontier-guards were greatly increased in strength along the entire length of the Soviet zonal border. Equally drastically, the Russians imposed major electricity cuts. Two days later Russian guards stopped an American military goods-train at Marienborn and removed a rail in front of it. The blockade of Berlin had begun.

The halting of all rail, road and water traffic between Berlin and the West had various implications and presented various options to the Western Allies. Over two million inhabitants of the British, French and American zones of Berlin were largely dependent for food on supplies from the west. By cutting off West Berlin from overland supply the Soviets had launched—in General Clay's words—'one of the most ruthless efforts in modern times to use mass starvation for political coercion.' For their part, the Western Powers—meaning to all intents and purposes the Americans and the British, for the French were in political crisis at home and vacillated weakly over Berlin—could do one of three things. They could give way to Soviet pressure, move their forces out of Berlin and abandon the West Berliners, who were staunchly anti-communist, to communist rule. For trenchant political as well as humanitarian reasons this option found favour with almost nobody on the Western side. 'We have lost Czechoslovakia,' General Clay warned the Department of the Army. 'Norway is threatened. When Berlin falls, West Germany will be next.' Berlin had to be held in order to sustain the morale of the peoples of Western Europe. Alternatively, the Allies could slug it out with the Russians. At the very beginning of the confrontation General Clay favoured the use of tanks to force the Allies' overland entry into Berlin. 'I am still convinced,' he reported in June, 'that a determined movement of convoys with troop protection would reach Berlin and that this might well prevent, rather than build up, Soviet pressures which could lead to war. Nevertheless, I realize fully the inherent dangers in this proposal, since once committed we could not withdraw.'

One of the most cogent reasons for not using force on the ground was the fact that Stalin had seventeen Red Army divisions deployed in the Soviet zone, while the US Army in Germany had been drastically weakened by demobilisation and redeployment since the end of the war, and neither the British nor the French, heavily committed to colonial wars and policing actions in other parts of the globe, were in a position to contemplate a new war in Europe so soon after the last one. In general the armed forces of the Soviet Union, now the world's greatest land-power, were stronger in men and conventional weapons than the combined forces of the USA, Great Britain, Canada and France. Sending an armoured convoy down the autobahn was not recommended, the American Defense Secretary, James Forrestal, reported on 28 July, 'in view of the risk of war involved and the inadequacy of United States preparation for global conflict.' But he added: 'contingency planning for an armoured convoy would go ahead in case every other solution were to fail, and in case evaluation showed that the armoured convoy was likely to get through, and in case the United States decided the risk of war for the Berlin cause was acceptable.'

This left the Allies a final option—to vault over the Russian blockade and supply Berlin by air, an idea first put forward by Lt.-General Albert Wedermeyer, former US Commander in China, whose forces had been supplied by an air-lift over the Himalayas during the war. This option raised two objections. The first was that technically it might prove impossible to supply West Berlin's needs—which amounted to 4,500 tons a day in food alone—purely by air. General Clay was one of those who simply could not believe that a major metropolis could be relieved for an indefinite period from the air alone. The American Ambassador in Moscow, Walter Bedell Smith, Eisenhower's wartime Chief of Staff at SHAEF, was another. Even if the Berliners could be saved from starvation, he cabled Washington, the economic life of West Berlin could not be supported by food alone. 'Time is still working entirely in favour of the Soviets if they desire to make the position of the Western Powers untenable.'

The second objection was that the Russians might attempt to cut the air corridors from the West, just as they had cut the land corridors—though there were few who believed that the Soviets would risk such a serious escalation of the crisis by sending up fighters against US Air Force and RAF transport aircraft, which would be tantamount to an act of war. The Soviets were doubtless well aware that American bombers capable of flying deep into the USSR had been adapted to carry nuclear weapons. They may have suspected, if not actually known, of American contingency plans, the first drawn up less than two months after the surrender of Japan in September 1945, for a nuclear air-attack on key cities in the Soviet Union. A revised plan, code-named Charioteer and drawn up by the Joint Chiefs of the Joint Intelligence Group at about the time of the start of the Soviet siege of Berlin, envisaged dropping 133 atom bombs on 70 Soviet cities and industrial centres, including eight on Moscow and seven on Leningrad, thus destroying the political and administrative centres of the USSR, the whole of the Soviet petroleum industry, 30–40 per cent of all other industry and nearly seven million members of the work force.

All in all, it was not fear of what the Soviet Air Force could do but what the Allied Air Forces could not do that worried the critics of the air-lift option to the Soviet blockade. On 26 June 1948 the Commander of the US Air Forces in Europe ordered the air-lift to begin. He had 70 aircraft and he lifted 225 tons a day. With another thirty aircraft he would be able to lift another 275 tons. But this was still only one-ninth of the daily total of 4,500 tons which was considered necessary simply to keep the population of West Berlin alive—not counting fuel for domestic heating, raw materials and normal consumer goods. The chances of an air-lift succeeding seemed slim. But there was, finally, no alternative.

The British and Americans were resolved to stick it out. To retreat, Murphy told the American Secretary of State on the evening of the first supply flights into Berlin from Western Germany, 'would be the Munich of 1948'—a craven admission of lack of courage to resist Soviet pressure short of war. The same day the British Foreign Secretary, Ernest Bevin, recommended that the Combined Chiefs of Staff in Washington and London make a joint assessment of the military situation while the Allied authorities in Berlin looked at the logistics of feeding the civilian population by air. A force of heavy American bombers should be sent over to Europe, he suggested, as evidence that the Western Allies were in earnest. President Truman concurred, as did Secretary of State Marshall. The problem over Berlin was not one of currency but of four-power government. The Russians wanted the Allies out of Berlin: it was as simple as that. The Soviet position was made plain at a subsequent meeting between Stalin and the three Western Ambassadors in Moscow. Stalin told the Ambassadors that Germany was now divided into two states with two capitals—Berlin and Frankfurt. Since Berlin was no longer the capital of the whole of Germany but only of Eastern Germany he could not accept the introduction of a separate West German currency in West Berlin. The Soviet government would only lift the blockade if the Western Powers accepted East German currency as the only legal tender in Berlin—meaning Soviet control of the whole of the city. This the Western Powers would on no account agree to. 'We are going to stay, period,' President Truman declared.

On 1 July Britain and America publicly committed themselves to the support of the West Berliners. Three weeks later, when all attempts at diplomacy with the Soviet authorities in Berlin and Moscow had failed, the National Security Council in Washington authorized the transfer of seventy-five Skymaster transport planes to reinforce the air-lift and the construction of a third airport (which was built in only three months) at Tegel in the French sector. The air-lift was on. To run it the Chief of the Air Staff of the US Air Force, General Vandenberg, sent for the most experienced air-transport officer in either the American or British air forces—General William H. Tunner.

Tunner had learned his business in World War Two when he had been in charge of a remarkable operation which had kept the American forces in China supplied by air 'over the hump'—across the Himalayas—from India. He arrived in Berlin on 28 July at a time when the tonnage being flown into the city was still far below the minimum required. He recalled later: 'My first overall impression was that the situation was just as I had anticipated—a real cowboy operation. Few people knew what they would be doing the next day. Neither flight crews nor ground crews knew how long they'd be there, or the schedules that they were working. Everything was temporary. I went out to the Wiesbaden Air Base, looked around, then hopped a plane to Berlin. Confusion everywhere.'

A successful air-lift, Tunner knew, was an unglamorous exercise in pure efficiency measured in maximum turn-round of aircraft and unbroken build-up of tonnages. Planes were either in the air or at the loading and unloading ramps. Crews were either flying or resting in order to fly again. There were no heroics, just getting on with the job. Tunner's first act was to make sure the air-lift was under a single command. The Combined Air-Lift Task Force was an Anglo-American operation under his command, with an RAF officer, Air Commodore G. W. F. Meren, as his deputy. His second act was to lay down a set of guiding principles for the conduct of the air-lift to be observed by all aircrews and all airfields. The first principle was that aircraft would fly at three-minute intervals all round the clock. The second was that if a plane could not land in Berlin at its first attempt it should fly straight back to the west. The third was that all pilots would fly under the same set of rules at all times—namely instrument rules, i.e. flying by instruments as if in fog. The fourth was that pilots would not be allowed to leave their aircraft in Berlin but would take off for the return leg as soon as the plane had been unloaded.

There were technical problems peculiar to the air-lift. One was lack of repair facilities, so that if a four-engined transport came in with one engine dead it would have to take off and fly out with only three engines on the return leg. Another was navigation. The approach to Tempelhof left a lot to be desired. Lt. Gail Halvorsen of the US Air Force, who became renowned among Berlin children as the 'chocolate bomber', because of his custom of dropping bags of sweets through the signal chute of his C54 transport, recalled getting in to the American air base at Tempelhof in the south of the city: 'As we came in looking for this place all we could see were bombed-out buildings all around. Then we spied this grass field—it seemed more like a pasture than an airfield—and came over the homing beacon. We came right on over the top of an apartment building and over a little opening in the barbed wire fence and there we were. It kind of reminded me of the feeling that a crop duster would have in western America, landing on a highroad or in the pasture he's dusting.'

There were three air corridors allowed for Allied flights into Berlin—two inward and one outward bound, each of them only 32 kilometres wide and patrolled by Yak fighters of the Red Air Force, which often buzzed Allied transports or held mock dog-fights near the air lanes. In the early weeks of the air-lift there were only 160 aircraft, most of them small twin-engined C47s and Dakotas with only $2\frac{1}{2}$ or $3\frac{1}{2}$ ton cargo capacity. But gradually bigger aircraft, such as C54 Skymasters with a 10 ton cargo capacity, began to arrive from American bases all over the world and the daily tonnages started climbing. In July it had averaged 2,226 tons or just under half the necessary minimum; in August it rose to 3,839 tons; by October, at 4,760, it had exceeded the minimum requirement for the first time. During the winter months the main worry was not food but fuel. West Berlin needed three times as much coal as it did foodstuffs to keep the populace from freezing to death, as well as diesel oil and petrol amounting to nearly 100,000 tons (flown in by British civil airlines planes). By the spring of 1949 the air-lift was in full stride and running as efficiently and tidily as a railway freight line. There were now over 400 aircraft—250 American, more than 150 British, and all makes from Skymasters to Dakotas—shuttling back and forth between the three airfields in Berlin and the airfields in the American and British zones, one plane every three minutes, twenty-four hours a day. At the peak of the air-lift a plane was landing or taking off from Berlin's airfields every thirty seconds round the clock and daily tonnages were averaging 8,000 tons. 'The sound of the engines,' wrote one Berliner, 'is music to our ears.'

At Easter 1949 General Tunner mounted what he called his 'Easter Parade'—an all-out effort to achieve a record lift and convince the Soviets of the futility of their action. Between noon on Easter Saturday and noon on Easter Sunday, the air forces flew 1,398 sorties and carried just under 13,000 tons of supplies into the blockaded city. In the course of over 550,000 sorties in thirteen months the planes from the West brought in over 500,000 tons of food—much of it in super-lightweight form, such as dehydrated eggs and potato, boneless meat and saccharin—and over 1,500,000 tons of coal. The planes also brought in special cargoes—feed for the animals in the Berlin Zoo, special diet packs for nursing mothers, the sick and the elderly, chocolate for Christmas, newsprint for West Berlin's free press, two million seedlings to replace the trees that had been cut down, Volkswagens for the Berlin police. The planes did not always leave Berlin empty. Nearly 175,000 people were air-lifted out of the city, most of them children and TB patients, along with thousands of tons of manufactured goods stamped 'Made in Blockaded Berlin'.

Still the Berliners did not have an easy time, especially during the bitter winter months. There were drastic power-cuts and the Berliners had to learn to live yet again by the light of candles and oil-lamps. Food was strictly rationed and fresh vegetables were scarce. Materially it seemed that little had changed since the end of the war—people were still cold and hungry, they still lived in ruins, still had to forage from the bomb-sites and chop down trees in the parks for firewood. But in reality they knew, the Allies knew and the Russians soon learnt that the Berlin air-lift had brought about an historic change. It could not be regarded simply as a colossal exercise in logistics, the US Air Force's major operation in Europe at the time, and the greatest relief operation in aviation history. Nor could it be looked upon as just a great Allied victory. It was Robert Murphy who first pointed out that the air-lift had actually achieved little except demonstrate that a big city could be kept going from the air by anyone who had the resources to afford it. Politically, diplomatically, the Allies had won nothing from the Russians. The problem of West Berlin was the same before the air-lift as it was after it, and the city remained an island in a Soviet sea. What *had* changed was the relationship between the members of the Allied Occupation and the people of Berlin—and by implication the people of Western Germany as a whole. Whatever the political motivations of their leaders might be, the American and British soldiers and airmen looked upon the air-lift as a humanitarian mission, and began to see their ex-enemies as comrades in adversity. 'The air-lift,' said one German housewife, 'was the intermediary between us and the rest of the Western world.' On 17 May 1949, General Clay reported to Congress: 'I saw the spirit and soul of a people reborn. This time the people of Berlin cast their lot with those who love freedom.' The attitude of the West Berliners to *their* ex-enemies can be judged by the fact that to this day a quarter of the population of West Berlin turn up on Air Force Day to give thanks for the air-lift and pay honour to the men who made it possible, including the forty-eight British and American airmen who lost their lives in twenty-four flying mishaps during the course of the operation.

The position of West Berlin is as precarious today as it ever was. But West Germany's alliance with the USA and the West sprang directly out of the circumstances of the Berlin blockade. That is the measure of the Allied victory and of Russia's loss.

A few days after General Tunner's 'Easter Parade' the Soviet Union threw in the sponge. The blockade had not only failed, it had hurt them. They had been made to look silly and suffered a moral defeat. The West Berliners had spurned all Soviet blandishments, and only twenty-thousand of them accepted the Soviet offer of East Berlin ration cards. The trade embargo between the Western zones and the Soviet zones had severely hampered the development of the East German economy, whereas the West German economy was beginning to take off in the wake of currency reform. On 12 May the siege was lifted. Vast crowds gathered to welcome the first Allied trucks that arrived overland from the West down the autobahn into Berlin. The locomotives of the first trains to roll in were garlanded with flowers. But the air-lift continued in full spate for another four months so that stocks could be built up in case the blockade was reimposed.

The year 1949 was the watershed, not just for Germany but for Europe as well. It was the year when Germany's future was decided and most of the world's political and military divisions were resolved. On 23 May, eleven days after the lifting of the Berlin blockade, the Federal Republic of Germany was created out of the Western zones. On 24 August the North Atlantic Treaty Organisation (NATO) was formed, in which the USA, Canada and most non-communist European countries pledged themselves to mutual assistance in case of foreign aggression. On 23 September President Truman announced that the Russians had successfully exploded their first atomic bomb and thus achieved nuclear parity with the West. Finally, on 5 October 1949, the German Democratic Republic was formally created out of the Soviet zone of Germany. Equilibrium of a kind was reached, with the frontier between the two halves forming the front line of the Cold War in Europe.

Could such an outcome of the Occupation of Germany been avoided? Shortly before his death, General Clay wrote to the present author outlining his views on the question:

I am sure that there was nothing that could have been done by military governments which would have altered events. Both General Eisenhower and I made every effort to know and to understand our Russian opposites, as did our British associates. Both in Germany and in the several Foreign Ministers' Conferences, every effort was made to find compromise positions which would give some promise of the Four-Power Control becoming effective, without any real results.

If the United States and the United Kingdom had maintained substantial military strength in Europe, the 'quadri-partite' military government might have succeeded. Soviet military strength would not have seemed so over-powering and the coalition governments of eastern Europe might have held on until replaced by elected governments. Freedom of movement and communication might have ensured the freedom of Europe. However, I must still ask—if quadri-partite military government had become effective for Germany as a whole, how and when could we have agreed to transfer power to a German government? It is doubtful if such a military government would have allowed Germany to become a full partner in the Marshall Plan or, if it had, to permit the rapid economic recovery which was so important to the recovery of western Europe. Certainly, the countries of western Europe would have been opposed to German economic recovery had not their own economies been brought to life again. Moreover, under Four-Power Control, could there have been a Germany invited to become a member of the Common Market and, without Germany, would there have been such a market?

I do know that when West Germany was established, it was hoped that someday there would be an equally free East Germany and that the German people would then determine their own future. That seems a rather dim prospect now but history is never measured in years or in tens of years. I still believe that what did happen was the best that could have been attained at the time without war for the then free people of Europe. It remains possible and, to my mind, probable that the Four Power agreement to keep Germany as a whole would have become effective had we maintained our strength in Europe. Whether that would have been good or bad for Europe is too speculative even to attempt to answer . . .

Sources

Chapter 1: *Pursuit*

German graffiti are from Padover 272, 226, 241 and SHAEF Psychological Warfare Division, Exhibits 13 and 18. The account of Homberg is from Moseley and Frank Gabell correspondence, 17 February 1953, Bentonville, Ar. (Ian Sayer Archive.) The bombing and surrender of Halberstadt is from Peter Saabor, interview with author, London 1974. The episode at Rohrbach is based on interviews with Christabel and Peter Bielenberg in Dublin and London, 1974; and on Christabel Bielenberg's own written account, *The Past is Myself* (1968). For an account of military events at Rohrbach in the last week of April 1945 see Hermann Riedel: *Ausweglos: Letzter Akt des Krieges im Schwarzwald* (1975). For an extended — and brilliant — description of the events at Salzwedel see Nowakowski, to which this account is indebted.

For a more detailed military account of the invasion of Germany see the official histories of Ellis (British) and MacDonald (American); the memoirs of Eisenhower, Montgomery, Bradley, Patton, Horrocks, de Guingand and other commanders; and the general accounts of Wilmot, North, Essame, Toland. Most of these discuss Eisenhower's decision on Berlin, as does Ambrose.

The British and American advance into Germany had the advantage of some gifted reporters (newspapers, radio, military official) including Moorehead, Mosley, Gordon-Walker, Chester Wilmot, Richard Dimbleby, Frank Gillard and Wynford Vaughan-Thomas (the last four in BBC *War Report*) and Padover — who have been referred to or quoted. For a more official view of spearhead Military Government in action see Donnison (British) and Ziemke (American).

Chapter 2: *A Fine Hell*

For the central narrative of this chapter — the first man to liberate Belsen — I have referred to Derrick Sington's own account, *Belsen Uncovered*, and interviews with his widow Gertrude Sington, a former inmate of the camp. The Kürstmeier quote is from Sington, p. 141 ff. The dead baby incident is from Gordon-Walker p. 40 — a different version is given by Richard Dimbleby in BBC War Report p. 402. The Peter Fabian quote is from my interview, London, 1974. For a succinct account of the cleaning-up operation at Belsen see Donnington, pp. 219 ff. For the rehabilitation of Belsen survivors see Herdman and Goodman, *The Survivors*, and Collis and Hogerzeil, *Staight On*. Among numerous discussions on the question of German collective guilt see Gollancz, *What Buchenwald Really Means*, written less than a fortnight after the discovery of the camp.

Chapter 3: *Storm* and Chapter 4: *End-Game*

Published sources include Bezymenski, Bernadotte, Boldt, Chuikov, Erickson, Fest, Haupt, Irving, Kempke, Kuby, O'Donnell, Riess, Ryan, Sevriek, Shtemenko, Thorwald, Tieke, Toland, Trevor-Roper, Tully, Ziemke. The names of the Berlin zoo animals are from Hans Georg-Kloes: *Von der Menagerie zum Tierparadis*. The anonymous diary quotations are from *A Woman in Berlin*. The account by Len Carpenter (pseudonym), one of the few Englishmen to witness the battle of Berlin, is from an interview with the author (Isle of Wight, 1974).

Chapter 5: *Victory*

Published sources include Bailey, Bradley, Butcher, Deane, Dönitz (*Wechselvolles Leben*), Eisenhower, Johnson, Lacqueur, Longmate, Maser, Murphy, Solzhenitsyn, Strong, Summersby, Thorwald, Toland, Voronov, Werth, Whiting. For the statistics of casualties and damage I have referred to: Balfour, Dollinger, *Fall of Nazi Germany* p. 422 (citing Putzger: *Historischer Weltatlas*, Bielefeld, 1963); Franck (citing *Statistisches Bundesamt*, Wiesbaden; Gerhardt Binder, *Deutschland seit 1945*, Stuttgart, 1969); Hans-Adolf Jacobsen and Hans Dollinger, *Der Zweite Weltkrieg*; Johnson, Lacqueur, La Farge, *Postwar World*, Part 1, pp. 12-13, Purnell's *History of the Second World War* (No. 93, 'An Overview'), Taylor, Urwin, Voznesensky.

Some of the original documents leading up to the surrender at Reims were collected by General Strong at the time and are now in the Ian Sayer Archives, Hounslow.

Chapter 6: *Last Rites*

Published sources include Brett-Smith, Brustat-Naval, Churchill, Djilas, Dollinger (*Fall of Nazi Germany*), Dönitz (*Memoirs*), Howley, Iakovlev, Lüdde-Neurath, Maginnis, Mee, Moran, Murphy, Schaeffer, Speer, Steinart, Truman, Whiting, Ziemke.

Chapter 7: *Hour Zero* and Chapter 8: *Stille Nacht*

Published sources include: Balfour and Muir, Brett-Smith, Byford-Jones, Clay, Davidson (*Death and Life of Germany*), Dickens, Donnison, Gollancz, Grosser, Grübe and Richter, Hilfswerk, Howley, Koch, Nabokov, Peters, Prinz, Sayer and Botting, Shirer, Ziemke. British Zonal Review No. 1 was useful. So were Public Record Office files WO. 171 4082, WO. 171 4654, WO. 171 4000 on matters ranging from railway bandits to deer shoots and SS roadbuilders in South Africa. I am grateful to Dr D. A. Spencer (diary) and Peter Fabian (interview) for vivid cameos of Germany's ruins, and to Elizabeth Carew-Hunt (interview) for examples of making-do in them. Also to Mrs M. H. Simpson for the letter from Dr Jessica Stolterfoht quoted here. Some of the recipes on p. 104 are from Marita Krauss: 'Die Frau in Münchner Trummeralltag' (in *Trümmerzeit in München*, ed. F. Prinz). For a brilliant photographic record of the shattered cities see Bauer (Munich) and Peter (Dresden); also the collection of colour stills from US Army newsreel films in Schwan and Steininger, *Besiegt, besetzt, geteilt*.

Chapter 9: *Exodus*

Sources for the Jewish Haganah movements across Europe: Bassak, Gitlin, Grossman, Proudfoot, Stone. Also a formerly Top Secret document, 'Illegal Emigration Movements in and through Italy' by CIC Agent Vincent La Vista, dated 15 May 1947 (US Archives 800. 0128 5-1547). Sources for DPs: Balfour and Muir, Donnison, Pierrepoint, Proudfoot, Ziemke. For German PWs: Eva Berthold, Will Berthold, Carell, Faulk, Sullivan. For expulsions: Arndt, Balfour and Muir, Böddecker, Byford-Jones, Dickens, Elliot, Franck, Franzel, Grübe and Richter, Hermann, Kaps, Kurth, Schieder, Thorwald, Zayas. Zayas's *Nemesis at Potsdam* is the most readily available account of the expulsions for an English-speaking audience, and I am indebted to it for the quotes from the three journalists and other references. A very full coverage of the flight and expulsions appeared in *Quick* magazine in a series of sixteen articles between 17 October 1974 and 6 February 1975, entitled *Die Flucht*. The two quotations from William Craydon are from an interview at Hitchin in 1974. The firing squad incident described by Stephen Patterson is taken from correspondence to the author dated 12 March 1975. For Russian repatriation see keyworks by Tolstoy and Bethell.

Chapter 10: *Raj*

Published sources in Bach, Balfour and Muir, Bower, Brett-Smith, Byford-Jones, Crawley, Davidson, Davis, Dickens, Dollinger (*Deutschland*), Franck, Gimbel, Gollancz, Grübe and Richter, Howley, Kahn, Kennan, Martin, Morgenthau, Nabokov, Peterson, Sayer and Botting, Stimson, Willis, Ziemke, Zink. Quoted interview material from Peter Bielenberg, Peter Fabian, Chris Leefe, Peter Saabor. Quoted letter material from letters by Phil May, Jessica Stolterfoht (to Mrs M. H. Simpson), I. Warner (to author). 'Hauptmann Toll' is from Peterson, the officers' mess menu from Gollancz. I am grateful to Patricia Meehan for the two quotes from Lord Cherwell and the women of Hamburg to Bürgermeister Petersen which were originally quoted in her television series *Zone of Occupation* (Programmes 4 and 2) in 1981. An unsigned, undated report by agent Guenther Reinhardt on the American Occupation of Germany (December 1947) gives a valuable insight into the Occupation style. The source for the Kissinger quote on p. 161 is Ralph Blumenfeld, 'The Formative Years of Henry Kissinger' (*The Observer*, 29 December 1974).

Chapter 11: *Vice*

Published sources: Bach, Balfour and Muir, Byford-Jones, Clay, Crawley, Davidson, Davis, Franck, Grübe and Richter (*Schwarzmarktzeit*), Koch, McGovern, Mee, Peterson, Radford and Ross, Rundell, Sayer and Botting, Trees (*Kaffee*), Ziemke. Also Marita Krauss: 'Die Frau im Münchner Trümmeralltag', and Margot Fuchs: 'Zucker, wer hat? Öl, wer kauft?' in *Trümmerzeit in München* (ed. Friedrich Prinz). The author is grateful to Chris Leefe and Len Carpenter for interviews extending over several days. The quote on p. 178 is from *Economic Survey of Europe since the War* (UN Dept of Economic Affairs, Geneva, 1953), that on p. 190

SOURCES

from Ratchford and Ross. I am grateful to Frank C. Gabell for first revealing the origins of the word 'motherfucker' in Occupation Germany, and to Dr D. A. Spencer for the Lilli Marlene 'frat' song recorded in his diary. The 'poignant affair' on p. 190 is from Byford-Jones, the scene of the naked Valkyrie is from McGovern. The quote on the VD epidemic is from the Chris Leefe interview (N.B. in later years it was sometimes doubted that there was a specifically Mongolian form of syphilis). I am grateful to Patricia Meehan for papers relating to the 4711 formula affair; also the Bückeburg castle affair, as a result of which, directly or indirectly, a number of distinguished careers in the RAF came to a sudden end. The Top Secret report referred to on p. 154 is entitled 'Illegal Trading in Germany' and dated 17 July 1946 (Foreign Office files, Public Records Office, London). Guenther Reinhardt (see *Raj*) makes a number of revelations about American misconduct.

Chapter 12: *Purge*
Published sources: Arendt, Bernstein, Bower, Brockdorff, Cooper, Crawley, Davidson, FitzGibbon, Friedmann, Fritsche, Fürstenau, Gilbert, Hearnden, Kurowski, Maser, Murphy, Neave, Nettl, Salomon, Sereny, Bradley-Smith, Trevor-Roper, Tusa, Wiesenthal, Ziemke, Zink. Tom Bower's meticulous and exhaustive *Blind Eye to Murder* must be considered the last word on war-crimes prosecutions to which anyone treading in its steps must be indebted. Ann and John Tusa's admirable *The Nuremberg Trial*, the latest addition to the enormous Nuremberg oeuvre, is probably the most satisfactory for the modern reader. There is no comparable book on denazification. The most authoritative is Justus Fürstenau's *Entnazifierung*, but this is heavy-going for the Anglo-American, and out of print. Also referred to: CIC Reports on Odessa, US zone, May–Sept. 1947; and CIC report 'Illegal Emigration Movements through Italy', 15 May 1947. Information about removal of German ammunition dumps is from Col. H. H. Cook (correspondence).

Chapter 13: *Reds*
The restrictions of time and space have precluded a comprehensive survey of the Soviet zone of Germany between 1945 and 1949. It is a huge subject and in the nature of things an opaque one. A few books but hardly any archival documentation of those days have emerged from that forbidding territory. To my knowledge Wolfgang Leonhard's is the only account written from the inside, with the possible exception of Klimov's *The Terror Machine*. Others — including Hornstein, Klimov, Knop, Löwenthal, Nettl and Schaffer — were written from the outside of the Soviet system. Of these Nettl is by far the most exhaustive and authoritative. Works on the airlift and its background include Arnold-Foster, Bennett, Clay, Davidson, Morris, Rodrigo and J. E. Smith. The quotations by Gen. Tunner and Lt. Halvorsen are from Mark Arnold-Foster's clear and knowledgeable account, to which I am indebted. The quotation on pp. 228–9 is from my interview with Captain Craydon (Hitchin, 1974) and from his letter to Major Sweeny. I am grateful to Brigadier Nigel Spiller for his lecture notes on Berlin airlift handling operations in which he took part. The quote on pp. 239–40 is from a letter written by General Clay to the author from New York on 16 December 1974. A valuable source is 'Background Letter June 1948–December 1949' (Control Commission for Germany, British Element, Wahnerheide, 1950) — not a letter but two substantial volumes containing a mass of information, including details of currency reform and events in the Soviet zone.

Bibliography

The following list includes books I have read or found useful. Among them are several works of fiction (marked with an asterisk) which give a more vivid insight into the feel of this bizarre period than many of the heftier tomes of academic scholarship. Articles, papers, documents, interviews, etc, are referred to in the previous section.

Stephen E. Ambrose: *Eisenhower and Berlin* (New York, 1967)
—*Eisenhower — The Soldier* (London, 1984)
Hartvig Andersen: *The Dark City* (London, 1954)
Ruth Andreas-Friedrich: *Berlin Underground 1939–45* (London, 1948)
Anon: *A Woman in Berlin* (London, 1955)
Hannah Arendt: *Eichmann in Jerusalem* (London, 1977)
Werner Arndt: *Ostpreussen, Westpreussen, Pommern, Schlesien, Sudetenland 1944/45* (Friedberg, 1980)
Mark Arnold-Foster: *The Siege of Berlin* (London, 1979)
Lester Atwell: *Private* (New York, 1958)

George Bailey: *Germans — the Biography of an Obsession* (New York, 1972)
Thomas A. Bailey: *The Marshall Plan Summer* (Stanford, Ca., 1977)
Michael Balfour and John Muir: *Four-Power Control in Germany and Austria 1945–46* (London, 1956)
Michel Bar-Zohar: *The Hunt for German Scientists 1944–60* (London, 1967)
M. Bassak: *Maapilim Buch* (Paris, 1949)
Richard Bauer: *Ruinen Jahre* (Munich, 1983)
BBC: *War Report* (London 1946)
Cajus Bekker: *Flucht übers Meer* (Frankfurt, 1976)
Cedric Belfrage: *Seeds of Destruction — The Truth About the US Occupation of Germany* (New York, 1954)
Lowell Bennett: *Berlin Bastion* (Frankfurt, 1951)
Folke Bernadotte: *The Fall of the Curtain* (London, 1945)
— *Instead of Arms* (London, 1949)
Victor Bernstein: *Final Judgement — The Story of Nuremberg* (London, 1947)
Eva Berthold: *Kriegsgefangene im Osten* (Königstein/Ts, 1981)
Will Berthold: *Parol Parole Heimat* (Bayreuth, 1979)
Nicholas Bethell: *The Last Secret* (London, 1974)
Lev Bezymenski: *The Death of Adolf Hitler* (London, 1968)
— *Tracing Martin Bormann* (Moscow, 1966)
Christabel Bielenberg: *The Past is Myself* (London, 1968)
Bird, Eugene K.: *The Loneliest Man in the World* (London, 1974)
Günter Böddeker: *Die Fluchtlinge* (Munich, 1980)
Gerhardt Boldt: *Hitler's Last Days* (London, 1973)
*Heinrich Böll: *Children Are Civilians Too* (London, 1973)
Meyrick Booth: *Prisoner of Peace* (London, 1954)
Douglas Botting: *The Aftermath – Europe* (Time-Life Books, Alexandria, Va., 1983)
— and Ian Sayer: *Nazi Gold* (London, 1984)
Margaret Bourke-White: *Dear Fatherland, Rest Quietly* (New York, 1945)
Tom Bower: *Blind Eye to Murder* (London, 1981)
— *Klaus Barbie — Butcher of Lyons* (London, 1984)
*Kay Boyle: *The Smoking Mountain — Stories of Post-War Germany* (London, 1952)
Omar N. Bradley: *A Soldier's Story — the Allied Campaign from Tunis to the Elbe* (London, 1951)
Richard Brett-Smith: *Berlin '45 — The Grey City* (London, 1966)
Werner Brockdorf: *Flucht Vor Nürnberg* (Munich–Wels, 1969)
Fenner Brockway: *German Diary* (London, 1946)
Fritz Brustat-Naval: *Unternehmen Rettung* (Herford, 1970)
Arthur Bryant: *Triumph in the West 1943–1946* (London, 1959)
Wilfred Burchett: *Cold War in Germany* (London, 1950)
Capt. Harry C. Butcher: *My Three Years with Eisenhower* (New York, 1946)
W. Byford-Jones: *Berlin Twilight* (London, 1946)
James F. Byrnes: *Speaking Frankly* (New York, 1947) .

Paul Carell and Günter Böddeker: *Die Gefangenen* (Frankfurt, 1980)
V. I. Chuikov: *The End of the Third Reich* (Moscow, 1978)
Winston S. Churchill: *The Second World War* (London, 1955)
Delbert Clark: *Again the Goose Step* (New York, 1949)
General Lucius D. Clay: *Decision in Germany* (London, 1950)
Sarah Mabel Collins: *Bitter Harvest* (London, 1951)

Robert Collis and Han Hogerzeil: *Straight On — Journey to Belsen and the Road Home* (London, 1947)
Control Commission for Germany (British Element): *Background Letter June 1948–December 1949* (Wahnerheide, 1950)
R. W. Cooper: *The Nuremberg Trial* (London, 1947)
*Geoffrey Cotterell: *Randle in Springtime* (London, 1949)
Aidan Crawley: *The Rise of Western Germany 1945–72* (London, 1973)

David J. Dallin and Boris Nicolaevsky: *Forced Labor in Soviet Russia* (New Haven, 1947)
Basil Davidson: *Germany — What Now? Potsdam to Partition* (London, 1950)
Eugene Davidson: *The Death and Life of Germany — An Account of the American Occupation* (London, 1959)
— *The Trial of the Germans* (New York, 1966)
Franklin M. Davis Jr.: *Come as a Conqueror — The US Army's Occupation of Germany 1945–49* (New York, 1967)
W. Phillips Davison: *The Berlin Blockade* (Princeton, 1958)
John R. Deane: *The Strange Alliance* (London, 1947)
Geoffrey Arthur Dickens: *Lübeck Diary* (London, 1947)
Milovan Djilas: *Wartime* (New York, 1977)
Hans Dollinger: *The Decline and Fall of Nazi Germany and Imperial Japan* (London, 1968)
— *Deutschland unter den Besatsungsmächten 1945–49* (Munich, 1967)
F. S. V. Donnison: *Civil Affairs and Military Government, North-West Europe* (HMSO, London, 1961)
Karl Dönitz: *Memoirs* (London, 1958)
— *Mein wechselvolles Leben* (Göttingen, 1968)

Raymond Ebsworth: *Restoring Democracy in Germany — the British Contribution* (New York, 1966)
Wolfgang Ecke: *Flight Towards Home* (New York, 1970)
Dwight D. Eisenhower: *Crusade in Europe* (London, 1948)
Gil Elliot: *Twentieth-Century Book of the Dead* (London, 1972)
L. F. Ellis: *Victory in the West*, vol. 2: 'The Defeat of Germany' (HMSO, London, 1968)
Julius Epstein: *Operation Keelhaul* (Old Greenwich, Conn., 1978)
John Erickson: *The Road to Berlin* (London, 1983)
H. Essame: *The Battle for Germany* (London, 1969)
Helmuth Euler: *Die Entscheidungsschlacht an Rhein und Ruhr 1945* (Stuttgart, 1980)

Henry La Farge (ed.): *Lost Treasures of Europe* (New York, 1946)
Henry Faulk: *Group Captives* (London, 1977)
Frances Faviell: *The Dancing Bear — Berlin de Profundis* (London, 1954)
Herbert Feis: *Between War and Peace — the Potsdam Conference* (Princeton, 1960)
Heinz-Dietrich Fischer: *Reeducations — und Pressepolitik unter britischem Besatzungsstatus* (Düsseldorf, 1973)
Jack Fishman: *The Seven Men of Spandau* (London, 1954)
Constantine Fitzgibbon: *Denazification* (London, 1969)
Heinrich Fraenkel: *A Nation Divided* (London, 1949)
Dieter Franck: *Jahre unseres Lebens 1945–1949* (Munich, 1980)
Emil Franzel: *Die Vertreibung Sudetenland 1945–1946* (Munich, 1980)
Oliver J. Frederiksen: *The American Military Occupation of Germany 1945–1953* (Frankfurt 1953)
W. Friedmann: *The Allied Military Government of Germany* (London, 1947)
Hans Fritzsche: *The Sword in the Scales* (London, 1953)
Hildegard Fritzsche: *Vor dem Tribunal der Sieger* (Preussich Oldendorf, 1981)
Justus Fürstenau: *Entnazifierung* (Neuwied, 1969)

John Kenneth Galbraith: *A Life in Our Time* (London, 1981)
James M. Gavin: *On to Berlin* (New York, 1978)
Hans Georg-Kloes: *Von der Menagerie zum Tierparadis*
*Sir Philip Gibbs: *Thine Enemy* (London, 1949)
Gilbert, G. M.: *Nuremberg Diary* (London, 1948)
John Gimbel: *A German Community under American Occupation — Markung 1945–52* (Stanford, 1961)
Murray Gitlin: *The Embarkation* (New York, 1950)
Victor Gollancz: *What Buchenwald Really Means* (London, 1945)
— *Our Threatened Values* (London, 1946)
— *In Darkest Germany* (London, 1947)
Samuel B. Goudsmit: *Alsos — The Search for the German Atom Bomb* (London, 1947)
*Harris Greene: *The Mozart Leaves at Nine* (London, 1961)
Alfred Grosser: *Germany in Our Time* (London, 1971)
Kurt R. Grossman: *The Jewish DP Problem* (New York, 1951)
Frank Grube/Gerhard Richter: *Die Schwartzmarktzeit* (Hamburg, 1979)
— *Flucht und Vertreibung* (Hamburg, 1980)
General Sir Francis De Guingand: *Operation Victory* (London, 1947)

*Hans Habe: *Aftermath* (London, 1948)
*— *Off-Limits* (London, 1956)
Carl Haensel: *Das Gericht vertagt sich* (Munich, 1980)
Leslie C. Hardman and Cecily Goodman: *The Survivors — The Story of the Belsen Remnant* (London, 1958)
Edwin Hartrich: *The Fourth and Richest Reich* (New York, 1980)
Werner Haupt: *Königsberg, Breslau, Wien, Berlin* (Friedberg, 1978)
W. Haupt: *Endkampf Im Westen 1945* (Friedberg, 1979)
Arthur Hearnden (ed.): *The British in Germany — Educational Reconstruction after 1945* (London, 1978)
Stewart Herman: *The Rebirth of the German Church* (London, 1946)
Hilfswerk of the Evangelical Churches of Germany: *Living Conditions in Germany 1947* (Stuttgart, 1947)
Russell Hill: *Struggle for Germany* (London, 1947)
Erika von Hornstein; *The Accused — Seven East Germans on Trial* (London, 1965)
General Sir Brian Horrocks: *A Full Life* (London, 1960)
Lali Horstmann: *Nothing for Tears* (London, 1953)
Elizabeth F. Howard: *Barriers Down — Notes on Postwar Germany* (London, 1950)
Frank Howley: *Berlin Command* (New York, 1950)

A. S. Iakovlev: 'The Capital Victorious' (in *Stalin and His Generals*, ed. Seiveryn Bialer, London 1970)
David Irving: *Hitler's War 1942–45* (London, 1977)
Rolf Italiaander, Arnold Bauer, Herbert Krafft: *Berlins Stunde Null 1945* (Düsseldorf, 1979)

Charles de Jaeger: *The Linz File (Hitler's Plunder of European Art)* (Exeter, 1981)
John Jahr Verlag: *Von Hitler zu Adenauer 1945–49* (Hamburg, 1976)
Karl Jering: *Überleben und Neubeginn* (München, 1979)
The Very Revd. Dr Hewlett Johnson: *Soviet Russia since the War* (New York, 1947)

Arthur D. Kahn: *Betrayal — Our Occupation of Germany* (Warsaw, 1950)
Dr Johannes Kaps (ed.): *The Tragedy of Silesia 1945–46* (Munich, 1952/3)
Ursula von Kardorff: *Diary of a Nightmare* (London, 1965)
Douglas M. Kelley: *22 Cells in Nuremberg* (London, 1947)
Frank Kelly: *Private Kelly* (London, 1954)
Erich Kempka: *Ich habe Adolf Hitler verbrannt*
George Kennan: *Memoirs 1925–50* (Boston, 1967)
Anna Kientopf: *Das Friedensfeindliche Trauma* (Lindhorst, 1954)
Gregory Klimov: *The Terror Machine — The Inside Story of the Soviet Administration in Berlin* (London, 1953)
Percy Knauth: *Germany in Defeat* (New York, 1956)
Hildegard Knef: *The Gift Horse* (London, 1971)
Werner Knop: *Prowling Russia's Forbidden Zone* (New York, 1949)
Thilo Koch: *Fünf Jahre der Entscheidung 1945–49* (Frankfurt, 1969)
Lev Kopelew: *Aufbewahren für alle Zeit* (Hamburg, 1976)
Wolf-Arno Kropat: *Hessen in der Stunde Null — 1945/1947* (Wiesbaden, 1979)
Erich Kuby: *The Russians and Berlin 1945* (London, 1965)
Fritz Kurowski: *Unternehmen Paperclip* (Munich, 1982)
K. O. Kurth (ed.): *Documents of Humanity* (Berlin, 1952)

Walter Lacqueur: *Europe Since Hitler* (London, 1982, revised)
— *The Terrible Secret* (London, 1980)
Count Hans von Lehndorff: *East Prussian Diary 1945–47* (London, 1963)
Rudolf Walter Leonhardt: *This Germany — The Story Since the Third Reich* (London, 1966)
Wolfgang Leonhard: *Child of the Revolution* (London, 1957)
Magnus Linklater, Isabel Hilton, Neal Ascherson: *The Fourth Reich — Klaus Barbie and the Neo-Fascist Connection* (London, 1984)
John Loftus: *The Belarus Secret* (London, 1983)
Norman Longmate: *When We Won the War* (London, 1977)
Fritz Löwenthal: *News from Soviet Germany* (London, 1950)
Walter Lüdde-Neurath: *Regierung Dönitz* (Leoni am Starnberger See, 1980)

Charles B. MacDonald: *The Last Offensive: US Army in World War Two* (Washington, 1973)
*Colin MacInnes: *To the Victors the Spoils* (London, 1950)
Sir Arthur S. MacNalty and W. Franklin Mellor: *Health Recovery in Europe* (London, 1946)
Maj.-Gen. John J. Maginnis: *Military Government Journal — Normandy to Berlin* (Boston, 1971)
Ethel Mannin: *German Journey* (London, 1948)
James Stewart Martin: *All Honorable Men* (Boston, 1950)
Werner Maser: *Nuremberg — A Nation on Trial* (London, 1979)
Richard Mayne: *Postwar — The Dawn of Today's Europe* (London, 1983)
Ian McDougall: *German Notebook* (London, 1953)
*James McGovern: *Fräulein* (London, 1957)
Finn McMahon: *Post Bellum Blues* (London, 1965)

Charles L. Mee Jr.: *Meeting at Potsdam* (London, 1975)
Tibor Mende: *Europe's Suicide in Germany* (London, 1946)
Drew Middleton: *The Struggle for Germany* (London, 1950)
Kurt Miller: *After Nazism — Democracy?* (London, 1945)
Rodney G. Minott: *The Fortress That Never Was* (New York, 1965)
Field Marshal the Viscount Montgomery of Alamein: *Normandy to the Baltic* (London, 1947)
— *Memoirs* (London, 1958)
Alan Moorehead: *Eclipse* (London, 1945)
Lord Moran: *Churchill — The Struggle for Survival* (London, 1966)
Henry Morgenthau Jr.: *Germany is our Problem* (New York, 1945)
Eric Morris: *Blockade — Berlin and the Cold War* (London, 1973)
Leonard A. Mosley: *Report from Germany* (London, 1945)
G. H. Mostar: *Im Namen des Gesetzes* (Hamburg, 1950)
Robert Murphy: *Diplomat Among Warriors* (London, 1964)

Nicolas Nabokov: *Old Friends and New Music* (London, 1951)
National Geographic Magazine: *Airlift to Berlin* (Washington DC, 1949)
Airey Neave: *Nuremberg* (London, 1978)
J. P. Nettl: *The Eastern Zone and Soviet Policy in Germany 1945–50* (London, 1951)
*Robert Neumann: *Children of Vienna* (London, 1946)
Jürgen Neven-du Mont: *After Hitler — Report from a German City* (London, 1969)
John North: *North-West Europe 1944–45* (HMSO, London, 1977)
Tadeusz Nowakowski: *Camp of All Saints* (New York, 1962)

James P. O'Donnell: *The Berlin Bunker* (London, 1979)
Official History of the Second Military Government Regiment (n.d.)
Alexandra Orme (Barcza): *From Christmas to Easter — A Guide to a Russian Occupation* (London, 1949)

Saul K. Padover: *Psychologist in Germany* (London, 1946)
Lord Pakenham: *Born to Believe* (London, 1953)
George S. Patton: *War as I knew it* (New York, 1947)
Richard Peter: *Eine Kamera klagt an* (Dresden, 1948)
William Peters: *In Germany Now* (London, 1946)
Edward N. Peterson: *The American Occupation of Germany* (Detroit, 1977)
W. E. R. Piddington: *Russian Frenzy* (London, 1955)
Albert Pierrepoint: *Executioner — Pierrepoint* (London, 1974)
*Theodor Plievier: *Berlin* (London, 1956)
Boris Polevoi: *The Final Reckoning — Nuremberg Diaries* (Moscow, 1978)
Norman Pounds: *Divided Germany and Berlin* (Princeton, 1962)
Friedrich Prinz: *Trümmerzeit in München 1945–49* (Munich, 1984)
Terence Prittie: *Germany Divided* (Boston, 1960)
Malcolm J. Proudfoot: *European Refugees — A Study in Forced Population Movements* (London, 1957)
*Mario Puzo: *The Dark Arena* (New York, 1953)

Tony Radspieler: *The Ethnic German Refugee in Austria 1945–54* (The Hague, 1955)
B. U. Ratchford and W. D. Ross: *Berlin Reparations Assignment* (London, 1947)
G. R. Rees (ed.): *The Case of Rudolf Hess* (London, 1947)
Guenther Reinhardt: *Crime Without Punishment* (New York, 1952)
Hermann Riedel: *Ausweglos — Letzter Akt des Krieges im Schwarzwald . . . Ende April 1945* (Vielingen – Schwenningen, 1976)
Curt Riess: *The Berlin Story* (London, 1953)
C. E. Bechhofer Roberts (ed.): *The Trial of William Joyce* (London, 1946)
Robert Rodrigo: *Berlin Airlift* (London, 1960)
Karl-Heinz Rothenburger: *Die Hungerjahre nach dem Zweiten Weltkrieg* (Boppard am Rhein, 1980)
Joseph Rovan: *Germany* (London, 1959)
Klaus-Jörg Ruhl: *Die Besatzer und die Deutschen: American Zone 1945–48* (Düsseldorf, 1980)
Bernd Ruland: *Geld wie Hen und nichts zu fressen* (Bayreuth, 1968)
Walter Rundell: *Black Market Money* (Louisiana, 1964)
Cornelius Ryan: *The Last Battle* (London, 1966)

Ernst von Salomon: *The Answers* (London, 1951)
Jacques Sandulescu: *Hunger's Rogues — On the Black Market in Europe 1948* (New York, 1974)
Heinz Schaeffer: *U-Boat 977* (London, 1952)
Gordon Schaffer: *Russian Zone* (London, 1947)
Theodor Schieder (ed.): *Documents on the Expulsion of the Germans out of East–Central Europe.* (4 vols., Bonn, 1961)
Stefan Schimansky: *Vain Victory* (London, 1946)
Hans Schlange-Schöningen: *Im Schatten des Hungers* (Hamburg, 1953)
Heinz Schön: *Ostsee '45* (Stuttgart, 1954)

Horst Schöne, et al: *Berlin 1945–48* (Leipzig, 1961)
Heribert Schwan and Rolf Steininger: *Besiegt, besetzt, geteilt* (Oldenburg, 1979)
— *Als der Krieg Zu Ende ging* (Berlin, 1981)
Gitta Sereny: *Into that Darkness* (London, 1974)
Arthur Settal: *This is Germany* (New York, 1950)
V. Sevruk: *How Wars End* (Moscow, 1969)
SHAEF: *The Psychological Warfare Division — Western European Campaign 1944–45* (Bad Homburg, 1945)
Tony Sharp: *The Wartime Alliance and the Zonal Division of Germany* (Oxford, 1975)
William L. Shirer: *End of a Berlin Diary* (London, 1947)
General S. M. Shtemenko: *The Last Six Months* (London, 1978)
Gerald Simons: *Victory in Europe* (Time-Life Books, Alexandria, Va., 1982)
Derrick Sington: *Belsen Uncovered* (London, 1946)
Bradley F. Smith: *Reaching Judgement at Nuremberg* (London, 1977)
Jean Edward Smith: *The Defense of Berlin* (London, 1963)
Alexander Solzhenitsyn: *The Gulag Archipelago* (Vol. I, London, 1974)
Albert Speer: *Inside the Third Reich* (London, 1970)
— *Spandau — The Secret Diaries* (London, 1977)
Stephen Spender: *European Witness* (London, 1946)
Martis G. Steinert: *Capitulation 1945* (London, 1969)
James Stern: *The Hidden Damage* (New York, 1947)
William Stevenson: *The Bormann Brotherhood* (London, 1973)
Gustav Stolper: *German Realities* (New York, 1948)
I. F. Stone: *Underground to Palestine* (London, 1979)
General Sir Kenneth Strong: *Intelligence at the Top* (London, 1968)
Stunde Null – und danach: Schicksale 1945–1949 (Leer, 1983–4): Band 1: 'Horst Wolf: Ich Sage die Wahrheit oder ich schweige (Ostpreussen bei der Roten Armee).' Band 2: 'Hildegard Rosin: Führt noch ein Weg zurück (3 Jahre in Köningsberg).' Band 3: 'Erich von Lölhöffel: Brief aus dem Spatzengarten (Flüchtelingsfamilie in Bad Harzburg).' Band 4: 'Lo Warnecke: Decke und Brot (In Mecklenburg, sowjetisch besetzte Zone).'
Matthew Barry Sullivan: *Thresholds of Peace — German Prisoners and the People of Britain 1944–48* (London, 1979)
Kay Summersby: *Eisenhower Was My Boss* (London, 1949)
Ben E. Swearingen: *The Plot that Saved Hermann Goering from the Gallows* (New York, 1985)

A. J. P. Taylor: *The Second World War* (London, 1975)
Eric Taylor and Willy Niessen: *Fronstadt Köln* (Düsseldorf, 1980)
Jürgen Thorwald: *Die grosse Flucht* (Stuttgart, 1979)
Jochen Thies and Kurt von Daak: *Südwestdeutsland Stunde Null: French Zone 1945–48* (Düsseldorf, 1979)
Wilhelm Tieke: *Das Ende zwischen Oder und Elbe — der Kampf um Berlin 1945* (Stuttgart, 1981)
Toland, John: *The Last 100 Days* (London, 1968)
Nicolai Tolstoy: *Victims of Yalta* (London, 1979, revised)
Wolfgang Trees: *Kaffee, Krähenfusse und Kontrollen* (Aachen, 1976)
— *Schlachtfeld Rheinland* (Aachen, 1976)
— Charles Whiting, Thomas Omansen: *Drei Jahre nach Null: British Zone 1945–48* (Düsseldorf, 1979)
Hugh Trevor-Roper: *The Last Days of Hitler* (London, 1973)
Harry S Truman: *Years of Decisions 1945* (London, 1955)
Andrew Tully: *Berlin: Story of a Battle* (New York, 1963)
John Frayn Turner and Robert Jackson: *Destination Berchtesgaden* (London, 1975)
Wilhelm K. Turner (ed.): Documents on the Expulsion of the Sudeten Germans (Munich, 1953)
Ann and John Tusa: *The Nuremberg Trial* (London, 1983)

D. W. Urwin: *Western Europe since 1945* (London, 1972)

Marshal N. N. Voronov: 'First Weeks of Peace' (in *Stalin and His Generals*, ed. Seiveryn Bialer, London, 1970)
N. Voznesensky: *The Wartime Economy of the USSR in the Period of the Fatherland War* (Moscow, 1945)

Patrick Gordon-Walker: *The Lid Lifts* (London, 1945)
James P. Warburg: *Germany — Bridge or Battleground* (London, 1947)
— *Germany — Key to Peace* (London, 1954)
Lo Warnecke: *Auf der Flucht: 1945 — der Treck aus dem Osten* (Bergisch Gladbach, 1980)
D. C. Watt: *Britain Looks to Germany* (London, 1965)
Ingeborg Wells: *Enough, No More* (London, 1948)
Alexander Werth: *Russia at War* (London, 1964)
Rebecca West: *A Train of Powder* (London, 1955)
— *The Meaning of Treason* (London, 1982)
W. L. White: *Report on the Germans* (New York, 1947)
Charles Whiting: *Finale at Flensburg* (London, 1973)

— †The End of the War — Europe April 15 to May 23, 1945 (New York, 1973)
— and Wolfgang Trees: *Die Amis sind da — wie Aachen erobert wurde* (Aachen, 1975)
— *Norddeutschland Stunde Null — April-September 1945* (Düsseldorf, 1980)
Simon Wiesenthal: *The Murderers Among Us* (London, 1969)
F. Roy Willis: *The French in Germany 1945–49* (Stanford, Ca., 1962)
Chester Wilmot: *The Struggle for Europe* (London, 1952)
Francesca M. Wilson: *Aftermath* (London, 1947)

Alfred M. de Zayas: *Nemesis at Potsdam* (London, 1977)
Earl F. Ziemke: *The Battle for Berlin: End of the Third Reich* (London, 1969)
— *Stalingrad to Berlin — The German Defeat in the East* (Washington DC, 1968)
— *The US Army in the Occupation of Germany 1944–46* (Washington DC, 1975)
Harold Zink: *American Military Government in Germany* (New York, 1947)
— *The United States in Germany, 1944–55* (New York, 1956)

Index

244